The Social Art

D1016424

The Social Art

Language and Its Uses
Second Edition

Ronald Macaulay

OXFORD
UNIVERSITY PRESS
2006

OXFORD
UNIVERSITY PRESS

Oxford University Press, Inc., publishes works that further
Oxford University's objective of excellence
in research, scholarship, and education.

Oxford   New York
Auckland   Cape Town   Dar es Salaam   Hong Kong   Karachi
Kuala Lumpur   Madrid   Melbourne   Mexico City   Nairobi
New Delhi   Shanghai   Taipei   Toronto

With offices in
Argentina   Austria   Brazil   Chile   Czech Republic   France   Greece
Guatemala   Hungary   Italy   Japan   Poland   Portugal   Singapore
South Korea   Switzerland   Thailand   Turkey   Ukraine   Vietnam

Copyright © 2006 by Ronald K. S. Macaulay

Published by Oxford University Press, Inc.
198 Madison Avenue, New York, New York 10016

www.oup.com

Oxford is a registered trademark of Oxford University Press

All rights reserved. No part of this publication may be reproduced,
stored in a retrieval system, or transmitted, in any form or by any means,
electronic, mechanical, photocopying, recording, or otherwise,
without the prior permission of Oxford University Press.

Library of Congress Cataloging-in-Publication Data
Macaulay, Ronald K. S.
The social art : language and its uses / Ronald Macaulay.—2nd ed.
p. cm.
Includes bibliographical references and index.
ISBN-13 978-0-19-518796-0 (pbk.)

1. Sociolinguistics.   2. Language and languages.   I. Title.
P40.M33 2006
306.44—dc22   2005049871

6 8 9 7 5

Printed in the United States of America
on acid-free paper

Language is a social art.
W. V. O. QUINE,
Word and Object

Preface to the First Edition

This book had its origin in a small book I wrote several years ago that is now out of print. *Generally Speaking: How Children Learn Language* was "intended to provide a reasonably up-to-date account of children's language learning, written in a form designed to be accessible to those who are unfamiliar with the topic and its jargon." More than ten years later it is no longer "up-to-date," and in contemplating a revision I saw an opportunity to expand its scope into an account of language in all its complexity. As a result the work has developed so that it bears very little similarity to its original plan. The first nine chapters of the present work owe much to the earlier work as they provide a way of introducing a certain amount of technical vocabulary, but they have been expanded to include more information about adult language. The rest of the book is new and is based on the kinds of examples that I have found successful in the past twenty-five years of teaching introductory courses. In order to keep the text as uncluttered as possible I have put all references at the end in a section on further reading.

Most of the information in this book comes from other scholars. I have tried to acknowledge specific examples but my debt is much greater than that. It has been my good fortune to have learned a great deal from teachers, fellow graduate students, colleagues, and friends. To all them I offer my sincere thanks. Special recognition must be accorded to Don Brenneis, Rene Coppieters, and Sarah Dart, for helpful comments and for their advice, support, and encouragement over many years. I am also grateful to Bill Bright for a very helpful review of an earlier draft, and, at Oxford University Press, to Cynthia Read, Paul Schlotthauer, and Brian MacDonald for their help and guidance.

Preface to the Second Edition

When I was writing this book more than ten years ago, I made a deliberate decision to avoid reference to the latest theories, mainly because such views tend to change quite rapidly and therefore earlier versions quickly go out of date. I wanted to write a book that would contain information that would be less susceptible to changes in fashion. On rereading it in preparation for this second edition I find little that I want to change, and consequently I have made relatively few changes in the text of the original chapters. I have, however, added two new chapters and an appendix examining some major theoretical issues in the study of language. These additions are intended to counteract some extreme views that have received more attention in the media than I believe is appropriate. Part of the problem is that the grounds for justifying theories are complex and cannot be easily explained to a non-specialist reader. As a result the claims are often treated in the media as well-grounded hypotheses that are generally accepted by scholars, although that may not be an accurate description of the situation. The new chapters are intended to show how there is considerable controversy about certain claims that have been developed through a complex process of reasoning rather than being based on generally accepted objective evidence.

My thanks to Lee Munroe and Don Brenneis for helpful comments and suggestions, and to Peter Ohlin at Oxford University Press for encouraging me to prepare this second edition and to Bob Milks for dealing with the production side.

Contents

The Social Art

Give a Dog a Name

"The world is full of obvious things which nobody by any chance ever observes."

Sherlock Holmes, *The Hound of the Baskervilles*

It is paradoxical that people know so little about the nature of language. Scholars from fields as various as philosophy, computer science, psychology, lexicography, and what is sometimes called "the science of language"—linguistics—have been studying language for a very long time. Their efforts have produced enough printed material to fill a fair-sized library. Yet little of what they have discovered has trickled down to the general public and debates over political, educational, and cultural issues such as literacy, bilingual education, or the alleged deterioration of the English language tend to be conducted in terms of the folk beliefs of the participants and with little reference to the "experts." This is perhaps as much the fault of the experts as it is of the general population. Linguists, in particular, have generally been mainly interested in the abstract nature of linguistic structure, which they have studied without reference to the people using it or the situations in which it is used. This approach has led to some remarkable discoveries about the nature of language but, not surprisingly, it usually takes some technical knowledge to appreciate their significance. In recent years more and more linguists have begun to look at the ways in which people use language, and many of their findings are more accessible to the lay public. This book is an attempt to summarize some of the results of both kinds of linguistic scholarship in a form that ordinary readers can understand.

The first question is, Where to begin? After all, language is almost as omnipresent as the air we breathe; yet just as it is difficult to tell much about the character of the atmosphere by looking at it, so it is hard to observe much about language while using it. There are exceptions, of course. Air pollution is easy to see and even easier to detect by other means. Language also draws attention to itself and, by taking note of what happens then, we may find out something. For example, we immediately notice when someone speaks differently from us, but what we notice will depend on our past experience. Thus one person might simply recognize the stranger as having a foreign accent, whereas someone else might identify him as having a French, German, or Russian accent. The differences in

3

the way the outsider speaks are what allows the hearer to "place" the speaker. Sometimes we are confused, puzzled, or even angry when a foreigner's speech is too close to our own because it makes it harder to remember that he may not share our beliefs and attitudes. Like most other aspects of language, a "foreign accent" may have its uses.

Another type of situation in which attention is drawn to language is when someone makes a pun (Q: *What do you get when you pour hot water down a rabbit hole?* A: *Hot cross bunnies.*) or points out an ambiguity (*Visiting relatives can be a nuisance*). One of the examples I give my students in the introductory linguistics class is a sentence that was used to test an automatic parser (that is, a computer program that analyzes the grammar of a sentence): *I saw the man with a telescope in the park.* After students have pointed out that there are various interpretations depending upon who has the telescope and who is in the park, I mention to them that the computer found another set of interpretations based on interpreting *saw* as the present tense of the verb *saw*, not as the past tense of *see*. This information is always greeted with groans, but I point out to them that they must have unconsciously rejected this interpretation on the grounds of implausibility, although they have no awareness of the process. This illustrates a fundamental point that will recur frequently throughout the book. Meaning is not something that belongs solely to the utterance that is spoken or the piece of writing. Meaning also depends on the person who hears the utterance or reads the text. This is a point that many people find hard to accept, but perhaps it will become more plausible as different examples are presented.

Because jokes about language are an example of speakers deliberately drawing attention to certain aspects of language, they can provide evidence about how we use and understand language. I begin with two cartoons by Gary Larson. Larson is a cartoonist who often shows animals behaving like humans and speaking English, but the two cartoons I want to discuss here show the relationship between humans and their pets. The first shows two pictures. The first is entitled "What we say to dogs" and shows a man shouting: "Okay, Ginger! I've had it! You stay out of the garbage! Understand, Ginger? Stay out of the garbage, or else!" The picture below is entitled "What they hear" and shows the man's words as "Blah blah GINGER blah blah blah blah blah blah blah blah GINGER blah blah blah blah blah . . ." The second cartoon shows a woman addressing similar remarks to a cat but in this case what the cat hears is blank. When I ask my students what these two cartoons show, they tell me, in patronizing tones, that the dog recognizes its name but the cat does not. I then ask them how they know that the dog knows its name. At this they look at me in astonishment: everybody knows that a dog recognizes its name. When I ask for evidence, they point out that the dog comes when called. But the fact that the dog comes when it hears the sound is no evidence that the dog recognizes this signal as its name. Moreover, we use the dog's name not only to call it but also to scold it, to stop it from doing something, to comfort it, and for a number of other reasons. We know that what is common to all these utterances is the dog's name, but how can the dog know this? It is likely that we say the name differently for different purposes: sharply for a reprimand or prohibition, gently for comfort. These are all different signals and there is no reason why the dog should be concerned about what they have in common. Even if the dog were to notice the common element, it would be incredible if it were able to identify this element as a name. The concept of a name is a purely human one and there is no reason to believe that any other creature could grasp this concept. Yet we act as if the dog knows its name and we find it hard to accept that it does not. This is probably because we want them to be more like us, to be almost human.

There are a number of basic points to be made from this example. The first is that we behave toward other people the way we do toward our dogs, that is, we expect them to understand what we have said in the way that we mean it. Usually this assumption seems to be justified, and humans have the advantage over dogs in that they can say that they do not understand or ask for clarification. As we shall see in later chapters, however, this assumption is not always justified, particularly not with young children.

The second point is that we probably attach more importance to words than is justified. In the case of the dog, we think of the name as the important signal although the tone of voice, what linguists call the intonation, may be much more important (see chapter 4). In some languages tone distinguishes words. In Chinese, for example, *ma* said with a high level tone means "mother," with a high falling tone it means "scold," with a low falling-rising tone it means "horse," and with a high rising tone it means "hemp." In English we do not use tone in quite this way but we all know that there can be a big difference between *no* said with a strong falling intonation, which might mean "definitely not," *no* said with a sharply rising intonation, which might mean "are you sure?" and *no* said with a falling-rising intonation, which might mean "maybe." Similarly, the particle *oh*, which does not have a clear dictionary meaning though it performs a number of useful functions, can express quite different responses depending on the intonation.

The third point is that language is only part of the communication. When we get dressed to go out, pick up the dog's leash while moving toward the door, and say, *Walkies?* the vocal signal is highly redundant. The dog probably recognizes our intentions long before the word is uttered. Similarly, we pay attention to how people look as well as to what they say. In this way we can often identify such notions as jokes, insults, flattery, sarcasm, or threats. In addition to facial expressions, gestures and posture are also ways of communicating. We also communicate with noises that are not words, for example, laughing or sobbing. The shepherd in sheepdog trials whistles to his dog to tell it what to do.

The most important point, however, is that the dog almost certainly does not notice details of the signal. For human beings who speak English there is an important difference between, for example, *walkies* and *talkies*, and this is parallel to the difference between *will* and *till* and between *wool* and *tool*. This is not because of any similarity in the difference of meaning between the pairs of words, but because the first word in each pair begins with a *w* and the second word in each pair begins with a *t*. The essence of human language is that it uses sounds that have no meaning in themselves to distinguish groups of these sounds that can have an associated meaning. Linguists call the sounds that can be used for this purpose *phonemes*. Each language has its own set of phonemes and its rules for combining them into sequences. Linguists call the groups of sounds that have an associated meaning *morphemes*. Many morphemes are what we think of as words, but some morphemes are parts of words. All human languages consist of sets of morphemes, which are made up of phonemes. Nothing we know about the ways in which animals communicate either among themselves or with human beings suggests that animals pay attention to the differences in sounds (phonemes) that are basic to all human languages. As we shall see, it takes children some time and effort to discover and use the phonemes of the language they will grow up to speak.

One of the ways in which the nature of language becomes clearer is by looking at what children do and what happens to them as they progress from being *infants* (literally "nonspeaking" from the Latin participle *fans* "speaking" and the negative prefix *in-*) to being fluent speakers who can use the language in all its marvelous variety and for an almost infinite number of purposes. There is, however, a danger in this approach. As adults, because we have a very strong notion of what it is to know a language, it is hard to put ourselves in the situation of imagining what it would be like to find out how language is organized without having that knowledge in advance. In fact, the task has been seen as so daunting that some scholars have argued that children must be born with a knowledge of the essential nature of language because they would never be able to work it out for themselves on the basis of the evidence provided by the environment in which they are growing up. The extent to which this is the correct view is a matter of dispute, but one thing is clear: a young child's language is like a foreign language to adults—but with the important difference that it is a language we can never learn. There are no instructors in child language listed in the yellow pages of the telephone directory. We can only observe, and observation is a very indirect way of finding out about language. Nevertheless, by looking at what children do when faced with the task of finding out how to become fluent speakers of a language, we may come to a clearer understanding of what it is we have succeeded in doing, though we have no recollection of how we did it.

Learning One's First Language

"A child is a strange thing," said Cassius. . . . "It is a natural thing," said his wife. "That is why it strikes a civilised person as strange."

Ivy Compton-Burnett, *The Present and the Past*

When we say that someone has learned a language, what has happened to that person? What has that individual done and what has been done to him or her? What has been learned and at what point can we say that the process is complete? What part do imitation and practice play in the learning process and what is the contribution of the environment? What is the importance of intelligence in language learning? Is there an age at which it is easier to learn a language and, if so, what is that age? Is there a difference between learning one's first language and learning a second one? Why does anyone learn a language? Questions such as these are critical for anyone interested in language development.

In the first place it is obvious that children do not create language totally anew nor do they learn language like a parrot by memorizing complete utterances, though in the early stages they may do a little of both. More often children's early utterances bear a clear relationship to utterances in the adult language while differing enough to show that they are not straightforward imitations, as can be seen in the following examples:

salt all shut	is it was a snake?
sleepy bed	her got hurt in the face
wear mitten no	anybody isn't here
I didn't did it	why kitty can't stand up?

It is extremely unlikely that the children who produced these remarks were repeating accurately something an adult had said. In fact, even when children are asked to repeat something exactly, they will often make changes by omitting words or parts of words and sometimes they will change the order of the words. The kinds of changes that children make depend upon the stage they have reached in their language development. Similarly, the length and complexity of the utterances that the children produce depend upon their stage of development. All children begin with one-word utterances, go on to two-word utterances, and gradually, as their language develops, they are able to produce (and understand) longer and more complex constructions. Moreover, the manner in which children's language develops is not haphazard but systematic and, to a certain degree, predictable, although there is considerable variation among children. Perhaps the most remarkable aspect of children's language development is that it follows a coherent pattern even though at times the forms are very different from those in the adult language.

In fact, it is curious that children are usually satisfied with a rough approximation to what an adult would say and do not try to perfect any single utterance before moving on to the next. One might expect children to practice a few phrases until they could say them as well as most adults, and then move to mastery of a few more phrases. But it is fairly obvious why this does not happen. If children concentrated on only a few utterances, they would be limited in the topics they could talk about. As it is, parents soon become fairly expert in interpreting what it is that their child has said, though they may not always get it right. Children do differ, however, in the accuracy with which they produce the sounds of the language they are learning. Some children seem happy with very rough approximations to the sounds in the adult language, whereas others come much closer to the adult model.

There is another, more fundamental, reason why children do not practice imitating adult utterances. If all they learned to do was imitate what had already been said, they would never become fluent speakers of the language. As adults we do not have a set of ready-made utterances (like a foreign language phrase book) from which to choose when we speak. Instead we have the ability to produce and understand utterances that we have never heard before. For example, to illustrate this point I once produced the following sentence:

> Karl Marx was playing bridge with Abraham Lincoln, Winston Churchill, and Mary Queen of Scots when Tarzan walked in.

I assumed that none of my readers had ever encountered this particular sentence before but I also knew that anyone who speaks English would be able to understand it. The ability to produce and understand utterances we have never heard before is sometimes referred to as *linguistic competence.*

One way of looking at linguistic competence is to think of it as a set of rules. Language is the prime example of human behavior that is both rule-governed and, at the same time, infinitely adaptable to new situations. What does it mean to say that language is rule-governed? Simply that it is systematic. Two simple examples may help to illustrate this point.

Suppose someone reads out the following lists of numbers to a group of people and asks them to repeat them after a short pause:

> 248163264128256
> 3927812437292187
> 416642561024409616384

Most people would probably not get much further than the sixth or seventh digit in each case, but one woman gets all three sequences right. Does this mean that she has a better memory than the others? Possibly, but there is another more plausible explanation and that is that she has grasped the secret of each sequence. This becomes more apparent if the figures are displayed like this:

2, 4, 8, 16, 32, 64, 128, 256
3, 9, 27, 81, 243, 729, 2187
4, 16, 64, 256, 1024, 4096, 16384

In each case the sequences of digits is produced by multiplying the first number by itself and then multiplying the answer by the original number and so on. Once the principle of organization is grasped, it would be possible to recognize and repeat even longer sequences of digits. Similarly, we are likely to find an utterance in an unfamiliar language difficult to repeat because we do not know the system by which it is organized.

The second example (table 2.1) illustrates the creative nature of linguistic competence. The rules of the Simple Language Device are very simple. Choose one item from column A and combine it with one item from each of the following columns and you will automatically produce an English sentence provided that the order A to F is maintained. With a total of only eighty words the Simple Language Device has the capacity to produce 531,441 sentences, enough for five books as long as this one. Of course, not all the sentences will be very plausible but that does not make them ungrammatical. The Simple Language Device has only a small number of words and one very simple rule for combining them into sentences. As adult speakers we have a much larger number of words and quite a few rules for combining them into acceptable utterances. It is easy to see how immense the creative capacity of our language is. If the Simple Language Device can produce over half a million sentences, it is not surprising that the capacity of our linguistic competence is infinitely vast. We can begin to grasp some of the complexity of this system by considering what confronts infants as they begin the long task of becoming fluent speakers of the language spoken by those around them. The next eight chapters will be devoted to various aspects of this task.

First, however, it is necessary to emphasize that, as adults, we can offer infants limited assistance in this task, however well-meaning we may be. Obviously, we

TABLE 2.1. Simple Language Device

A	B	C	D	E	F
Suddenly	several	naked	giraffes	ran	into the room
Slowly	six	hairy	Martians	jumped	out of the box
Without warning	those	bold	students	slipped	between the houses
Amazingly	some	blue-blooded	dalmatians	fled	from behind the trees
Reluctantly	the	laughing	duchesses	skipped	down the road
Carefully	a few	dark	boys	crawled	over the hill
Fortunately	a great many	bald	lawyers	darted	through the tunned
Cunningly	twenty-two	unscrupulous	octogenarians	danced	across the bridge
In due course	innumerable	dirty	feminists	limped	up the street

cannot use language to give explanations to a child who does not know the language. More important, we do not know what will be most useful to the child at a particular stage of development. Although researchers have discovered a great deal about the stages that children go through in their language development, we still have no clear understanding of how children find out what they need to know, and they are also incapable of telling us. This does not mean that how adults behave around children does not affect what happens, but it is not the only factor. Children are very actively engaged in developing fluency in a language and they succeed under a very wide range of different conditions. It seems to be as natural for children to learn to speak as it is for birds to learn to sing.

The Act of Communicating

Language then has the strange striking characteristic of not having entities that are perceptible at the outset and yet of not permitting us to
doubt that they exist and that their functioning constitutes it.

Ferdinand de Saussure, *Course in General Linguistics*

The first thing the child has to discover is that it is possible to communicate with
other beings. Children usually find this out fairly quickly when their cries produce some kind of response. Mothers and other caregivers also often set up small
communicative routines, such as peek-a-boo, in which the child learns to respond
to certain cues. Children also soon learn to recognize not only faces but also facial
expressions and to associate these expressions with different moods. It has also
been suggested that the early routine of feeding sets a pattern of turn-taking long
before the infant is capable of any kind of conversational exchange. Mothers are
often anxious to encourage any response from the infant that can be interpreted as
intentional communication. The following is an exchange between a mother and a
three-month-old girl:

MOTHER	DAUGHTER
	(smiles)
Oh what a nice little smile!	
Yes, isn't that nice?	
There.	
There's a nice little smile.	(burps)
What a nice wind as well!	
Yes, that's better, isn't it?	
Yes.	
Yes.	(vocalizes)
Yes!	
There's a nice noise.	

At this age the child is no more capable of understanding the language than the
dog is of grasping its name, but that does not prevent adults from talking to very
young children as if they could understand. Any kind of sound or facial expression,
sneeze, cough, burp, or yawn may be responded to as if the child had made a

conversational remark. The mother, of course, knows that these noises are not part of language. This is something the child has to find out.

As adults we know that communication can be through any of the senses (see figure 3.1). The most direct is touch. A punch on the nose, a hug, or a kiss conveys the message very directly. The extent to which Western societies believe that smell communicates can be seen in the perfume and deodorant business. Even taste can be used; we sugar the pill to make it palatable. The two most important senses for human communication, however, are sight and hearing.

We communicate visually in many ways from the decoration of our rooms to the car we drive, from the length of our hair to the clothes we wear. The role of uniforms in signaling authority is obvious. Posture and gait also can send messages; again, the military provides examples. By smiling, frowning, or looking puzzled, we can send important messages, but the most flexible visual signaling system (leaving aside writing, which is a special case, and will be dealt with in chapter 15) is through gestures. By pointing, beckoning, nodding, shaking a fist, waving, and so on,, we can express a large number of very specific messages. Most of these signals are conventional and may vary from society to society, but there are also involuntary gestures, such as scratching one's nose, rubbing one's eye, changing posture, or crossing one's legs, that may give indications of our impatience.

Not to be confused with these visual forms of communication are the varieties of sign language (such as American Sign Language) used by the hearing-impaired. Sign language systems are as complex and structured as spoken languages and as capable of dealing with the total range of communicative functions. At many scholarly conferences, sign language interpreters can be seen translating highly abstruse and dense spoken reports into sign. There used to be great prejudice against signing by those responsible for the education of hearing-impaired children because it was thought that they would make little effort to understand or use spoken language. However, recent scholarship has emphasized the crucial role of language acquisition for cognitive and emotional development, regardless of the channel used. As a result, hearing-impaired children are now encouraged to master any form of language in which they can find out and communicate about the world around them.

The primary channel for most human communication, however, is acoustic. In evolutionary terms it is easy to see why this should be the case. Auditory communication works in the dark and other situations in which the participants cannot see each other. Obviously, not all the sounds that we produce are part of language. In addition to the various sounds that our bodies produce involuntarily, we can clap our hands, stamp our feet, and whistle. The sounds that come out of the mouth, however, are most important, and here the child has to learn to distinguish between those sounds which are part of language and those which are not. Coughs, sneezes, belches, and yawns have to be ignored. The child also has to learn that there are differences in the noises that do not directly affect the meaning of what is said. In this respect, it does not matter how loudly or softly, how quickly or slowly, how hesitantly or fluently the noises are made, although such aspects are an important part of the total communication. Linguists call these aspects *paralinguistic features* and, while there are many ways in which their occurrence is more predictable than one might expect, they are not parts of the linguistic signal.

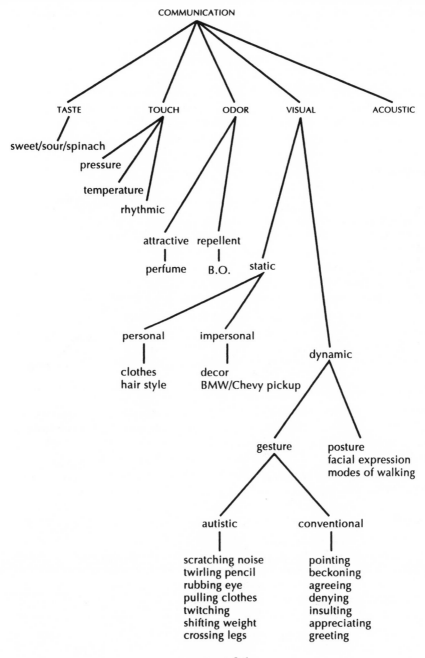

FIGURE 3.1a

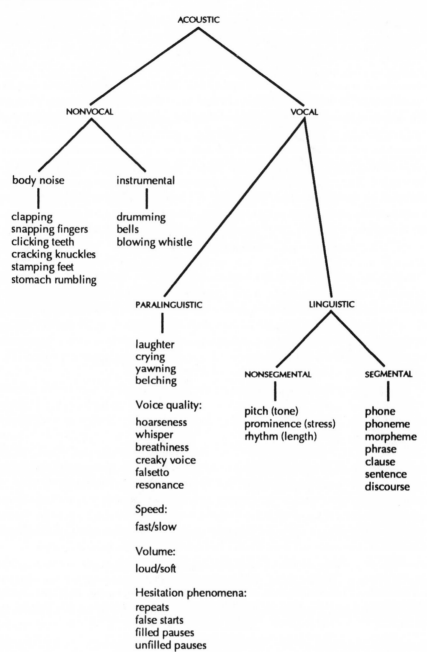

ACOUSTIC

NONVOCAL

VOCAL

body noise

instrumental

clapping
snapping fingers
clicking teeth
cracking knuckles
stamping feet
stomach rumbling

drumming
bells
blowing whistle

PARALINGUISTIC

LINGUISTIC

laughter
crying
yawning
belching

NONSEGMENTAL

SEGMENTAL

Voice quality:

hoarseness
whisper
breathiness
creaky voice
falsetto
resonance

pitch (tone)
prominence (stress)
rhythm (length)

phone
phoneme
morpheme
phrase
clause
sentence
discourse

Speed:

fast/slow

Volume:

loud/soft

Hesitation phenomena:
repeats
false starts
filled pauses
unfilled pauses

FIGURE 3.1b

The most important point is that the child has to discover the phonetic character of language. The discovery that a limited number of noises can be used to convey particular meanings is the essential first step in understanding the nature of language, since language is a mode of expressing meanings through sound. The child has to discover that communicative noises may differ from each other only partially (for example, *pin/bin/tin/din/sin/thin/fin/gin/chin/kin/win*). In these words there are two sounds [I] and [n] that are the same but the sound that precedes them in each case is different. A list of phonetic symbols is given on pp. 225–26. Each of these words has a distinct meaning and their individuality is signaled by the different initial sounds. Note that some sounds, *th* and *ch*, are represented by two letters but the writing system is misleading in this respect. (The relationship between writing and speaking will be examined in chapter 15.) Sounds that are capable of indicating a difference of meaning are called *phonemes*. The child must discover which sounds are phonemes in the language because each language has a different set of phonemes. Languages may differ in the kinds of sounds they use but also in the ways in which the sounds are used. For example, French and Portuguese have nasal vowels (vowels that are produced by allowing the sound to escape through the nose as well as through the mouth). These vowels are phonemes in French and Portuguese. In English vowels may be nasalized before or after a nasal consonant such as [m] or [n], but these nasalized vowels are not phonemes in English. They are merely variants of the oral vowels (that is, the vowels produced by allowing the sound to escape only through the mouth). Variants of phonemes are called *allophones* and many phonemes have two or more allophones.

For example, the phoneme /t/ in English has several allophones. (It has become conventional to write phonemes between slant lines /t/ and allophones between square brackets [t].) In a word such as *ton* the /t/ is pronounced with a slight puff of air after it like a very lightly pronounced /h/. This puff of air is called *aspiration*. The /t/ in the word *stun*, however, does not have this following puff of air, that is, it is not aspirated. It is a general rule of English that the sounds /p/, /t/, and /k/ are aspirated at the beginning of words but not aspirated after the sound /s/. This is something that most speakers of English do not notice because it is not a phonemic difference, but speakers of other languages are more likely to notice it. In particular, speakers of languages such as Thai and Korean, where the difference between aspirated and unaspirated consonants is phonemic, will notice it at once.

There is another allophone of /t/ that has become increasingly common in the speech of many inhabitants of British cities, and that is the glottal stop, which is produced by a closure in the vocal cords rather than in the mouth. (It is often heard in American speech in the word *mountain* and sometimes in *bottle*.) This is an allophone of /t/ in English, but in languages such as Arabic and Tagalog glottal stops are phonemic.

Learning the phonemic distinctions of the other language is one of the most important tasks in trying to master a foreign language. Until we have succeeded in that, there is a great risk that we shall not be able to make ourselves understood. However, until we have mastered, if we ever do, the allophonic variants, we shall have a "foreign accent."

The infant's first vocal noises are forms of crying and a variety of noises such as spluttering and burping. At about six to eight weeks the infant usually has a small repertoire of calls that are often described as "cooing," perhaps because of the frequency of [u] sounds in these vocalizations. These cooing sounds are apparently signs that the infant is comfortable, and it is likely that the infant is, to some extent, using them deliberately.

Gradually the young child begins to use a fairly wide variety of vocal noises, many of which sound very similar to syllables in adult speech, and often sequences of these noises have an intonation pattern that makes them sound like utterances in the adult language. This state is called *babbling* and precedes the point at which the child can be said to be using language. Many of the combinations of sounds produced in babbling are similar to those the child uses early in linguistic development, particularly in the frequency of single consonant-vowel (CV) syllables. It is possible that this babbling serves an important purpose in allowing children to practice using their speech organs in a way that will later be useful to them, although the role of babbling in language development is far from clear. In babbling it is not known whether the child is actually attempting to produce a particular sequence of sounds or cares how closely one syllable resembles or differs from another. In speech, even at the earliest stage, the child is apparently aiming at consistency in the use of a word, even though there will be much variation in the actual phonetic forms produced by the child for that word. The differences between babbling and speech are largely a matter of control.

A simple comparison may help to illustrate the difference. Even if you have never had a piano lesson in your life, you can sit down at a piano and produce sequences of notes simply by letting your fingers run over the keys. In this way you may produce short sequences that sound tuneful, though you may not be able to reproduce those sequences at will. However, when you take lessons and start to control your fingers so as to produce a certain sequence, you will probably need to limit yourself at first to a small number of sequences to get them right. You will no longer be producing the wide variety of "tunes" that you did when you were just running your fingers over the keyboard, but you have taken the first step that may ultimately result in your becoming an accomplished pianist. This roughly parallels what the child does in learning to speak—with the significant difference that not all of those who take piano lessons end up as pianists whereas all normal children learn to speak.

The order in which the child learns to produce sounds is predictable up to a point. It is probably not an accident that many of the words for mother, father, and other close relatives are similar in a wide variety of languages:

		MOTHER	FATHER
English		mama, mommy	papa, daddy
Russian		mama	papa
Romanian		mama	tata
Welsh		mam	tad
Bulgarian		baba ("grandmother")	
Turkish			baba
Pima	American	ma	mas
	Indian		
Laguna	Languages	nana ("grandmother")	papa ("grandfather")

The simplest sounds for the child to produce are apparently those produced with the lips, [p], [b], and [m], and those produced by putting the tip of the tongue against or slightly behind the back of the upper teeth, [t], [d], and [n]. The first syllables usually consist of one consonant followed by one vowel. It also seems to be the case that the easiest way for the child to make a short word longer is by repeating the same syllable. Thus words such as *mama, papa, dada*, and *tata* are relatively easy for children to produce, and it is not surprising that words of this kind should form part of the child's early vocabulary.

It also not surprising that sounds and combinations of sounds that are easy for children to produce should also be found widely in the languages of the world. All languages have syllables consisting of a consonant followed by a vowel (CV) but some languages (such as Samoan) have only CV syllables. English, on the other hand, has syllables with up to three consonants before the vowel (*spring*) and up to four after it (*sixths*). It is not the case, however, that any three consonants can occur at the beginning of an English syllable. As in so many other respects, there are rules and they are called *phonotactic rules*.

If a word in English begins with three consonants, the first consonant must be /s/ and the second /p/, /t/, or /k/. (Note that we are referring to sounds, not letters, so /k/ may be spelled with a *c*.) The third consonant will also be one of a small set but the rule is slightly more complicated. Thus we have words such as:

split
strike
scream

but not

*zblit
*zdrike
*zgream

There are also rules for combinations of two consonants in English. Combinations of two or three consonants are not possible in many languages, whereas other languages have combinations of consonants that are not possible in English. The examples in the list marked with an asterisk (used to indicate a form that is not found in the language) are quite easy to pronounce, so what combinations occur in a language is not simply a matter of pronounceability. Some consonants are, however, inherently easier than others to pronounce.

A simple experiment will demonstrate this. If I ask you to bring thumb and index finger together until they are touching lightly, you will not find this a difficult task. But if I ask you to bring them together until they are about the thickness of a piece of paper apart, you will find this much more difficult. The reason is that the peripheral muscles in the first case simply have to send back a message to the brain saying that contact has been made; in the second case the messages are more complex and contradictory: "Closer!" "Not so close!" "Closer again!" In fact, in trying to keep your finger and thumb separate at about the thickness of a piece of paper, you will probably bring them in contact from time to time and then over-correct by opening them much wider than you want.

Certain consonants, for example, [p], [b], [t], [d], [k], and [g], are produced by making a firm closure in the mouth that interrupts the air-stream coming from the lungs. They are known as *stop consonants*. This closure is caused by bringing the lips together for [p] and [b] or making firm contact between part of the tongue and the roof of the mouth for the others. Children generally find sounds such as these relatively easy to produce and they are found in most of the world's languages. Other consonants are produced by bringing, for example, the tip of the tongue close to but not actually touching the roof of the mouth to produce the [s] and [z] sounds. Sounds of this kind are called *fricatives* and they require more complex muscular control. Children usually do not begin to use them until they have succeeded with some of the stop consonants. The most difficult consonants include [l], [r], and [č] (the first sound in *chin*), [ǰ] (the first sound in *gem*), [š] (the first sound in *ship*), [ž] (the middle consonant in *measure*), [θ] (the first sound in *thumb*), and [ð] (the first sound in *them*), though not necessarily in that order. It is not surprising that young children often at first avoid words that contain more difficult sounds, even though the objects they refer to must be quite familiar to the children (for example, *finger* and *thumb*, *juice* and *cheese*). It is also not surprising that some of the sounds that English-speaking children find difficult do not occur in all the languages of the world. For example, children learn the /l/ and /r/ sounds relatively late, and these sounds are not found in all languages. Japanese, for example, has only /r/ and Cantonese only /l/. Even in English there are important dialect differences in the use of these two sounds.

If you put your hands over your ears and pronounce the sounds [ssss] and [zzzz] in succession you will notice an obvious difference. In the production of the [zzzz] sounds you will hear a buzzing in your ears that does not occur during the production of the [ssss] sounds. This buzzing is actually produced in the throat by the vibration of the vocal cords, which are the "lips" at the top of the windpipe that, among other things, prevent food from getting into the lungs. Just as when you close your lips firmly air cannot enter or leave your mouth, so when the vocal cords are tightly closed nothing can enter or leave the lungs. However, if you close your lips lightly and blow you will produce a noise that is often considered rude. In a similar fashion, when the vocal cords are loosely closed and we force air out of the lungs, we produce the buzzing sound that distinguishes [z] from [s]. This buzzing sound is known as *voicing*, and speech sounds are mostly classified as either *voiced* (with the vocal cords vibrating) or *voiceless* (with the vocal cords apart, allowing the air to pass out freely).

The difference between voiced and voiceless sounds is fundamental to human language, and all languages use both kinds of sounds, although the kinds of sounds and the ways in which they are used vary from language to language. Vowels are generally voiced but consonants can be either. In the early stages, children learning English do not make a systematic distinction between voiced consonants ([b, d, g, v, z]) and their voiceless counterparts ([p, t, k, f, s]). For example, they will use either [p] or [b] apparently indifferently. This is because they have not yet learned to make the phonemic distinction between /p/ and /b/. Gradually they learn to make this distinction, at first at the beginning of words, then in the middle of words, and finally at the end of words. Similarly, adults learning a second language will have difficulty in making a distinction between a pair of voiced and voiceless consonants if their own language does not have this distinction.

Children often substitute sounds that they find easier to produce for those they find more difficult. For example, one two-year-old girl said [nam] for *thumb* and [bap] for *lamb*. These examples also show how it is not only individual sounds that children find difficult but also combinations of sounds. Both [n] and [m] are nasal consonants produced with the air passing out through the nose; both [b] and [p] are oral consonants produced with the air passing out through the mouth. At the same stage she also said [u:pud] for *apron*. This was not because she could not pronounce [n] but because at that time she had difficulty in pronouncing a word with both a nasal and an oral consonant.

In omitting certain sounds or in replacing one sound by another, children are not behaving perversely or being careless about the sounds they use. They are in the process of mastering a highly complex set of integrated muscular movements, and it takes time to learn to coordinate the movements correctly. As adults we have been doing this so long and so well that we do not realize what an achievement it is. It is only when we try to learn new sounds or new combinations of sounds in another language that we find out how complex the whole business is.

Children, however, may be aware of distinctions in the sounds adults make even when they cannot make them themselves. One boy who regularly said *mouse* for *mouth* would not accept that pronunciation from his father, and there were many examples showing that he could distinguish pairs of words in adult speech that sounded the same when he said them. This ability to discriminate sounds helps to explain why, when children learn how to make a new distinction in their speech, they usually do not extend it in the wrong places. Thus when this boy finally succeeded in saying *mouth* instead of *mouse*, he did not at the same time begin to say *houth* instead of *house*.

The process of mastering the system of speech sounds in a language takes time and may not be fully achieved until the age of seven or eight, but the basic system is usually well established by about four. Until it is fully established, strangers may have difficulty in understanding what the child says, and part of the motivation for the child to speak more clearly may be increased contact with adults and older children outside of the immediate family. The rate at which this happens depends more upon the child than on any efforts of adults to insist on the correct pronunciation. As with many other aspects of language development, children have to find their own way, and the amazing thing is that they do it very well.

Prosodic Features

It ain't what you say but the way that'cha say it.

Popular song by Sy Oliver and James Young

In singing the pitch of the voice rises and falls as the singer follows the melodic line. In fact, for many people this is the most important part of singing; we often enjoy a song in another language even if we cannot understand the words. In speech, most people tend to take the opposite view and think of the words as the only important part and the melodic line as mere decoration. Possibly because of the powerful influence of the alphabetic writing system (see chapter 15), even linguists have tended to concentrate on the segmental aspects of speech, that is, on the individual sounds (phonemes), words, parts of words (morphemes), and ways of combining them into larger units (syntax). There are, however, other aspects of speech that are as important as—and, in many cases, may be more crucial than— the sounds and words themselves. Utterances may contain very different messages depending upon the tone of voice in which they are delivered (see chapter 10). Most of the factors that contribute to the tone of voice have been investigated under the heading *prosodic features* (or *suprasegmental features*).

One of these features is the *length* (duration) of a sound. This can be a feature of both consonants and vowels. It is customary in marking -long consonants to double the symbol, for example, [tt], but with vowels a colon is often used to indicate length, for example, [i:], though sometimes the vowel is doubled [ii]. (The latter method is usually chosen in tone languages when there may be different tones on each part of the vowel.) Length can be used to indicate differences of meaning, as in these examples from Tewa, an Azteco-Tanoan language spoken in New Mexico:

/si/	"six"	/si:/	"intestine"
/su/	"arrow"	/su:/	"wild spinach"
/te/	"wagon"	/te:/	"tree"

In Italian, double consonants can distinguish words as in:

| fato | "fate" | fatto | "done" |
| poro | "pore" | porro | "wart" |

A Portuguese tenor told me about his embarrassment during his opera debut at La Scala. By holding on the [l] sound in *su questo cielo* ("under this sky"), what he sang sounded to the Italians like *su questo ucello* ("under this bird"). He said the audience burst out laughing and the soprano singing with him found it hard to continue. In languages where length is not used to distinguish words, it can be used for expressive purposes, and the singer had transferred this practice from his native Portuguese into Italian, where it is not appropriate.

Length is not significant for distinguishing words in English but in most dialects of English* there is a difference between vowels that can occur in a monosyllable without a following consonant and those that cannot. For example, the vowels in the words in (a) are all slightly longer than those in (b):

a.	bee, beat	[i]
	bay, bait	[e]
	new, nude	[u]
	go, goad	[o]
	law, laud	[ɔ]
b.	bit	[ɪ]
	bet	[ɛ]
	bat	[æ]
	boot	[U]
	cot	[ɒ]

The vowels in (b) can occur only in *closed syllables*, that is, those syllables that end in a consonant, but even in closed syllables the vowels in (a) are slightly longer. The vowel in *beat* is slightly longer than the vowel in *bit*. Other factors, however, affect the length of vowels. Vowels made with the tongue higher in the mouth tend to be shorter than those made with the tongue lower in the mouth. The vowel in *seed* will be slightly shorter than the vowel in *sawed*. Vowels also tend to be shorter before voiceless consonants than before voiced consonants (for example, the vowel in *leaf* is shorter than the vowel in *leave*), and shorter before stop consonants than before fricatives (*seed* versus *seethe*). These differences in length are very slight but they probably help the listener to decipher the signal, particularly in noisy conditions. Vowels also tend to be longer when stressed.

Stress (or prominence) is the degree of force with which a sound or syllable is perceived to be uttered. It is a subjective notion because speech sounds have different carrying power. While there is disagreement as to how many degrees of stress are significant in English, it is generally agreed that there are at least three: primary, secondary, and weak. All three occur in words such as *elevator* with primary stress on the first syllable, secondary stress on the third syllable, and weak (or the absence of) stress on the second and fourth syllables. Stress can have a grammatical function, as in the following pairs of words in English:

---

*A notable exception is Scots, where there are different rules for lengthening vowels. This can cause problems for speakers of other dialects even when the phonetic quality of the vowels does not.

NOUN	VERB
INsult	inSULT
TORment	torMENT
CONvict	conVICT

Stress can also distinguish compounds from free phrases:

the WHITE House	the white HOUSE
BLACKboard	black BOARD
FOREpaws	four PAWS

In English stress also plays an important role in intonation.

Intonation is the rise and fall of the pitch of the voice during an utterance. Differences in pitch are caused by differences in the rate of vibration of the vocal cords, producing variation in the fundamental frequency of the vocal tone. It is generally the case that women's voices are higher in pitch than men's, about an octave on average. This is caused by the fact that the vibrating part of the vocal cords is about a third longer in men than in women. This is one of the few significant differences in speech that has a physiological origin. The sex difference does not exist before puberty. It is the lengthening of the vocal cords at puberty that causes boys' voices to "break." The absolute differences in pitch, however, are not what is important for language but the variations in pitch during an utterance.

Differences in pitch (or tone) can be used to distinguish words or morphemes (lexical tone) and to distinguish phrases or sentences (intonation). As was illustrated in chapter 1, in the Chinese language words that are the same in segmental form— for example *ma*—can have different meanings depending upon the tone. Many languages in different parts of the world, including Africa, Asia, and both American continents use tones in this way. Tonal distinctions are not common in Indo-European languages.

The use of intonation, however, is widespread. There are three important attributes of intonation. It is meaningful (it makes a difference which intonation you use). It is systematic (we learn a limited number of pitch patterns as part of language acquisition). It is language specific (the intonation patterns are not the same in different languages and similarities can be misleading). We can usually make allowances for a foreigner's inability to reproduce exactly the sounds of our language but we may misinterpret "mistakes" in intonation as signaling a particular attitude.

In English, intonation has three functions: grammatical, accentual, and attitudinal. Grammatical differences can be illustrated by the following example:

When he approaches the girls don't pay any attention to him.

Printed like this there is no way to know which of two possible utterances was produced. By punctuation, which is sometimes (but not always) a guide to intonation, we can distinguish two possible versions:

a. When he approaches, the girls don't pay any attention to him.
b. When he approaches the girls, don't pay any attention to him.

In (a) the pitch of the voice will drop at the end of *approaches* and jump up at *the girls*. In (b) the pitch of the voice will continue dropping while saying *the girls* and jump up at *don't*.

Another example of a rather different kind is:

John hit Peter and then Harry hit him.

In this form it is not clear whether Harry hit Peter or John, since *him* could refer to either. However, in speech there would be no ambiguity:

    a. John hit Peter and then HARRY hit him.
    b. John hit Peter and then Harry hit HIM.

In (a) it is clear that Harry hit Peter and in (b) that he hit John. This is because of a general principle in English that *new information* is stressed and *old information* is unstressed. In (a) the new information is that Harry also hit Peter, and the old information is that it was Peter (*him*) that was hit. In (b) the new information is that the person that was hit was John. The same kind of principle can be seen in the following exchange:

It would be very odd if Peter said *My NECK hurts* since it is clear that the topic is his neck. It is thus old information and should not receive stress. On the other hand, if John had simply said *How are you feeling?* Peter might appropriately say *My NECK hurts* because his neck had not been mentioned before and is thus new information. A more amusing example is:

If you think you've got PROBLEMS, come and SEE us.

In contrast to:

If you think YOU'VE got problems, come and see US.

These examples all show the interaction between stress and intonation. It is easier to illustrate these than many others because there is no simple way of indicating intonation in the writing system, but stress is not always critical. For example, if someone says *Would you like coffee or tea?* there is a big difference depending upon whether the pitch of the voice falls or rises on the word *tea*. If it falls, then you are being offered a choice between coffee and tea. If the pitch of the voice rises on both *coffee* and *tea*, then this is a kind of listing intonation in which there may be more alternatives to follow. In which case, if you want a beer or a fizzy drink, you may wait before responding to the question in the hope that more alternatives will follow.

Intonation can also be used in English for emphasis:

It was a very big SPIDER.
It was a very BIG spider.
It was a VERY big spider.
It WAS a very big spider.

This kind of emphatic intonation is not possible in many other languages (for example, French, in which most syllables receive the same amount of stress). Sometimes the emphasis carries with it other implications:

JACK likes fish. (John doesn't)
Jack likes FISH. (he doesn't like meat)
Jack LIKES fish. (it's not true that he doesn't like it)

Intonation is also used to indicate attitude:

I can't FIND one. (and I'm cross about it)—falling tone on *find*.
I can't find one. (perhaps you can)—falling-rising tone on *I*
I CAN'T find one. (I've tried)—falling tone on *can't*
I can't find ONE. (not even one)—falling tone on *one*
I can't find ONE. (there's one that I can't find)—falling-rising tone on *one*
I can't find one. (are you calling me a liar?)—rising from *I* to end
I can't FIND one. (and I don't care)—rising slightly from *find*
I can't FIND one. (very angry)—very low throughout

By intonation we signal how sure, sincere, and serious we are. In conversation we also use intonation to give turn-taking signals about whether we wish to continue speaking or are willing to have someone else take over, whether we wish to introduce a new topic or continue on the same one, and whether we expect agreement or opposition. We also can express politeness or rudeness, interest or boredom, sympathy or revulsion through intonation. In fact, intonation is probably the first aspect of language children (and dogs!) learn to respond to, and this may explain why it continues to play such an important role in the communication of emotion.

Learning About Words and Their Structure

I gotta use words when I talk to you.

T. S. Eliot, *Sweeney Agonistes*

Learning to perceive and produce the sounds (phonemes) of a language is one of the fundamental tasks in becoming a fluent speaker but it is only a means to an end. The sounds themselves are meaningless. Children have to realize that some of the noises made by adults refer to various aspects of the world in which the children find themselves. They have to notice that certain combinations of sounds occur repeatedly and that the adults seem to attach some significance to these combinations, for example, *Daddy, milk, down, no*. At first the child probably only has the vaguest glimmerings as to the significance these noises have for adults. It is also difficult for an adult to guess at what significance the child attaches to the utterance. One father was pleased that his daughter seemed to understand the question *Where is the baby?* by turning and looking at herself in the mirror, but she did exactly the same when he asked *Where is daddy?* We are back to the problem of the dog and its name.

It is not only with children and animals that there is a problem of knowing how much is understood. As adults we take it for granted that the people we are speaking to understand what we are saying in the way that we intend, and we are dismayed or shocked if we find out that they have not. It is, however, very difficult to know whether someone has understood or not. Take a very simple example. Suppose you are in a strange town and you stop and ask someone for directions. Very often the directions are so complex that you have difficulty in following them. Do you usually say: *I'm sorry I don't understand. Could you tell me again?* Perhaps you always do, but I know that I often simply thank the speaker and move on in the direction I think I have been told to go, hoping that things will become clearer as I go and leaving the direction giver the sense of having been helpful. I suspect that young children are frequently in this situation of not understanding clearly what an adult had said, but by luck or good judgment they usually succeed in behaving the way we expect and thus we assume that they understand.

As soon as they begin to speak, however, children can test their understanding, for example, by saying *milk* (or some approximation to the sound that the adult interprets as *milk*) and the adult either responds by saying *Yes, that's milk* or by giving the child some milk, or acting in some other way that confirms the relationship between the sound and the object. This is where the dog fails; no matter how loudly, repeatedly, or insistently it barks, we will not suddenly recognize its vocal production as *walkies* or some other word in our language. Parents are often anxious to report their child's "first word" but what this means is the first sound that the parents identify as corresponding to a word in the adult language. Very often parents are so impatient to hear this first word that they decide that a certain babbling sequence is *Daddy* or *Mummy* or *Nana*. However, such sequences do not become "words" until they are used repeatedly and consistently with the same reference. A word is neither the meaning alone nor the sound alone but the conventional association of the two.

That the sound alone does not constitute the word can be seen in the number of words that have the same sound, for example, *right, write*, and *rite*, but very different meanings. Words that sound the same but have different meanings are called *homophones*. The fact that we spell them differently makes it easier to recognize them in writing but in the spoken language they can be distinguished only by the context in which they occur. Surprisingly, there seldom seems to be a problem in knowing which word is used except in artificially constructed examples such as *The sons raise meat*, which is indistinguishable from *The sun's rays meet*. The example, however, illustrates an important point that cannot be stressed too much: the hearer is not simply a passive receptor for a message transmitted by the speaker. The hearer has to interpret the signal and decide, for example, whether the third word is the verb *raise* or a noun *rays*. The words themselves do not always come with clear labels saying "I am a verb" or "I am a noun."

In many languages, however, there are parts of words that help to identify the part of speech. In English, for example, the suffix *-ly* often indicates an adverb, *quickly, happily*, (but not always: *friendly*), *-ment* often indicates an abstract noun, *enjoyment*, and *-er* often occurs with nouns formed from verbs to indicate the person doing the action, *painter, speaker* (but not always, *hammer, bigger*). These parts of words that have a consistent meaning or function are called *morphemes*. Morphemes are of various types. Some morphemes are words that cannot be divided up into meaningful parts, for example, *dog, father, artichoke, rhinoceros*. These are free morphemes because they can occur alone without other morphemes attached to them. Free morphemes are sometimes classified into two categories: content words such as those just illustrated, and function words such as *to, the*, and *because*, but the distinction is not always easy to maintain. Morphemes such as the suffixes *-ly, -ment*, and *-er* or the prefixes *un-* and *dis-* that must be attached to another morpheme are known as bound morphemes, of which there are two types. Some, like these suffixes and prefixes, are used to make new words from existing ones. For example, from the verb *employ* we can create the nouns *employer, employee*, and *employment*. These kinds of bound morphemes are called derivational morphemes, and languages differ in the ways in which they can create new words in this manner. In English we often create new words by using Greek or Latin words as in *telephone* from the Greek words for "distant" and "speaking";

in German the corresponding word *Fernsprecher* was created by using the German words for "far" and "speaker."

Children do not have to concern themselves with derivational morphology. It is enough if they can identify a sequence of sounds as a word. This may not seem to be a very difficult task, but as adults we have become accustomed to the notion of words as separate from each other. This is partly because in the written form words are separated from each other by a space. In speech there may be no pause between words and it is only because hearers know where the pauses could occur that they can tell which words are being said. There is no audible difference between *an aim* and *a name* in normal speech, but the hearer will usually have no difficulty in deciding which the speaker intended because only one will be appropriate in the context. A problem arises only when the context fails to distinguish between two possibilities. For example, if I say *I saw Joe Nash yesterday* you might respond *I don't know Joan Ash. Who is she?* As adults we are most likely to experience this kind of situation when we are listening to someone speaking in a language which we know up to a point but not very well. Other examples in the history of the language show that hearers failed to recognize where a word began. The word *apron* belongs with *napery* and *napkin* but has lost its initial consonant, whereas *nickname* (from Middle English *ekename* "an additional name") has gained one. However, children seldom make mistakes of this kind and, if they do, they are likely to be corrected.

Children also have to notice that words occur in different forms: *cat/cats/cat's, walk/walks/walking/walked, big/bigger/biggest*. The suffixes *-s, -s, -s, -ing, -ed, -er*, and *-est* in these words belong to the category of grammatical morphemes. Note that *-s* is listed three times. Just as with free morphemes (or words), there can be homophones in bound morphemes. The *-s* of the plural in *cats* is different from the *-s* in *he walks*, which marks the subject of the verb as third-person singular, and also different from the possessive *-s* of *the cat's eyes*. Similarly, the *-er* of *bigger* is not the same as the *-er* of *singer*.

Languages vary as much in their morphology as in their phonology. In many languages there is grammatical gender, that is, every noun belongs to a formal class that affects the form of other words accompanying it. In Spanish, for example, masculine nouns often end in *-o* and feminine nouns in *-a*. The articles and adjectives accompanying the noun must agree with it in number and gender, so that in Spanish we have:

los hermanos buenos	"the good brothers"
las hermanas buenas	"the good sisters"

Here the *-o* signals masculine gender and the *-a* feminine gender, and the *-s* signals plural not only on the nouns but also on the articles and the adjectives. It is not only people or animals that have gender in Spanish but all nouns so that we have:

los libros buenos	"the good books"
las mesas buenas	"the good tables"

Some languages such as German have three genders, masculine, feminine, and neuter, and English speakers are sometimes surprised to find that *das Mädchen* "the girl" is neuter. Gender systems are not simply ways of indicating sex, however, but part of a grammatical system of marking which words are to be associated together. This can be seen very clearly, for example, in Swahili, which has seven noun classes (see chapter 28).

Gender systems, and grammatical morphology in general, are one of the most intriguing aspects of linguistic structure. Some languages have very complex morphology, which can be very difficult for adult learners to master. Languages that are easier for adults to learn, particularly pidgins and creoles (see chapter 32), have little or no grammatical morphology. Children do not find the task impossible but progress gradually through different stages of acquisition. The age at which children pass through these stages varies from child to child, but the order tends to remain more or less the same. Children usually learn the morphemes that have a fairly clear meaning (for example, the plural *-s*) before those whose significance is less obvious (for example, the third-person singular *-s* on present-tense verbs). Children also learn those aspects of language that are straightforward and regular before those that are complex and irregular.

In fact, this concern for regularity often leads children to make "mistakes" at a certain stage in their language development because they have not learned that there are irregularities in the adult language. For example, children learning English will often go through a stage when they say *comed* and *goed*, even though earlier they may have used the forms *came* and *went* correctly. The explanation for this apparent regression is that the child has learned the rule for forming the past tense of verbs such as *played* and *walked* and applies the same rule to all verbs, including the so-called irregular verbs (which are a residue of an earlier stage of the language). Mistakes of this kind are very helpful for understanding the process of language development because they show that children are not simply imitating what they hear but working out a system for speaking.

Discovering the Structure
of Language: Syntax

It takes much time and many steps for a child to arrive at ideas which
to us seem simple.

Hippolyte Taine, *"Acquisition of Language by Children"*

Children begin by producing utterances that consist of a single word, go on to
two-word utterances, and gradually develop the ability to produce longer and
more complex utterances. It is possible that this process is the result of the child's
developing short-term memory as a consequence of rapidly increasing brain size.
Human infants are born very immature in contrast, for example, to young horses
or sheep. For obvious survival reasons a young foal must be able to keep up with
its mother as the herd moves about. The human infant, like the kitten or puppy, is
helpless at birth and needs careful protection, nourishment, and preparation before
being allowed to venture forth alone. Unlike the kitten and the puppy, though, the
most spectacular development in the human infant during the period of immaturity
is the increase in brain size. During the first two years the infant's brain increases
ten times, and then continues growing until about the age of puberty. As it increases
in size the brain also becomes more complex. It is apparently this long period of
brain increase that allows the process of language development to proceed as
smoothly as it does.

At the one-word stage, children are particularly concerned with commenting
on the presence or absence of people and things. They also comment on their
disappearance and reappearance. At just under eighteen months old, one girl used
the following words most frequently: *there, up, more, down, no, gone,* and *baby.*
Contrary to what many people might have expected, most of these words are not
"naming" words (that is, nouns), though four months later she was using many
more nouns much more frequently.

Even at this stage there are indications that children use words with some
awareness of their grammatical function in the adult language. For example, it is
not uncommon for an exchange such as the following to take place:

CHILD: Daddy.
MOTHER: Where's Daddy?
CHILD: Gone.
MOTHER: Yes, Daddy's gone to the office.

Children at the one-word stage seem to distinguish people who can do things (agents) from the actions themselves and also from the things that can be acted upon (objects). They also seem to be aware of the notion of place. It is possible that children's understanding of these relationships helps them to work out the syntax of adult utterances.

The number of words the child knows gradually increases, but the rate of increase varies greatly. One girl who had a vocabulary of ten words at the age of thirteen months had increased that number to fifty words by the age of fifteen months. Another girl who knew ten words at the age of thirteen months did not reach a total of fifty words until she was twenty-two months old. The kinds of words the child learns may also vary. Some children are more interested in words that refer to objects or people, whereas others seem more concerned about the kinds of language that are useful in social interaction.

As the child's vocabulary increases, combinations of two words begin to emerge. These combinations are not random but usually have a structure that can be interpreted in terms of syntactic relations in the adult language. Some examples are given in table 6.1.

Children do not begin using all of these constructions at once. The first constructions are likely to be those that draw attention to the presence (*There doggie*), absence (*No milk*), or recurrence (*More cookie*) of an object or person. Then appear those constructions that involve people as agents (*Daddy go*), actions (*Dig hole*), and locatives (*Sit table*). These are followed by possession (*Mommy hair*) and attribution (*Doggie sad*). Many of the child's utterances can be understood only by guessing what is intended from the context, as for example when *Throw Daddy* is interpreted as *Throw it to Daddy*. The ability of adults to interpret the child's

TABLE 6.1. Syntactic Structures in Children's
Two-Word Utterances

Agent + action	Possessor + possession
Nicky bark	Lion song
Mommy push	My book
Action + direct object	Adjective + noun
Read book	Dead bee
Clean nose	Happy pumpkin
Action + place	Object + attribute
Sit chair	Knee wet
Walk street	Shoe tied

Note: In these examples the spelling does not indicate the child's pronunciation; which is often very different from the way an adult would say the words.

utterances successfully may be an important factor affecting the speed of the child's language development, because frequent failure to communicate is likely to be discouraging, whereas successful communication is rewarding in itself. On the other hand, in many societies adults make little attempt to interpret a child's unclear utterances, and the children manage to develop normal language just the same.

During the one-word and two-word stage it often becomes apparent that the child has a grasp of more complex structures but cannot express them in one utterance, perhaps because of short-term memory limitations. Thus the child may say *Daddy read* followed closely by *Read book* but does not put them together to produce the three-word utterance *Daddy read book.* The three-word stage will not be far away then, however. By the time the child is regularly producing utterances of three words and more, language development proceeds at a rapid rate. Up to the three-word stage, the child omits all the short, unstressed words such as articles or auxiliaries (function words) and also all the grammatical morphemes that indicate such notions as plurality, possession, or tense. This stage of the child's language is sometimes called *telegraphic speech* because of its similarity to the form of a telegram. Since the cost of telegram was calculated on the number of words, it became a common practice to omit unimportant words while preserving the normal word order. This is what children at this stage do. Gradually, they begin to use the omitted words and morphemes.

In English the first grammatical morpheme to be regularly used is the progressive *-ing* suffix as in *Daddy working,* but it is much later before the child consistently uses an auxiliary verb as well, as in *Daddy's working.* It is hardly surprising that children should learn to use this form early as it is so important. In English there are two forms of the present tense. There is what is sometimes known as the *simple present* as in *John paints.* This form of the verb, despite its name, is not used to refer to something that is happening at the present moment. Instead we use the *present progressive* form, *John is painting,* for this purpose. The simple form *John paints* indicates either an ability that John has or an activity that he engages in regularly. This kind of observation is much less likely to be made by young children than a reference to something that is happening in the child's presence. There are, however, some verbs, known as *stative verbs,* that do not occur in the progressive form even when referring to the present moment. For example, we do not say **Peter is knowing her name* or **Mary is resembling her mother.* (The asterisk indicates that these examples are considered ungrammatical.) Interestingly, children do not make the mistake of using the *-ing* suffix with stative verbs.

The prepositions *in* and *on* are learned early, as is the plural morpheme, followed by the possessive morpheme as in *Daddy's shoe.* However, children are more likely to use the possessive morpheme correctly in utterances where it clearly distinguishes the meaning as in *That Daddy's.*

Children generally learn things that are obviously meaningful before those whose meaning is more obscure. For example, the plural morpheme *-s* in *dogs* and *cats* carries a much more obvious meaning than the third person singular *-s* in *He sings.* The latter morpheme is somewhat an anomaly in English and it is hardly surprising that both children and foreigners have difficulty in mastering it. It is only in the present tense that we make a difference between the third-person singular *He sings* and the other persons, *I sing, we sing,* and so on. In the past tense there is no difference, *He sang* versus *I sang,* nor with certain auxiliary verbs, for example, *He can* versus *I can, He must* versus *I must.* The third-person singular present-tense morpheme is a survival from the time that English was an inflected language with several suffixes to distinguish person and number (see chapter 26). There are also dialects in which this suffix has been lost or is rarely used.

Children also learn those aspects of the language that are simple and regular before those that are more complex or irregular. For example, most nouns in English form their plural by adding a single sound [s] if the final sound in the word is a voiceless consonant as in *cats, cups,* and *socks.* If the final sound in the singular form is voiced then [z] is added as in *dogs, knobs, beds, guns,* and *eyes.* However, words that end in a sibilant ([s, z, š, ž, č, or ǰ]) form their plural by adding a whole syllable [əz] as in *kisses, sneezes, wishes, garages, witches,* and *edges.* Children learn to use the simpler plurals in [s] and [z] before they learn to use the more complex plurals in [əz]. The notion of complexity is here based on the kinds of difficulties children appear to encounter, because adults may not be good judges of what is simpler or more complex for children. In fact, because there is no independent way of measuring simplicity or complexity in a language, claims that one language is easier or more difficult than another are not based on objective evidence. Since languages serve the same function in all societies, it is likely that they are equally complex, though one aspect (phonology, morphology, or syntax) may appear to be simpler in one language compared with another.

Languages, however, tend to have their own types of regular patterns or rules so that the child, having mastered the rule for one structure, is often able to find the same or similar rules elsewhere in the language. The rule for forming regular plurals also applies to the other two *-s* suffixes, the possessive morpheme and the third-person singular present morpheme. Since they have the same phonetic form, this is perhaps not surprising, and the similarity could account for the survival of the verbal suffix, which is the only inflectional suffix in the present tense remaining from the older system. A similar kind of pattern to the *-s* morpheme can be found in the rule for forming the past tense of regular verbs. Verbs with a voiceless final consonant take [t] as the past-tense morpheme, for example, *walked, missed,* and *slipped* (the spelling is misleading as can be noted from the fact that *missed* and *mist* are homophones). Verbs with a final voiced sound take [d] as the past-tense morpheme, for example, *tugged, showed,* and *rubbed.* The exceptions are verbs that end in [t] or [d] and add another syllable [əd], for example, *wanted, ended.* Although the past-tense morpheme is different phonetically from the plural morpheme, the principle is the same: a voiceless consonant is followed by a voiceless consonant, and a voiced sound is followed by a voiced consonant. As adults we have mastered these rules so effectively that we automatically apply them to new nouns and verbs without having to think about it. However, we know that there are exceptions to the general rules (for example, *feet, mice,* and *sheep; came, broke,* and *cut*). There are historical explanations for these so-called irregular forms, but this information is not available to the learner who must simply learn the exceptions. As pointed out earlier, children often have learned some of the irregular forms before they learn the rules for forming the regular plural or past tense. Thus, a child who has previously been using *feet* and *broke* correctly may later say *foots* and *breaked.* This process, which is sometimes called overregularization (though in fact it is simply regularization), shows that the child is not merely repeating what adults say but has developed rules for forming plurals and the past tense. The exceptions to the rules must be learned later. Children thus will follow an independent course in their language development, even if it means replacing a form that is correct in the adult language with one that is incorrect. The "mistakes" are a sign that the child's language development is progressing rather than the reverse.

Languages differ greatly in their morphology. Some languages have sets of grammatical morphemes that indicate whether a noun is the subject or object of a verb and other syntactic relationships. Old English was one such language (see chapter 26) but modern English retains this distinction only in the pronoun system (*he* versus *him*). English uses prepositions instead of suffixes for some of these relationships.

English also uses what are called *articles* to accompany many nouns. Some languages (Japanese, Russian) have no articles and others (French) use them rather differently. In English there are two articles: the definite article *the* and the indefinite article *a/an.* The rules for using these articles are extremely complex and this is one of the places where even a very fluent nonnative speaker of English may make mistakes. Children do not begin using the articles until they have learned some of the easier grammatical morphemes. This might surprise some people since the articles are very frequent in the language the children hear, more frequent in fact than most of the grammatical morphemes they have already learned. This is another clear indication that children do not simply imitate exactly what they hear.

In order to understand some of the complexity in the rules for using the articles, it is necessary to make a distinction between *mass nouns* and *count nouns.* Mass nouns are those that refer to materials in bulk or abstract concepts, for example, *milk, wheat, music, honesty.* Such nouns do not normally have a plural form, and they also do not usually occur with the indefinite article. We do not usually say *a wheat or **an honesty.* Count nouns, as their name implies, are those nouns that have a plural, for example, *cat, pen, singer, joke.* When these nouns are used in the singular they must be accompanied by an article. We would immediately recognize the following as examples of a foreigner's English:

I saw cat here yesterday.
I need pen to sign this.
He is very good singer.
She always makes joke out of it.

The difference in meaning between the definite and the indefinite articles is rather different from what their names might suggest. If I say *I saw a cat here yesterday,* that is no less definite than if I say *I saw the cat here yesterday.* In each case I am referring to a particular cat I saw. The difference is that in the second case, when I refer to *the cat,* I expect you to know which cat I mean. In the first case, when I say *a cat,* I have no such expectation, though you may know the cat very well. This is an example of how the speaker must take into consideration what the hearer knows (or can be expected to know). The importance of such expectations and the relationship between speaker and hearer will be examined later (see chapter 10).

The use of the articles, however, does not always indicate reference to a particular individual or object. For example, if I say *Mary wants to marry a handsome millionaire,* there is an ambiguity. It is possible that there is a particular individual, Henry Pearson, who is both very rich and good-looking, and that Mary wants to marry him. (His desires are irrelevant.) It is also possible that Mary has never seen far less met anyone of this description and she still could have this desire. It may even be a fact of the world that all handsome men are poor and all millionaires are ugly. This would not prevent Mary from wanting to marry a handsome millionaire any more than someone else can be prevented from wishing to see a unicorn. A similar ambiguity can occur with the definite article. Some years ago it would have been perfectly accurate for someone to say *The President of the United States is a respected figure,* even when Richard Nixon, the holder of the office at that time, was in disgrace. The phrase *the President of the United States* can either refer to the office itself or to the person occupying that office. These examples again illustrate a point that cannot be overemphasized. Meaning is not something that is expressed unequivocally by the language: all utterances require interpretation and some of the most important parts of the meaning are not conveyed directly by distinct forms. As a French philosopher referring to written language once remarked, much of the meaning lies in the spaces between the words.

More Syntax

Syntax is a faculty of the soul.

Paul Valery, *Analects*

Languages are fairly economical communication systems. One of the ways in which they achieve this economy is by using the same forms for different purposes, as we have seen with homophones such as *right, write, rite,* and so on, or with expressions such as *a handsome millionaire.* Another is by avoiding unnecessary repetitions. For example, suppose I tell you *I saw an elderly man with a long grey beard, a squint, and a limp carrying a tattered umbrella yesterday* and I wish to inform you of something this individual did, I do not need to say *and the elderly man with a long grey beard, a squint, and a limp carrying a tattered umbrella suddenly began shouting obscenities.* In fact, you would think it odd if I said that instead of *and he suddenly began shouting obscenities.* The word *he* can be used to replace a long phrase such as *an elderly man with a long grey beard, a squint, and a limp carrying a tattered umbrella.* Words of the type of *he* are called *pronouns,* although this is really a misnomer since what the pronoun replaces is not simply the noun *man* but the whole noun phrase of which it is a part. The crucial point here is that, in order to use and understand what the pronoun *he* refers to, both the speaker and the hearer have to recognize that *an elderly man with a long grey beard, a squint, and a limp carrying a tattered umbrella* is a single unit, of a particular kind. Utterances do not consist simply of sequences of words; the words are grouped into phrases and it is these phrases that are the units of syntax.

Let us take another example of avoidance of repetition. Suppose I wish to tell you *My sister recently bought a very large house with a beautiful garden and my brother recently also bought a very large house with a beautiful garden.* It is obvious that there is a lot of repetition here that would normally be avoided by saying *My sister recently bought a very large house with a beautiful garden and so did my brother.* Here *so did* has replaced the verb phrase *recently bought a very large house with a beautiful garden.* Just as words such as *he* can replace a noun phrase, the verb *do* can replace a verb phrase. The hearer, however, must be able to identify what *he* and *do* have replaced. If I begin a conversation by saying *So did he* you are unlikely to know who and what I am talking about. The process of referring back to something said earlier is called *anaphora,* and *he* and *so did* are anaphoric expressions. We use a variety of anaphoric expressions to avoid repeating what we have already said. For example, in *John went to live in the very depths of the country and while he was there he fell ill,* the word *there* is an anaphoric expression replacing *in the very depths of the country.*

We can also use pronouns in anticipation of a later noun phrase as in *Before he came in to fix the leaking boiler, the plumber turned off the water at the mains.* This anticipatory use of pronouns, which is known as *cataphora,* is much rarer than anaphora and there are complex rules about when a cataphoric expression can be used.

There is one further use of pronouns that must be mentioned here. We cannot use a simple pronoun referring back to the subject of a simple clause. If I say *John identified him,* the pronoun *him* must refer to someone other than John. If I had intended otherwise I would have to say *John identified himself.* Pronouns such as *myself, himself,* and so on are *reflexive pronouns,* and a number of complex rules govern their use. Normally, the reflexive pronoun refers to the subject of the clause, as in *John gave Mary a picture of himself,* but with "picture" nouns we can also say *John gave Mary a picture of herself,* although *Mary* is not the subject of the clause.

Children begin to use pronouns quite early, the first anaphoric pronoun usually being *it.* At about the same time come two pronouns that are not anaphoric but refer to the speaker and listener, *I/me* and *you.* These are called *indexical expressions* or *deictic expressions,* meaning those that point to something (see also chapter 10). What is peculiar about these expressions is that the person they refer to changes with the speaker (for this reason they have also been called *shifters*). Learning these two pronouns requires an immense imaginative leap and it is not surprising that children sometimes display some confusion about their use. One two-year-old boy used to say *Carry you* when he wanted one of his parents to carry *him.* It is clear where this confusion arose. His parents would say to him *Do you want me to carry you?* Either he did not understand the meaning of *you* or he thought that the verb was *carryyou;* in either case he had not mastered the distinction between *I/me* and *you,* though he would do so soon. Blind children take longer to learn this distinction, perhaps because they often speak by repeating what an adult has said. In the case of the pronouns *I* and *you,* repeating what the speaker has said confuses the reference to self and to the person addressed. The fact that sighted children generally master the distinction fairly easily is another piece of evidence that they are not simply imitating what is said to them.

As anyone who has been around young children who have just begun to speak knows, they generally like to ask questions. There are two kinds of questions they have to learn how to produce. There are *yes/no questions* such as *Are you hungry?* that can be answered by a simple *yes* or *no.* There are also *wh-questions,* which begin with one of the *wh*-question words, *who, what, where, why,* and so on (also *how*). For example, *Who did you see?, What are you eating?, Where is the key?, Why is this wet?,* and *How old are you?* To none of these questions can you appropriately reply simply *yes* or *no.*

In English it is possible to ask yes/no questions by allowing the voice to rise instead of fall at the end of what would otherwise be a statement: *You're coming?*

Children find this an easy way to start with, and most of their early yes/no questions are asked through rising intonation. For adults, generally only short questions are asked in this way. Most yes/no questions are formed by putting the auxiliary verb before the subject as in:

Are you coming?
Can you see it?
Has the plumber arrived?
Would the owner of the green Mercedes that is blocking the entrance please move it?

In order to be able to ask questions of this type, the child has to identify two things. One is the auxiliary verb and the other is the subject. There are only a few auxiliaries in English: *be* and *have* (in all their forms); *can/could, may/might, must, shall/should, will/would.* For the child it is simply a matter of learning to identify them, and children seem to find this relatively easy. Knowing what the subject is again requires an ability to recognize abstract structures without any overt marking. In the final question in the preceding list, the subject is *the owner of the green Mercedes that is blocking the entrance,* and there can be even more complicated subjects. Children generally begin with fairly short subjects such as pronouns or people's names but as soon as they start to ask questions with other nouns as subjects they have to be able to recognize the whole phrase that makes up the subject.

There is another challenge that faces learners of English, whether young children or foreigners, in learning to ask questions and that is what happens when there is no auxiliary. If we want to ask the question about whether John sings we cannot say **Sings John?* Nor if we want to know what he sang can we say **What sang he?* Instead we say *Does John sing?* and *What did John sing?* In other words, if there is no auxiliary, we supply one in the form of *does* or *did.* If I want to know whether you sing, however, I say *Do you sing?* The choice of *do, does,* or *did* depends upon the form that the verb (in this case *sing*) would have taken in a statement.

Children begin to use *do, does,* and *did* in questions at about the same time as they are learning to use these forms in negative statements. This is hardly surprising since the same principle is involved. When there is an auxiliary we form a negative statement by adding *not* (or more usually the contracted form *n't* in speech) after the auxiliary as in:

He is singing   He isn't singing
He would sing   He wouldn't sing
He has sung   He hasn't sung

But when there is no auxiliary we do not say **He singsn't* or **He sangn't* but *He doesn't sing* and *He didn't sing.* Here is another example of something that children have to work out for themselves because, at the stage when they are trying to learn it, they could not possibly understand any explanation that an adult might give, and most adults probably could not give a very clear explanation anyway.

There is one kind of question in English that requires a more complex awareness of structure than many people might think. When we want to check up on an assertion, we often add what is called a *tag question*. Tag questions are formed by adding a short question after a statement. If the statement is affirmative, the tag is usually (but not always) negative; if the statement is negative, the tag is almost always affirmative:

> John is singing, isn't he?
> John isn't singing, is he?

In order to form a tag question the speaker must (1) identify the subject and determine its number and gender (if singular); (2) find the auxiliary (if there is one); (3) identify the tense of the verb if there is no auxiliary; (4) determine whether the statement is affirmative or negative:

> Mary and Peter are coming, aren't they?
> Your cousin is beautiful, isn't she?
> You and I know better, don't we?
> The news hadn't reached them, had it?
> You understand the question, don't you?
> They attended the meeting, didn't they?

This apparently simple construction thus requires an understanding of both pronoun and verbal anaphora and the English auxiliary system. Given this complexity, it is remarkable that children begin to use tag questions by the age of four, though they will not fully master the process till much older. At this time, however, children are ready to start learning more complex constructions.

Still More Syntax

Linguistics works continuously with concepts forged by grammarians without knowing whether or not the concepts actually correspond to the constituents of the system of language.

Ferdinand de Saussure, *Course in General Linguistics*

Syntax is what governs the relationship between the structural units (noun phrases, verb phrases, and so on) in an utterance. Languages differ in the ways in which they signal these relationships. In some languages there are many morphemes which indicate the relationships. In English, which in its modern form has few such morphemes, word order is of vital importance. In the utterance *The boy next door loves the girl across the street* the subject of the verb *loves* is *the boy next door* and the object of the verb is *the girl across the street* (in this case the beloved object). These relationships are signaled by the order of the words (or rather of the phrases made up by the words). From these relationships we can tell that it is the boy who loves and the girl who is loved. *The girl across the street loves the boy next door* is a quite different utterance and may, alas, not be true even when the first utterance is. The order subject-verb-object (SVO) is the basic order of these syntactic units in English. Almost half the languages in the world (including European languages such as French, Russian, and Hungarian) share this basic word order. Slightly more of the world's languages (such as Japanese and Turkish) have the basic order SOV with the verb at the end. A very much smaller number (including Irish, Welsh, and Hebrew) have the verb first, VSO. The other three ordering possibilities are found, but rarely. In every language there are also complex rules for the order of constituents in particular constructions and in some of these the basic word order is changed.

Children learning English seldom make mistakes in the basic word order. This is perhaps not surprising because they would have difficulty making themselves understood if they did not get the order of the elements right. There may also be cognitive reasons why subjects tend to occur first in a majority of the world's languages. The subject of a verb is usually who or what we are talking about (the topic or theme), and it is reasonable that this topic should be mentioned early. In *John is a good singer* the topic is *John* and the rest of the utterance says something about him. There is also a tendency to mention people before things so that instead of saying *A number 11 bus knocked John down* we are more likely to say *John was knocked down by a number 11 bus.* This construction, in which the object in the first utterance becomes the subject in the second, is called the passive. Children initially have difficulty with this change from the normal order and will often understand an utterance such as *Mary was kissed by John* to mean that Mary kissed John. However, they are less likely to misunderstand *The apple was eaten by John* because they know that it is people who eat apples, not the other way round.

Children also have difficulty with other utterances where the basic word order is distorted. One of these cases is with relative clauses. A *relative clause* is one that adds information about a noun rather in the way that an adjective does. In *The man who sold you that car must have been a crook* the relative clause is *who sold you that car* and identifies the man you are talking about. Relative clauses of this type are called restrictive relative clauses. There are also relative clauses which do not need to identify their antecedent that are called nonrestrictive relative clauses, as for example, *John, who lives in the New Forest, has invited us down there for the weekend.* In this case the hearer presumably knows who John is, but the speaker does not know if his residence is known to the listener. In writing, nonrestrictive relative clauses are usually set off by commas, which are not used with restrictive relative clauses. In speech it is intonation that makes the difference, but nonrestrictive relative clauses are rare in spoken language. A pair of utterances that shows the contrast is:

a. My sister who lives in London told me about it.
b. My sister, who lives in London, told me about it.

In (a) the restrictive relative clause tells the listener which of my sisters I mean; in (b) I have only one sister. Thus it is important to get the intonation or punctuation right in an utterance such as *My wife, who is now forty, is expecting our third child,* at least in a monogamous society.

In restrictive (but not in nonrestrictive) relative clauses, the relative pronoun can be *that* instead of *who* and it may be omitted if it is the object of the verb in the relative clause:

The man you saw here yesterday has agreed to buy my house.

These constructions cause some initial problems for children because the subject of the main clause, *the man,* is separated from its verb, *has agreed,* by the relative clause, *you saw here yesterday.* As in all language it is not the order of the words alone that is important but the structures of which the words form part.

The basic unit in syntax is the clause. Many utterances consist of a single clause, but there are also rules for combining clauses into larger units. The simplest way is by using a coordinate conjunction, *and, but, so,* and *or.* These may seem rather insignificant items but they represent a vast step forward from anything that we can imagine in even the most sophisticated form of animal communication, and they are probably more complex than many people realize.

The most frequently used coordinating conjunction in speech is *and,* which is about three times as frequent as *but,* with the other two fairly rare. Repeated use of *and* is common in narratives as in this example from an interview with a Scottish coal miner telling me about his trip to New York:

2067	we went on the Queen Elizabeth
2068	we left Southampton
2069	*and* we went over to le Havre
2070	*and* we went from le Havre to Ireland
2071	*and* we left Ireland
2071	*and* then across the Atlantic tae [to] America tae New York
2072	*and* we were conducted tours roond [round] New York sort of thing
2073	we were all roond New York
2074	*and* then we flew back
2075	come back across in the plane
2076	*and* we got to Gatwick
2077	I think
2078	it was Gatwick aye Gatwick
2079	*and* I think
2080	she thought
2081	I was running away fae [from] her at that time
2082	I don't like the aeroplanes no no no no
2083	I was ready for the toilet
2084	when we landed

The whole narrative from line 2069 is carried by clauses introduced by *and;* the clauses in lines 2074, 2076, 2078–79 are asides or elaborations. *And* does not occur in the last three lines where the speaker explains his behavior.

And often has the implication of "and then." For example, there is a difference implied between (a) and (b):

a. John went to the bank and stole some money.
b. John stole some money and went to the bank.

There is a natural inference that the sequence of events corresponds to the order of the clauses, though *and* need not imply this:

Yesterday I worked very hard and I had an excellent lunch at the club.

This does not imply that I worked hard only before lunch.

But is logically very similar to *and* with the difference that the second clause says something that is contrary to what might have been expected. *John is a lawyer but he is honest* implies that lawyers are not usually honest. *So* is the coordinating conjunction of consequence: *It was late so I told him to go home.* The first clause gives the reason for the second. The same information could have been provided by saying *I told him to go home because it was late.* The difference is that the clause beginning with *because* is a subordinate clause.

There are several different kinds of subordinate clause. The use of subordinate clauses is particularly characteristic of written language, where they can be combined into extremely long sentences. In speech there is seldom more than one subordinate clause and often coordinate clauses are used where a subordinate clause could have been used. For example, in making a threat it is less common to say something like *If you do that, I'll kill you;* it is much more likely that the speaker would say something like *You do that and I'll kill you.*

There are also a number of constructions with nonfinite verbs. Finite verbs are those that are marked for tense. For example, *sings* in *he sings* and *is* in *he is busy* are in the present tense; *sang* in *he sang* and *was* in *he was busy* are in the past tense. Nonfinite verbs are infinitives (for example, *to sing* in *he likes to sing*) or gerunds (*singing* in *he likes singing*) and they do not change when the tense of the finite verb changes (*he liked to sing when he was younger*). Nonfinite constructions are another way in which languages can be economical. For example, *John expected that Mary would sing* can also be expressed as *John expected Mary to sing* and *John expected that he [John] would sing* as *John expected to sing*. In *John expected Mary to sing* it is clear that it is Mary who would be singing, and in *John expected to sing* it would be John. In *John promised Mary to sing,* however, it is again John. Expressions of the latter kind cause problems for children until the age of about seven or eight. Similarly, children may have difficulty with the difference between *Peter is eager to tease* and *Peter is easy to tease.* In the first case, Peter likes to tease, but in the latter it is easy to tease Peter. A different kind of infinitive occurs in *Harry is likely to win,* which is equivalent to *It is likely that Harry will win.* The different kinds of infinitives illustrate the kinds of difficulties children encounter in learning to master a language. It is not true, as is sometimes claimed, that children master the syntax of the language by the age of five. There are some complex constructions that will not be fully learned until much later but by five children will be able to use and understand most of the syntactic structures they need for ordinary conversation. Whether they will always understand them in the same way as adults is another question that will be explored in the next chapter.

Semantics
— meaning

A definition is the enclosing of a wilderness of ideas within a wall of words.

Samuel Butler, *Notebooks*

The most important aspect of language is meaning, which is mainly studied under the heading semantics. It is the most important because all linguistic communication depends upon some common understanding of what is being said. For the most part we take it for granted that other people who speak the language understand an utterance in the way we do. This assumption is most dangerous in talking with children. Just because a child uses a word adults can identify as one in their own vocabulary, it does not follow that the word has the same meaning for both adult and child. In fact, it would be truer to say that words *never* have exactly the same meaning for adults and for young children, because words take part of their meaning from their relationship to other words, and when the child knows only a few, those words are likely to have a wider meaning than they do for adults. One girl used the word *papa* to refer not only to her father but also to her grandfather and her mother, and later to any man. Children often use the word *doggie* to refer to a wide range of animals. Partly this is because children usually begin by learning words that are neither very specific nor very general. For example, a child is much more likely to learn the word *dog* than the more specific *poodle* or the more general term *animal,* even though *dog* may be used with the general sense of animal and the only dog that the child knows is a poodle. As children learn more words, they become able to distinguish verbally between dogs and cats or horses and thus show that they know the difference between them.

In the early stages many of the child's words name things of interest to the child. Often this is in response to the caregiver's prompting, either in the form of direct questions or by giving the child the chance to supply a suitable response.

MOTHER: Now we're putting on baby's . . .

CHILD: Shoe

MOTHER: That's right, baby's shoe.

The first words that children learn in this way usually refer to things that children can handle or that move. For example, the names of animals are very common among the child's earliest words, and so are words for food. Words for furniture, buildings, and places that might appear to be prominent in the child's environment seem to be of less interest. Some words that one might expect would interest the child, such as *finger, thumb,* and *juice,* are often learned relatively late, presumably because they contain sounds that are difficult for the young child to produce.

As the child's vocabulary develops the risk of misinterpretation by an adult increases. It is a slightly disturbing fact that children usually learn to say *no* before they learn to say *yes,* and there is sometimes a stage when children will use *no* not only with its obvious meaning but occasionally when they mean *yes.* Similarly, it has been shown that children may go through a stage when they interpret *less* as meaning *more* and *before* as meaning the same as *after.* At a later stage children may still be unclear as to the difference between *ask* and *tell.*

What may strike adults as odd is that children seldom say that they do not understand the meaning of a word. Instead, they behave as if they understood it perfectly even though careful questioning may reveal that they have either a very vague or a totally misleading notion of the meaning. There are several factors that help us to make sense of this attitude. The linguistic signal is only part of the communication situation. If we say *Hand me that book,* we may accompany the utterance with a look or a gesture that conveys much of the intention without the words. Second, ordinary language is highly redundant. For example, in the written language we can often guess at the meaning of a sentence without vowels:

    a. tbrnttbthtsthqstn

This is fairly easy to interpret but it would be even easier with spaces between the words:

    b. t b r nt t b tht s th qstn

Of course, it is easier because this is a familiar quotation but even an original sentence can often be interpreted:

    c. ths sntnc s wrttn wtht vwls

It is a different matter if the consonants are omitted and only the vowels are left. Few of my students find (d) as easy to interpret as (a) or (b), although the sentence is equally well known:

    d. ayaaiea

Even with spaces between the words it is hard to guess at its sense:

    e. ay a a ie a*

In speech, however, it is the vowels that carry more information, partly because sounds such as the voiceless stop consonants [p,t,k] are not sounds at all but short periods of silence; what we hear as these consonants are the ways in which the vowels change before and after these brief silences.

---

* It is *Mary had a little lamb.*

CP True

interesting

It has been estimated that the redundancy in much written English is about 50 percent. In other words, you need only perceive roughly half of what you read in order to get the message. It is this redundancy that makes proofreading so difficult. As practiced readers we have become so skillful in letting our eyes skip quickly over the text that we find it hard to slow down and look at every letter.

The redundancy makes language a very efficient system of communication even in very noisy conditions because we can often guess at the meaning of words from the context even if we have not heard them very clearly. Children must be doing this all the time though they are probably not aware that they are doing so. For example, take the following sentences:

- a. The boy put out the light before he went upstairs.
- b. After the boy put out the light he went upstairs.
- c. The boy put out the light and went upstairs.

The three sentences mean the same and it is not necessary to understand the words *before* and *after* to know what happened, since the order of events is the same as the order in which they are mentioned. Children need have no difficulty in understanding any of the sentences even if they don't know the meaning of *before* in (a) and *after* in (b).* This is a very simple example but the situation must be a very common one for children.

Sometimes the context does not help the child to grasp the difference in meaning between two words. The following sentences have a similar intent:

- a. Tell John to open the window.
- b. Ask John to open the window.

The difference is in politeness, so it is not surprising if children come to think that *ask* and *tell* have the same meaning. One investigator found that, when she gave one of a pair of children the instruction *Peter, ask Mary what time it is,* Peter might answer *I don't know what time it is,* showing that he interpreted *ask* as meaning "tell." This kind of confusion was found among children as old as six years of age. It is, however, the kind of confusion that is unlikely to become obvious without some kind of testing. I can remember being puzzled when my own children said *I want to ask Mummy something* and proceeded to tell her something, but I did not understand the source of the confusion.

It has been suggested that there are three factors that affect how a child interprets what an adult says. One is the child's knowledge of the language and understanding of the utterance. A second factor is the child's estimate of what the adult wants. A third factor is how the child perceives the situation that the adult is talking about. This is most likely to happen when children are in the process of learning a particular aspect of language but are not yet secure enough in their awareness of its meaning to feel confident that they have understood it correctly, particularly if their interpretation in any way conflicts with their estimate of what the speaker wants or their general perception of the situation. Thus two-year-olds who are not

---

* The difficult case is *Before he went upstairs the boy put out the light* because the order of the clauses does not correspond to the order of events.

yet secure in their interpretation of the distinction between *in* and *on* will interpret an instruction using one of these prepositions as *in* if the apparent reference is to a container but as *on* if the apparent reference is to a flat surface, because one normally puts things in a container and on a surface. Similarly, slightly older children may interpret a passive sentence such as *John was kissed by his mother* as *John kissed his mother* because normally the agent comes before the verb, but they will not interpret. *The apple was eaten by John* as *The apple ate John* because that is not likely. Children generally interpret what they hear in terms of what makes sense in that particular situation.

As children's vocabulary increases they will gradually become aware of other semantic features. They will discover that a word can have more than one meaning, as in *bank* referring to a financial institution or the boundary of a river. Such words are called *homonyms;* if they sound the same, whether or not they are spelled the same way (for example, *see* and *sea*), they are called *homophones;* if they are written alike but sound different (*lead* as a verb and *lead* as a metal), they are called *homographs.*

At about the age of seven or eight, children become interested in linguistic jokes that depend on such similarities. For example:

Q: Why is the sun like good bread?

A: Because it isn't light until it rises.

Here the joke depends upon the difference between *light* versus *dark* and *light* versus *heavy.* Other adjectives that can be distinguished by their opposites are *dry* versus *wet* or *sweet,* and *old* versus *young* or *new.*

A few adjectives imply the negative of their opposite. If I say *Elvis is not dead,* this is equivalent to claiming *Elvis is alive.* If I say *This room is not big,* however, it does not necessarily follow that the room is small; it could be medium-sized. Adjectives like *big* and *small* are gradable, because things can be bigger or smaller. It is only in a metaphorical sense that we can talk about someone (or something) being more dead or more alive. Adjectives like *big* and *old* also have the characteristic that they can be used in a neutral sense, whereas their opposites cannot. If I say *How big is it?* or *How old is she?,* I am not implying that it is big or that she is old. In fact, I could ask the latter question about a baby. But if I say *How small is it?* or *How young is she?,* there is a definite implication that it is small and she is young. This implication holds for both senses of *old; How new is it?* implies that it is new. Children generally learn the neutral term first, that is, *long* before *short, wide* before *narrow,* and so on.

In addition to words with very different meanings, that is, homonyms, there are also words with meanings that may be related in some way, such as the word *head* in the following examples:

a. Mind you don't bump your head.
b. He has a fine head of hair.
c. I bought a large head of lettuce.
d. He owns over fifty head of cattle.

e. She went right to the head of the queue.
f. You must clean the head of the tape recorder.
g. He is the head of a very large company.

While some of these could be considered metaphors, many are such common expressions that they seem part of the meaning of *head*. Distinguishing between polysemous words like *head* and homonyms like *bank* is the dictionary maker's dilemma. The dictionary maker has to decide whether to list them as separate words or as single words with multiple meanings. As speakers of the language we do not have to worry about this, but both kinds of words illustrate the economical use of linguistic forms for a variety of functions. It is probably not an accident that words with a wide range of meanings tend to be short. Words that are used more frequently tend to be shorter than those which are less commonly used. A word such as *anthropomorphize* is likely to have many fewer meanings than a word like *head*.

Children also come to learn that certain words have reciprocal meanings. For example, from *Peter bought the bicycle from John* we can infer *John sold Peter the bicycle.* There is a reciprocal relationship between *buy* and *sell*. Similarly, *Harry is David's son* means also that *David is Harry's father.* Young children have difficulty with terms of family relationship and the notion of reciprocity. For example:

ADULT: What is a sister?

CHILD: A babysitter. She watches TV with her boyfriend.

A more complicated example:

ADULT: What is a wife?

CHILD: A wife is a mommy—a other mommy's mommy.

ADULT: What do you mean?

CHILD: A wife is a daddy's mommy.

ADULT: What is a husband?

CHILD: A husband is a mommy's mommy.

Traditionally the study of semantics has concentrated mainly on what might be called the dictionary maker's notion of meaning, that is, definitions that are paraphrases using different words. In practice, this is only a part of the meaning that expressions have for speakers. It is also a misleading view of meaning because dictionary meanings are irrelevant to most everyday objects, which is why many dictionaries supplement the definitions with illustrations. It is unlikely that anyone would expect to distinguish *coriander* from *tarragon* or a *wolf* from a *coyote* on the basis of dictionary definitions. Moreover, we need not even know the precise meaning of words to be able to use them quite confidently. Most of us know more names for plants, animals, and metals, to take only three simple examples, than we could probably identify if challenged, but this does not inhibit us from using the words. There is an even more fundamental problem in attaching too great significance to dictionary meanings and that is the implication that normal use of language consists of combinations of words in their literal meanings. As we shall see in the next two chapters, this is far from being the case.

At this point it becomes less profitable to look at language from the perspective of children's language development. As they grow older, their language and behavior come more and more to resemble those of adults. The subsequent chapters will examine some of the ways in which people use language and the variety of forms that have evolved to meet these needs.

Pragmatically Speaking

> I am sitting with a philosopher in the garden; he says again and again
> "I know that's a tree," pointing to a tree that is near us. Someone else
> arrives and hears this, and I tell them: "This fellow isn't insane. We are
> only doing philosophy."
>
> Ludwig Wittgenstein

It is mainly philosophers, linguists, and other exotic breeds who are concerned with the literal meaning of simple statements. Ordinary people are more interested, as the philosopher J. L. Austin put it, in "how to do things with words." Austin pointed out that we can do a variety of things when we speak. We do such things as asserting, denying, questioning, requesting, promising, threatening, offering, wagering, thanking, apologizing, insulting, flattering, welcoming, congratulating, excommunicating, declaring war, christening, and dismissing someone from a job. In some cases we actually perform the act by speaking, as when you make a promise or when the judge sentences you to a spell in prison. However, the act is valid only if certain conditions are met. I cannot legitimately promise something that is beyond my capabilities to accomplish and I cannot sentence you to prison unless I have been given that authority.

Austin also pointed out that the linguistic form need not bear a direct relation to the purpose for which it is being used. The obvious linguistic form for giving orders is the imperative (for example, *Sit down!*) but speakers can use different ways of expressing a message:

a. Have you tidied your room yet?
b. This place really is untidy.
c. Can you tidy your room?
d. Would you mind tidying up a bit?
e. It's time to put this place straight.
f. Please tidy your room.
g. If you don't tidy your room, I'll . . .
h. Get this place tidied up.

All these utterances can be used for the same purpose of getting you to tidy up your room. They include statements, questions, and imperatives. The form of the utterance may affect its politeness but the overall message remains the same.

The same form can be used for different purposes. If I say *The bull is about to charge,* I might only be making an uninvolved statement but I might otherwise be giving a warning. Young children have difficulty with remarks such as *I'm sure the cat likes you pulling its tail,* which are meant ironically. But even adults sometimes have difficulty with questions of the form *Why don't you tell him?,* which might simply be an inquiry about your reasons for not telling him but might also be a suggestion that you should tell him. Once at a public talk the person next to me said, with a gesture to someone in the row in front, *Do you know who that is?* I said *No, who is it?,* thinking I was about to be enlightened but it turned out to be a genuine query.

The import of an utterance may not be established until the addressee has responded, as in the following examples:

A: Where are the reimbursement forms?

B: I'll get one for you.

A: Where are the reimbursement forms?

B: Over there in the corner.

In the first example, B treats A's utterance as a request for a form rather than as a request for information. In the second, B treats A's utterance as a request for information. It is not difficult to imagine that B in the first example feels more respectful or more friendly toward A than B in the second example. This kind of exchange underlines the interactional nature of verbal communication and how it is not simply a matter of what the speaker says.

Sometimes there is a conventional interpretation, as in questions such as *Can you pass the salt?, Have you got a match?,* and *Do you know the time?,* which are not usually interpreted as requests for information but rather for action. Although they have the form of yes/no questions, a simple *yes* as a response would be interpreted as aggressively rude. There is a similar interpretation in this telephone exchange:

A: Is Peter there?

B: I'll get him for you.

B takes A's query as signaling that he wishes to speak to Peter but A may have simply wanted to know if Peter was there and continue *No, I just wanted to know if he was there.*

Often there is no obvious connection between the literal meaning of an utterance and the way it is interpreted, as in the following exchange, presumably shouted out:

A: That's the telephone.

B: I'm in the bath.

A: Okay.

[handwritten margin note: Great example]

A's first remark is not simply intended to inform B that the telephone is ringing, it is a request to answer it. B's response is not intended only to inform A about where he is but to explain why he cannot comply with her request. A's response shows that she accepts this as a reason for not answering the telephone. Exchanges of this kind are so common that we do not even notice the extent to which we have gone beyond the meaning of the utterance, but imagine trying to program a computer to draw such inferences.

All interpretations of a speaker's remarks have to be made in the context of normal expectations, unless there is some reason to believe that something strange is going on. The normal expectations are that the speaker is well intentioned and not trying to mislead the hearer. Thus the speaker is expected not to exaggerate and say something like *The car's a total wreck* when there is only a slight dent in the fender. On the other hand it is misleading to reply *Two daughters* to a question *Have the Browns any children?* when you know that they have also three sons. We expect people to say no more but also no less than they know (or believe) to be the case.

This does not mean that you should never tell a lie, but normal conversational exchange is possible only on the assumption that generally people are trying not to mislead their hearers. There are, of course, times when we feel obliged to tell a lie in order not to upset someone, but such tactics would not work if the hearer always suspected insincerity.

There are also many occasions when people do not wish to speak too clearly because they do not want to be held responsible. This may happen in negotiating, quarreling, gossiping, insulting, or threatening. *You wouldn't want your son to have an accident, would you, Mr. Jones?* is not a simple request for confirmation of an obvious attitude, as its literal interpretation would indicate, but a much more alarming type of message.

A remark that might seem harmless enough can also take on greater significance from the context in which it occurs. The mate on board an oil tanker was annoyed when he found that the captain had entered in the ship's log *The mate was drunk last night,* although he did not dispute the accuracy of the report. The next day the mate entered in the ship's log a statement that was also true, *The captain was sober last night,* but by making the entry the mate managed to imply that this was an unusual state of affairs.

An FBI agent explains how in the agency's rating system a rating of *satisfactory* does not mean what one might think:

Attempting to explain the FBI's rating system, Mullany testified that about 90% of the FBI's 8,000 agents received ratings of excellent. He said a satisfactory rating "would be somewhat of a warning to an agent that he was not performing to the level of other agents." Porter's own testimony in the Miller trial suggested that the "satisfactory" ratings he gave to Miller reflected an even lower assessment. He said he tried to have Miller fired on at least three occasions for poor judgment, bad work habits and failure to keep his weight in line with FBI standards.

(*Los Angeles Times*, November 21, 1985)

So *satisfactory* meant "unsatisfactory."

Remarks can also make accusations indirectly as in *When are you going to stop bothering me?*, where I imply that we agree that you have been bothering me. This kind of tactic is often used in quarrels. Many kinds of remarks contain implications or presuppositions of this kind. If I say *It was John that offended Mary*, I am indirectly asserting that somebody offended Mary as well as saying who did it. If I say *It was Mary that John offended*, I am indirectly asserting that John offended someone as well as saying who it was. Statements of this kind, which take something for granted while appearing to be saying something else, are a common feature of polemical language (see chapter 20).

Unlike written communication (see chapter 15), speech always takes place on a specific occasion in a particular place with known interlocutors. In order to speak appropriately it is essential for the speaker to take into consideration what the hearer knows or can be expected to know. We have already seen this in the use of the articles. The difference between *I bought a car yesterday* and *I bought the car yesterday* is that in the latter case the speaker expects the hearer to know which car he bought, whereas in the former there is no such expectation.

Certain expressions cannot be fully interpreted without knowing who said them, where, and when. Charles Fillmore once observed that the least informative message to find floating in a bottle on the ocean would be *Meet me here tomorrow at the same time with a stick this big.* The expressions *me*, *here*, *tomorrow*, *the same time*, and *this* all require reference to aspects of the situation in which the message was produced. Such expressions are called *deictic* elements, from the Greek word for pointing, because they all "point" to aspects of the situation.

The essence of deictic elements is that they take their point of reference from the speaker (or writer). The referents of the first- and second-person pronouns *I*, *you*, and *we* change with a change of speaker (see further chapter 30). *Here* and *this* can be used for reference closer to the speaker in contrast to *there* and *that*. Similarly, *come* and *bring* often refer to motion in the direction of the speaker in contrast to *go* and *take.* There are exceptions, however. We may say *Can we come over?* and *What can be bring?* in both cases indicating movement in the direction of the hearer. Other deictic elements with a spatial orientation are *on my left* (*right*) and *facing me* and so on. Some deictic elements may take their reference from other than the speaker or the addressee. *I took Mary home* can mean either that I took her to my house or to hers.

There are also temporal deictic elements. *Now* takes its reference from the time of speaking (or writing) in contrast to *then* as do *today*, *yesterday*, *a week ago*, *last year*, *next month*, and so on. In English there is a deictic verb form. If I say *I lived in Lisbon for five years* it is clear that I no longer live there, but if I say *I have lived in California for twenty years* then I am also indicating that I still live there. The use of the *have -ed* form (often misleadingly called the perfect tense) is a constant problem for foreign learners of English, but young children begin to use it correctly by the age of four.

Deictic elements are among the most obvious aspects of language that bring attention to the interactional nature of language. What aspects of the situation speakers need to take into consideration may vary from society to society. When we travel abroad, we may see people greeting each other in various ways: bowing, embracing, kissing, shaking hands, and so on. Some of these forms of greeting will not differ much from those we are familiar with in our own society but others will be very different. So it is with language, but before we look at the diversity elsewhere, it is necessary to examine the variety to be found in our own speech community.

Theories of Language Development

The map appears to us more real than the land.

D. H. Lawrence

The distinguished linguist James McCawley once remarked in a talk, "When you
hear a linguist use the word *theory* you should put your hand on your wallet."
In the past half century a great many people have been in danger of losing their
wallets. The Fagin figure in this dubious enterprise has been Noam Chomsky,
whose own theories of children's language development have spawned many rival
versions. (See the appendix for an account of Chomsky's work.) Fifty years ago
Chomsky attacked the then-current theories of children's language acquisition. The
prevailing view claimed that children learned by attempting to imitate the speech
of adults and were reinforced to improve their early inadequate efforts by rewards
and punishments. Chomsky argued that there was no way that infants could develop
language by this method since language is too complex for such an approach.
Instead, he argued that human beings are born with an innate knowledge of how
language is structured and use this innate knowledge to work out how to acquire
competence in the language to which they are exposed. Chomsky initially called
this innate knowledge a *language acquisition device (LAD)* but latterly has referred
to it as *universal grammar (UG)*. Central to this notion is the claim that all languages are basically the same, though they differ in many superficial characteristics.

For almost fifty years now, Chomsky has been revising his theories of universal
grammar and in the process has gained but also lost many supporters. It is unclear
at present what the verdict of posterity will be on Chomsky's theory of language
but it would probably be fair to say that in recent years the widespread support he
once enjoyed has been receding. Nevertheless, he has had an immense impact on
the field of linguistics and also on studies of children's language development.
While there have been many studies carried out by investigators who espoused
Chomsky's theories that have produced interesting information, on the whole
Chomsky's influence on this topic has been unfortunate. There are a number of
reasons for this.

The most basic problem with Chomsky's influence on the study of language development is that Chomsky vehemently rejects the notion that communication is central to the notion of language. Chomsky's theory of language describes a system in the brain that cannot be studied directly but can only be inferred from external evidence. This might not be a problem except that Chomsky has chosen to argue from invented complex examples of English that probably nobody has ever said and for which it is even hard to imagine a context in which they might be said. At best, these examples illustrate the kind of knowledge that well-educated, literate adults may possess, but they do not exemplify the kind of language that is used in normal conversation or the kind of expressions that young children are exposed to at the time when they are developing their language skills.

The second important problem with Chomsky's influence is his view that language consists of a set of abstract structures that can be described in a quasi-mathematical notation. There are certain advantages to such an approach if one is trying to characterize the complexity of human languages, but it always has to be stressed that such an approach is an idealization, not a description of any actual language. Linguists who claim otherwise are the kind of wallet thieves that James McCawley warned against. Too many investigations of children's language development in the Chomskyan paradigm have focused on the learning of abstract structures, as if that is what children are striving to do.

The third problem with approaching children's language development in this way is that many of the kinds of features that the investigator has wanted to study do not occur frequently in naturally occurring situations. Consequently, many accounts of children's language development are based on specially devised procedures or tests. While these tests do provide some information on what the child has or has not learned, they are not necessarily a good guide to how the child uses language in a normal situation.

What is missing from this approach is the generally accepted notion that children develop language because they are interested in communicating. However, if your view of language assumes that communication is irrelevant to language development, you may come up with some rather strange theories. Probably only Chomsky's immense prestige allowed so many scholars to adopt a position that is contrary to common sense.

Fortunately a great many studies recently have shown how intensely infants from their earliest existence focus on ways to communicate with adults and try to understand what the adults are trying to communicate to them. Long before anything that could even remotely be called language, children are engaged in the process of communication. At an early age infants will direct their gaze to the place that an adult is looking at. This shared experience lays the basis for the infant to identify what the adult may be referring to by producing certain noises. Infants also seem to realize that adults are making an effort to communicate with them and they try to understand that. It is clear from observational studies that children's language development then proceeds by accretion from one-word utterances to more complex expressions.

Part of the problem arises because linguists see language in terms of the kinds of analytical accounts they have developed to describe its structure. These accounts bear the same kind of relationship to language use as a two-dimensional map does to the actual countryside. Maps can show details and relationships that would be hard for someone to notice while walking around. However, there are many aspects of the scene that will not be recorded on any map. The map will not tell us about the plants and animals that we see, the temperature or wind direction, or the sounds that we hear. The map contains information that is not directly available to us by observation but the experience of walking through the countryside is much richer in many ways. Similarly, linguists' descriptions of language contain information that is not available to the speaker through introspection but the act of speaking (and hearing) is much richer than any linguistic description. Accounts of children's language development that focus on the structural aspects of language see the process as similar to that of internalizing a map, and (following Lawrence's observation) treat the map as more real than the language people use. Developmental psychologists, on the other hand, see young children as exploring the world into which they have been born and building up their own sense of where things are through a language that develops and becomes more complex as their knowledge and ability increase.

Another problem is that linguists have succeeded in showing how language is much more complex than it appears on the surface. However, this complexity has been revealed by pushing language creativity to its limits, particularly in terms of subordination and embedded structures. In their everyday casual conversation most speakers use few complex structures. Arguments about linguistic structure have used the grammaticality of sentences such as *Who did Sara ask why everyone likes cats?* versus the ungrammaticality of **What did Sara ask why everyone likes?* It is difficult to imagine a real-life situation in which the first sentence would be asked and obviously nobody would attempt to ask the second. Children do not need to internalize a map that distinguishes between these two sentences.

Linguists in their accounts (map-drawing) also deliberately ignore those aspects of communication that are not linguistic. These include the features that are often called paralinguistic (see chapter 3). However, we all know, as functioning human beings, that it is not simply the linguistic information that affects us when interacting with others. There are all kinds of signals such as tone of voice, voice quality, facial expressions, and posture that often communicate more directly than any words that accompany them. The infant (and young child) will be paying as much attention to these signals as to the linguistic content. As adults we process a great deal of information about the speaker (age, gender, social position, mood, attitude, etc.) whenever we hear someone speak. To focus on the words alone is to ignore what may be the most important aspect of the communication. For children finding out about a language, however, successful understanding of a general sense of what is being communicated can help to establish the meaning of words.

Linguists analyze language in terms of discrete elements such as phonemes, morphemes, words, and clauses, but there is no reason to believe that children's early language is similarly organized. One of the major mistakes in looking at children's language development has been to measure their success in terms of the adult language. Moreover, even linguists have apparently been too prone to think of language in terms of its written form. Chomsky famously claimed that linguistic theory was concerned with an ideal speaker-listener in a completely homogeneous speech community who never made any "mistakes." Such speakers do not exist but the description better fits those writers who publish in the mainstream press. However, people do not speak like this and certainly not to young children. Judging children's language development against the standard of the written language is a mistake. If young children are assumed to be aiming at the written standard language with all its complexity then it is not surprising that appeal has been made to innate knowledge. Such theorists often used the term "poverty of the stimulus" as a basis for claims about innate knowledge. The argument was sometimes based on the failure of computer programs to learn complex structures on the basis of a set of examples. Such studies showed that a computer could not infer a complex syntactic structure from a set of examples illustrating that structure. Consequently, it was argued, young children would not be able to do this either. However, the argument continued, since as adults the speakers are able to use such constructions they must have been born with knowledge of this structure.

The Russian psychologist Alexander Luria drew a distinction between what he called classical science and Romantic science. He claimed that classical scientists reduce the richness of living reality to abstract schemas, while "Romantics" aspire to a science that retains the wealth of living reality. He saw the development of computers as creating a grave danger of reducing the reality of human cognitive activity to mechanical models. Attempts to characterize Universal Grammar exemplify such a model.

Nobody denies that human beings are born with brains that will enable them to develop competence in a language. The difference of opinion comes over the details of how that brain is structured. Those who argue for the notion of Universal Grammar or a Language Instinct (often referred to as nativists) believe that the innate ability contains specific knowledge of syntactic constructions that are crucial to adult competence in the language. Those who take a developmental approach (sometimes referred to as empiricists) believe instead that human beings are born with a range of cognitive abilities that will enable the infant to work out how to communicate in the language but these cognitive abilities are not narrowly focused on syntactic structures.

Much work is at present being done on the structure of the brain and eventually it may be possible to identify more precisely how the brain develops and processes language. At the present time, however, despite frequent claims in the media, there is insufficient evidence from studies of the brain to show whether the linguists or the developmental psychologists are correct. It is clearly too early to claim that any theory is seriously supported by this kind of evidence. Keep your hand on your wallet.

Variety

"It is called a tundish in Lower Drumcondra," said Stephen, laughing, "where they speak the best English."

James Joyce, *A Portrait of the Artist as a Young Man*

Imagine a distant horizon against which can be seen as yet unidentifiable moving objects. As one gets closer it becomes possible to see that the objects are indeed human beings but other than that they are indistinguishable. Getting closer still, it is possible to draw certain conclusions about the age, sex, race, and even perhaps the nationality and relative social status of the individuals. Finally, through such attributes as facial features and fingerprints, it is possible to determine that each individual is unique. Such identifications are made visually, but we can also draw similar inferences from what we hear. At one extreme we may simply realize that the sounds we hear belong to human language; at the other we may recognize that it is a friend speaking. Between the universal and the unique, a number of categories can be identified from speech. In this chapter we shall examine some of the group characteristics of speech, but first it is necessary to recapitulate some of the basic features of language.

The primary purpose of language is communication and, whatever the origin of language may have been, there is no doubt that the specialization of the vocal tract for spoken language was a very successful evolutionary development. The tongue and the vocal cords are capable of rapid and minute variations of position and tension, and the human ear is remarkably skillful in detecting slight variations in the sounds produced by the vocal tract. Compared with the vast range of sounds that the vocal tract is capable of producing, languages are extremely parsimonious systems. Very few languages use an inventory of more than one hundred discrete units of sound, although the vocal tract is capable of producing and the ear able to discriminate more than one hundred times that number. However, this under-utilization of the resources of the vocal tract has some advantages, of which the most important is probably the range of variation permitted within each speech sound. In fact, the distinctive speech sounds of a language are not narrowly defined sounds but rather categories with fairly loosely defined boundaries. Thus, for example, a vowel sound in a particular language is only loosely categorized by the features *high* (meaning that the tongue is raised), *front* (meaning that the highest part of the tongue is near the tip), and *unrounded* (meaning that the lips are spread). Within certain limits, the vowel may vary considerably in phonetic (acoustic) quality. The essential point for the language system is that, in its variation, it should not encroach on the territory of another vowel with which it is in contrast (that is, another phoneme in the language). For example, in English where there are two high, front, unrounded vowels, /i/ as in *heat,* and /ɪ/ as in *hit,* the variation in the quality of each vowel is limited by the necessity for it to remain distinct from the other. On the other hand, in Spanish, where there is only one phoneme that is a high, front, unrounded vowel /i/ as in *si* ("yes") and *mismo* ("same"), the range of permissible variations is greater.

Another aspect of language that is extremely important in this connection is redundancy. As we have seen in chapter 9, languages are characterized by considerable redundancy in their signaling systems. What this means is that it is not essential to hear (or, in the case of written communication, to see) every detail of the signal to comprehend the message. In many cases, it is possible to guess accurately what the missing part of a signal contained because the possibilities are limited. For example, a businessman receiving the typewritten message *Please telephone Mr. Brxwn as soon as possible* would have little difficulty in deciding that he should contact Mr. Brown. However, if the message had been *Please telephone 5533621 as soon as possible* and if there had been an error in the sequence of digits, the recipient would have had more difficulty in guessing where the mistake lay, unless he knew the number already. It is the redundancy of language that makes it possible to read a page full of misprints successfully or to understand what is being said under very noisy conditions that drown out part of the signal. This high redundancy of speech makes it possible for the hearing-impaired to lip-read, because not all speech sounds are distinguished by the visual form of their articulation. This redundancy also allows successful communication to take place between two speakers even if they have very different accents.

The human ear is a very sensitive instrument that can discriminate a thousand times the number of differences found in the phoneme system of any language. One of the first tasks children have to face in learning their first language is to ignore very obvious differences in speech sounds that are not important (that is, not phonemic). Thus, for example, it is obvious that the word *cat* uttered by a five-year-old boy, by a fifteen-year-old girl, by a thirty-year-old man, and by a seventy-year-old woman will sound different in each case. A machine asked to say whether the utterances were "the same" or "different" would have no hesitation in finding them different. However, young children who are discovering what language is really like have to learn to ignore such differences and realize that differences of pitch of the voice, small differences of phonetic quality, and differences of voice quality are irrelevant and that the essential characteristics of the word *cat* are not affected by these various differences. This is such an obvious characteristic of language that we are likely to take it for granted, but it represents an important imaginative leap for the child.

The acute sensitivity of the ear, combined with the rather limited use any language makes of the acoustic productivity of the speech organs, means that a great deal of information can be conveyed in speaking that is distinct from the linguistic message contained in the utterance. Although most of this information concerns the speaker, it is not restricted to that side of the communication situation. One can often tell something about the person addressed from the form of speech used and also about the social relationship between speaker and addressee. The acoustic quality of the utterance may indicate the physical proximity of the speaker, for example, by whispering or shouting. Any utterance will in this way provide information in addition to the linguistic content of the message. An obvious and important part of this additional information concerns the speaker.

At the extreme, it is probably correct that no two people speak in exactly the same way. We are generally recognizable by our voices in much the same way as we are recognizable by our physical appearance, and although we occasionally confuse one person with another, as in the case of identical twins, it is normally easy to distinguish individuals by their appearance and to identify them by the way they speak. Speakers we have not met before inevitably give clues about themselves. Even on the telephone (or in the dark), where there are no visual clues, it is usually possible to make reasonable guesses as to whether the speaker is male or female, old or young, and, in many cases, to gain some impression of the individual's mood. Such characteristics are not usually affected by any deliberate choice, conscious or unconscious, on the part of the speaker. Thus, in much the same way as we can infer quite a lot about strangers from their appearance, we can also (and often with much greater accuracy) tell a great deal from the way they speak.

Language serves many functions in addition to being the major vehicle for conveying information from one human being to another. Through language we also communicate our hopes, fears, anxieties, dreams, and, to some extent, our emotions. Language also serves as an identification card, enabling a stranger to make a reasonable guess about "where we are coming from" (in both a literal and a metaphorical sense). The clearest case is where two individuals speak different languages, where it is obvious to each that the other comes from "somewhere else." This kind of recognition also happens within a specific language; differences within a language are called dialect differences.

Linguistically it is impossible to draw a clear line between a *dialect* and a *language*. All languages, except the original ur-language, were dialects at one time. French, Italian, Spanish, Portuguese, and Romanian are the descendants of the language spoken by the Romans and so could be said to be dialects of Latin. That they are not usually so described is because France, Italy, Spain, Portugal, and Romania are separate countries. However, the varieties of language spoken on either side of the Spanish-Portuguese frontier are probably closer to each other than either is to the languages spoken in Madrid and Lisbon respectively. The notion of a language is a political one. Max Weinreich said that a language is a dialect with an army, but it would probably make more sense in developed countries to say that a language is a dialect endorsed by a national government and promulgated through a state educational system. More important, perhaps, languages in literate societies have a standard orthography; dialects are seldom written down.

The kind of complexity that is involved in using a language can be seen in figure 12.1. This diagram is intended to be read as a kind of flow chart from top

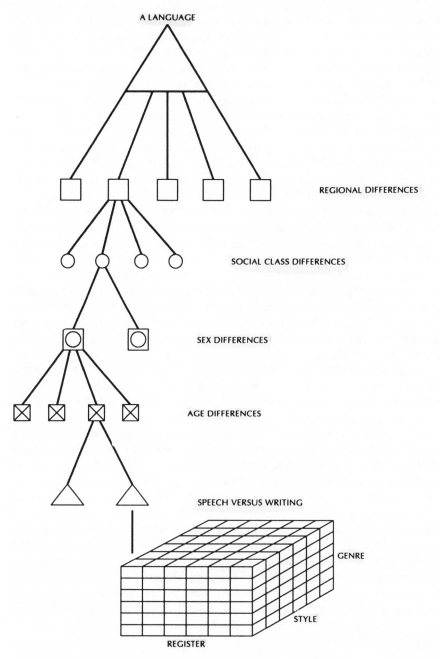

FIGURE 12.1

to bottom, although the interaction between the different factors is not simply that shown by the order of the items. The top triangle represents the common core shared by all speakers of the language named (for example, "English," "Spanish," "Japanese"). The first line down, *regional differences,* refers to all variations that can be explained horizontally (spatially), that is, because of geographical location, such as the differences between the speech of those who live in London, Liverpool, and Newcastle in England or between the speech of the inhabitants of New York, Atlanta, and Chicago in the United States. Such variation is studied under the heading of *regional dialects* (although until recently dialectologists were more interested in rural dialects than urban ones). The second line, *social class differences,* refers to the variation that is related to the vertical axis of a socially stratified society. *Sex differences* include not only those aspects of language (such as the natural pitch of the voice) that are related to physiological differences but also any that are the result of socialization into gender roles. *Age differences* are both those features that depend upon date of birth and those that accompany the aging process. The final line above the box, *speech versus writing,* does not refer to acts of speaking or writing but to the characteristics of spoken language or written language to the degree that these typically differ. The six aspects of language (common core, regional, social class, sex, age, and medium of expression differences) make up those factors that affect the form of language that an individual uses. The range of variation that these aspects of language encompass in any speech community will depend upon such factors as natural geographical barriers, population movement, social mobility, sharpness of social stratification, degree of separation of gender and generational roles, and the importance of literacy. The language a speaker uses will depend not only on the distribution of these factors in the community but also the accidents of individual experience and personality.

The part of figure 12.1 that is contained in the three-dimensional box is an attempt to indicate the kind of variation that is implicit in any use of language (whether spoken or written). The dimension of *register* refers to the encyclopedic knowledge represented in the speaker's vocabulary. The dimension of *genre* includes not only the obvious types such as narrative, sermon, conversation, and so forth, but also all types of written and spoken uses of language. Finally, the dimension of *style* refers not only to differences of formality but what Dell Hymes has called "tone" (for example, jocularity versus seriousness, politeness, sincerity, enthusiasm).

Dialects can vary in any aspect of language: pronunciation, morphology, syntax, vocabulary, and so on. Some of the variety that results from differences of geographical location, social position, sex, channel (speech versus writing), genre, style, and register will be illustrated in the next few chapters.

Regional Dialects

I wouldn't like to have an English accent. I think it's a very daft one.
They pronounce words correctly but they don't sound very nice.

Fifteen-year-old Glasgow schoolboy

It is impossible to think back to a time when any language was homogeneous.
Even when, if it was the case, there were very small groups speaking the same
language, there must have been some variety. Language is heterogeneous by its
very nature and the existence of differences creates the possibility of combining
certain features into new groupings. To take a parallel from another field, there are
now several hundred recognized breeds of dog but all dogs have as their common
ancestor the wolf. Through centuries of selective breeding, the wolf has evolved
into such different creatures as the Great Dane, the dachshund, the poodle, and the
Lakeland terrier. Certain features of size, color, temperament, and so on have been
selectively reinforced or suppressed. So it is with language. Although we have no
idea what the ur-language was, or even whether there was only one, we know
enough about language diversification to know that languages can change dramat-
ically with changing circumstances. Most European languages can be traced back
to a hypothetical single ancestor (see chapter 27), yet speakers of Russian, Greek,
Welsh, French, and English do not consider themselves as speaking the same language, though they will find occasional resemblances among the words of the
different languages.

As was pointed out in the previous chapter, there are several sources of linguistic differences and one of them is geography. The nineteenth-century French
scholar Gaston Paris observed:

> Varieties of common speech blend into one another by imperceptible gradations.
> A villager who might know only the speech of his village would easily understand
> that of the neighbouring village, with a bit more difficulty that of the village he
> would come to by walking on in the same direction, and so on, until finally he
> reached a point where he would understand the local speech only with great dif-
> ficulty.

Because of this notion of gradual variation, many linguists have despaired of using
the term *dialect* in any well-defined sense. Yet there are often linguistic features

that show clear regional variation. For example, the Old English vowel in such words as *stān* and *bān* has become the vowel in *stone* and *bone* in most varieties of modern English. North of the River Humber in northeast England, however, this vowel developed differently so that Scottish children may be heard saying:

> Sticks and stanes may break my banes
> But names will never hurt me.

The line dividing two areas that differ by a single feature such as this is called an *isogloss*. Where a number of isoglosses coincide there is a strong likelihood of a dialect boundary. For example, there are more isoglosses at the border between England and Scotland than for a considerable distance on either side of that border. In this case the language differences coincide with a difference in national identity. Similarly, it is not surprising that there should be a number of features that distinguish the speech of the South in the United States from that of the North. Noah Webster, fifty years after the United States gained its independence from Britain, was at pains to show the independence of American English by spellings such as *theater, color, defense,* and *jeweler* in contrast to *theatre, colour, defence,* and *jeweller*. There are nowadays many forms and expressions that distinguish the two varieties. For example:

BRITISH	AMERICAN
pavement	sidewalk
petrol	gasoline
boot (of a car)	trunk
motorway	freeway
goods van	freight car
biscuit	cookie
lift	elevator
queue	line
handbag	purse

There are also morphological differences. The past tense of the verb *fit* is *fitted* in British English and *fit* in American English; the past participle of *got* is *gotten* in the United States and *got* in Britain. Britons say *different from* in contrast to American *different than*. With increased travel and two-way traffic in television entertainment, many people are aware of such differences, but I find that my students in California do not understand the British colloquial expression *ticked off* as in *The supervisor called me in and I was ticked off* (that is, "reprimanded") because for them it means "annoyed." In England when I tell people that my daughter *went to school in Santa Cruz,* they are surprised to learn that she went to university there. Most Americans, however, have learned that in Britain *public school* refers to an exclusive private school. There may still be confusion with *grammar school,* which in the United States is for younger children and in Britain for older pupils, and *prep school,* which prepares pupils for a public school in England and for college in the United States. Finally, *colleges* in Britain, unlike those in the United States, do not grant baccalaureate degrees.

Does this mean that British English and American English are different dialects? In one sense, yes, but the term seems inappropriate for such large areas that have a great deal of geographical variation within them. Languages and dialects have both a unifying function and a separatist function. They help a group of people see what they have in common with each other and how they differ from "others." In the past, before the existence of passports or other identifying documents, language was one way of distinguishing not only friend from foe but also those from whom a suitable marriage partner could be chosen. Dialects still serve this function. It is part of what it means to be English or American to speak in a certain way, just as it is part of what it means to be Scots, Welsh, Texan, or a New Yorker.

Dialects can differ with respect to any characteristic of language. The most obvious is pronunciation. In the Old Testament it is recorded that the men of Gilead asked the Ephraimites to say the word *Shibboleth;* if they could not say it correctly but said *Sibboleth* instead, they were killed. Things are not usually so serious nowadays, but a Caribbean woman who was attempting to enter the United States illegally from Canada at Niagara Falls was stopped when she claimed to have been born in "Booffalo" on the grounds that anyone who was born in Buffalo would know how to say it. Single sounds, however, can give an important clue as to geographical origin. In England north of a line approximately from the Wash to the Bristol channel, the vowel in words such as *come* and *much* is pronounced as if spelled *coom* and *mooch.* This was an important factor when advertisements for traveling salesmen often contained the warning *Northcountrymen need not apply.* In the United States the word *greasy* is usually pronounced with an [s] north of the Mason-Dixon line and with a [z] south of it. In Scottish dialects, where the effects of the Great Vowel Shift are different from its impact in England, words such as *down* and *mouse* are pronounced *doon* and *moose.*

In the Potteries area of England, according to Peter Trudgill, there is an interesting pattern of vowels:

bait is pronounced like beat
beat is pronounced like bait
bought is pronounced like boat
boat is pronounced like boot
boot is pronounced like bout
bout is pronounced like bite
bite is pronounced like "baht"

According to Trudgill, in this dialect, *it seems the same* is pronounced like *it sames the seem.* In practice, even substantial differences like this need not always cause difficulty in understanding because it will often be clear from the context which word is being used. Only occasionally does a word occur in an ambiguous context. I once bought a freezer from someone who had grown up in New Jersey. He warned me that there was *a plastic pen* in it that sometimes rattled. Knowing that he had young children who were quite lively, the presence of a plastic pen did not seem surprising to me. It was years later that I realized that he had been talking about *a plastic pan.*

There can also be morphological differences between dialects, for example, in negation. In Scottish dialects the contracted negative is frequently *-nae* rather than

-n't as in *the foreman there he didnae want a lassie* and *it cannae be broken*. In some dialects *ain't* is used for all contracted forms of the negative with *be* and *have*, instead of *isn't, aren't, hasn't,* and *haven't*. For example, *there ain't nothing over there* and *I ain't got one single flea in my hair, they're all married*. In Somerset dialect *I be* can occur for *I am* as in *he's older than what I be and I ben't taking her down there*. In both England and the United States there is variation in the past tense of *see* in local dialects. In the north and part of the southwest of England *seed* is used, in the southeast *seen* is more common, while in many places *see* is used as a past tense. A similar kind of distribution is found in dialects in the eastern United States with *see* (for the past tense) commonest in northern parts, *seen* in midland areas, and *seed* in the southern part.

Syntactic differences in dialects have been studied less than other aspects, partly because it is more difficult to collect information on syntax. In Ayr in Scotland I recorded speakers using emphatic forms of syntax such as *he was some man him, it was Jimmy Brown was the fireman, it was him that led the band,* and *that's me seen it*. In Irish English there are similar but different constructions: *it was a great race was that, it is looking for more land a lot of them are, it's badly she'd do it now*. In Alabama speakers have a distinctive verb form with *done* as in *I think that Mr. K has done passed away* and *they had done operated on her for appendicitis,* where the sense is like "already." In Hawick in Scotland double modals are found as in *he might could do it for you* where the use of both *might* and *could* reinforces the notion of possibility. Such combinations are also found in the southern United States: *I might should turn over to Ann and it shouldn't oughta take us very long*. The persistence of such forms despite the efforts of teachers and other authorities to discourage them is a reminder that the actual standards for "correctness" are set by the people who speak the language.

The greatest differences, however, are found in vocabulary, particularly in the kinds of words that are learned directly from other people rather than in school or from books. Words for farm equipment, birds, animals, and plants have traditionally varied from region to region. For example, in different parts of Scotland the foxglove is known as *bloody finger, fairy finger, witch's pap, trowie glove, bloody man's finger, lady's finger, witch's thimble, fairy thimble, dead man's bell,* and *dead man's finger*. The references to *finger* translate its Latin technical name *digitalis purpurea*.

When I was growing up in Ayrshire, I often got a *skelf* in my finger and I thought that was the word all Scots used for a splinter. When the first volume of the *Linguistic Atlas of Scotland* came out, I found that this word was only one of many; those in the north of Scotland called it a *stab* or a *stob,* while further south it was known as a *spale* or a *spelk*. When I went to California, I learned a number of new words. It took me some time to find out that *submarine* was a special kind of sandwich, but even longer to discover that the same sandwich had other names in other parts of the United States—a *hoagie* in Philadelphia, a *po' boy* in New Orleans, a *grinder* in New England, a *hero* in New York City, a *wedge* or a *torpedo* in other parts of New York State, and a *zep* in Norristown, Pennsylvania.

Local customs can also give rise to local words. In Scotland the last corn sheaf cut at harvest was considered important enough to justify its own name. In the northeast it is known as the *clyack,* further south it is the *maiden,* in central Scotland it is the *kirn,* and in the southwest it is the *hare.* It does not have a special name south of the Scottish-English border.

There is one dialect that is not usually considered such and that is the standard dialect. There is probably no expression referring to a variety of language that is more liable to misuse and misinterpretation than *Standard English.*

Part of this is because of the ambiguity in the word *standard.* It can be used in reference to a model for imitation or as a basis for comparison, as in *setting a standard,* but it can also be used in the sense of "normal, average" as in *standard model.* Use of the term Standard English can imply that it is both the measure of excellence and the normal form of language to be used. Consequently, forms of language that are labeled "nonstandard" are assumed to be inferior and abnormal, and thus this label is simply a euphemism for "substandard."

There are many people who will insist that Standard English is the best possible form of English because it is (1) the most logical, (2) the most regular, and (3) the most beautiful. Each of these views is questionable. (1) Languages are neither logical nor illogical, though the users of the language can be. (2) Those dialects in which the third-person singular *-s* inflexion has been lost are more regular (in this respect) than Standard English. (3) There is no objective criterion by which the beauty of a language can be measured.

Beliefs in the superiority of Standard English in these terms would be harmless were it not that they can lead to prejudice against a large proportion of the population in both the United States and Great Britain. Standard English is a form of language based on that used by the educated minority in both countries. It is promulgated through the educational system and sustained largely through the editorial staff of the media and major publishing houses. Dennis Preston has clearly expressed the value of such a variety:

> Surely one of the functions of a standard is to convey serious information in a variety which implies that the speaker or writer is well-informed and which disallows a caricature of the message itself on the grounds that it is delivered in "incorrect" language.

It is as a "neutral" variety that Standard English is useful, to avoid the distracting impact of local variants. In this sense, Standard English is a nonregional dialect and that is why it is being considered in this chapter. However, it also has social class associations since it is identified with the speech of the middle and upper classes, and in that sense belongs in the next chapter. I once suggested that a better term would be *Common English,* and then deviations would be examples of *Uncommon English,* which they often are in the case of local dialect expressions, though none the worse for that.

There is another reason for considering Standard English in this chapter. It had its origin in a regional dialect. There were major dialect differences in Old English, which continued into Middle English. In the fourteenth century the administrative center of England moved to London, taking with it an East Midland form of speech that became the basis of what is known as Chancery English, the form in which official documents were written. This written form laid the foundation for the administrative language of the court and ultimately led to what we now call Standard English. Even today it is largely the written form that determines what is accepted as standard.

John Earl Joseph points out that the common view puts a high value on the notion of a standard language:

> The myth of a Golden Age that is so deeply embedded in Western culture includes as one of its facets that in the harmonious time all people shared a common tongue, and that the subsequent diversity of language and dialects accords with a diminution of all positive virtues from their primeval absoluteness. In so far as standardization represents a cultural effort to restore language to its pristine state, its goal will be to overcome dialectal diversity by providing the ideal medium for communication among all members of the unit of loyalty.

The importance of Standard English in the educational system has been a controversial subject. James Sledd expresses one view forcefully: "Upward mobility is impossible for underdogs who have not learned middle-dog barking." The importance of attitudes to language will be examined in the next chapter.

Social Class

Education is seldom obtained by stealth
Learning requires no small amount of wealth.

William Telford

Over the past thirty years it has been shown quite clearly that in socially stratified societies there are systematic differences in the way people from different
backgrounds speak. This is not a new phenomenon but goes back at least as far as
Chaucer's time. The invention of the portable tape recorder, however, has made it
possible to investigate social differences in language more closely and to show
exactly which features vary and under what circumstances. Briefly, the most common method has been to record samples of speech from people of different social
backgrounds in a single community and to search the tapes for features of language
that vary. Such features are labeled *linguistic variables*. For example, in New York
City it is common to hear [t] instead of [θ] in words such as *think* and *three*. This
usage is not equally frequent among people from all social backgrounds but is
more common among those lower down the social scale. The extent to which this
is true can be shown by taking the contexts in which a choice is possible between
[t] and [θ] and counting the number of times [t] occurs. By converting this score
to an average, it is possible to produce an index for this variable for each individual
whose speech has been recorded. The indexes for individuals at the same socioeconomic level can then be combined and averaged to produce a score for that
section of the community. The results for the (th) variable can be seen in figure
14.1.

It can be seen from figure 14.1 that the line slopes downward from the lowest
socioeconomic level to the highest. In other words, as you go up the social ladder
you are less likely to find people using [t] for [θ]. There is thus a correlation
between socioeconomic level and the use of the (th) variable. Other correlations
may appear. For example, in Glasgow the use of a glottal stop for [t], particularly
before a vowel or a pause, is generally condemned by teachers and others in positions of authority. However, most Glaswegians use glottal stops to some extent
as table 14.1 shows. The roman numerals refer to three social class groupings based
on occupation. I is the professional and managerial level; II the lower white-collar
occupations; and III the manual workers. It can be seen that the use of glottal stops

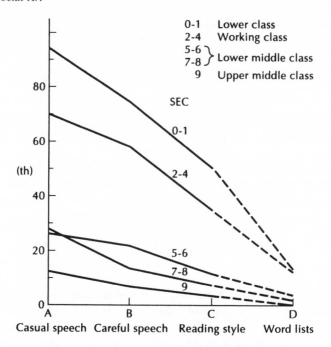

0-1   Lower class
2-4   Working class
5-6 ⎱
7-8 ⎰ Lower middle class
  9   Upper middle class

SEC

0-1

2-4

5-6

7-8

9

A   B   C   D
Casual speech   Careful speech   Reading style   Word lists

FIGURE 14.1 *Class stratification of /th/.* (From Labov, 1966. By permission of the Center for Applied Linguistics).

increases from Group I to Group III. It can also be seen that in each group women use fewer glottal stops than men. This is most obvious in Group II. The question of sex differences in language is examined in chapter 18. There is also an interesting difference depending upon the age of the speaker as shown in table 14.2. At ten years old the children I interviewed in Glasgow speak more like each other regardless of family background than the fifteen-year-olds or the adults. In other words, social differences in language increase with age rather than decrease. If this is true elsewhere, then it would mean that education, far from having a leveling effect actually has a stratifying effect.

There is no evidence that normal human beings are significantly different at birth in their potential for developing language. The language children learn does not depend upon any characteristics of their genetic parents but on the language

TABLE 14.1 Percentage of Glottal Stops

	I	II	III
All adults	10.3	27.1	84.0
Men	11.3	41.6	90.7
Women	9.3	12.5	77.2

TABLE 14.2. Percentage of Glottal Stops

	I	II	III
Adults	10.3	27.1	84.0
15-year-olds	14.9	69.2	87.4
10-year-olds	57.5	84.3	83.9

they hear around them at the time they are learning to speak. Infants adopted soon after birth into families speaking a totally different language from that of their natural parents will learn the language of their adoptive parents. The language, education, race, and social position of the natural parents are totally irrelevant. It is therefore rather surprising that there is such a close relationship between family background and success on language tests in school.

A large number of studies in different countries have shown that family background is a very important factor in predicting success at school. Children from lower social-class groups on average do worse at school than those from higher social-class groups and part of the reason appears to be language. In the United States most high school students applying for admission to colleges and universities take a standardized achievement test (SAT) administered by the College Entrance Board. Every year statistics are compiled showing the average SAT scores achieved by students according to family income. Figure 14.2 shows that there is an almost perfect match between the rise in parental income and the rise in average scores. These figures are based on nearly a million responses and the correlation has remained constant over a number of years, so it is not a matter of chance.

A large-scale survey of seven-year-olds in Britain found that children in the lowest social-class group were twenty months behind those in the highest social-class group in reading skills. Moreover, the chances of an unskilled manual worker's child being a poor reader were six times greater than those of a professional worker's child, and the chances that the manual worker's child would be a nonreader were fifteen times greater.

It should be stressed that there is no evidence to show that this lack of success among children from certain kinds of backgrounds has anything to do with natural ability. On the contrary, there is considerable evidence to show that many of those children who fail at school are as capable as many of those that succeed. One study in the United States failed to find any differences in intelligence among newly born children that could be related to social class differences among the parents. It is also important to emphasize that a poor score on a language test need not indicate that a child is nonverbal. All normal children develop normal skills under normal conditions but the kinds of topics they talk about and the ways in which they will talk about them depend upon the environment in which they are growing up. A test that classifies as nonverbal a child who can be heard communicating effectively through language with other children outside of the classroom has simply failed to tap that child's linguistic competence.

Some Italian adolescents who had been considered failures in the state school

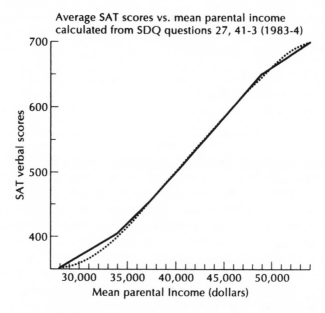

FIGURE 14.2 *Average SAT scores versus mean parental income (calculated from SDQ questions 27, 41–43 [1983–84]).*

system were taken into an "alternative" school. As a group project, they wrote a book in which they commented on the shortcomings of the educational system in their country. It is a book that is full of perceptive and insightful comments. One of their remarks refers to the importance of language: "Languages are created by the poor, who go on renewing them for ever. The rich crystalize them in order to put on the spot anybody who speaks in a different way. Or in order to make him fail exams" (*Letter to a Teacher,* by the School of Barbiana). Language tests may prove to be discriminatory for a variety of reasons having to do with linguistic, cultural, and social differences.

However, the influence of language differences on success in the school is not limited to tests. Teachers' expectations may affect a child's academic progress and such expectations are often based on the child's use of language. Children who speak up, articulate clearly, speak fluently, use the same language forms as the teacher, both answer and ask questions, and appear to understand what is said to them are generally judged to be brighter and more likely to succeed, and most teachers would be able to point to many examples where their judgment had been confirmed by the child's subsequent success. However, the teacher's judgment, expectations, and consequent behavior may have been an important ingredient in that success. This is fortunate for the child rewarded in this way but unfortunate for those of the child's peers who have been judged less favorably, for whom the expectations have been lower, and for whom the teacher's attitude may have produced less positive results.

Unfortunately, there are cultural and social differences in the use of language that may mislead the teacher in judging the child's potential. In some cultures, children are not encouraged to question adults or volunteer remarks in their presence. A child from such a background might easily appear sullen, uncooperative, or dull to a teacher who has different expectations about "normal" speech behavior from a child of that age. Conversely, in other cultures children may be encouraged to show off in front of adults and they may seem to be impudent and undisciplined to a teacher who does not expect this.

Differences in "good manners" and what is considered appropriate behavior should not and probably would not affect success in school were it not for the important fact that so much of language development is cumulative. The more you know, the easier it is to increase that knowledge. The better you read, the easier it will be to read more widely and more quickly. Learning one thing is often the essential springboard to learning something else. Thus the child's early experiences in school may be of critical importance for future linguistic and intellectual development. It is tragic if differences between the child's form of speech and the teacher's either create serious problems of communication between them or lead the teacher to underestimate the child's potential.

Since the teacher's expectations can affect children's progress in academic subjects, the dangers inherent in making superficial judgments are obvious. Unfortunately, it is too easy to find evidence of negative attitudes toward certain forms of speech. One investigator in the United States asked a group of trainee teachers to evaluate the speech of some Anglo-American, African-American, and Mexican-American children. They saw the children on videotape and heard them on an accompanying audiotape. What the trainee teachers did not know was that excerpts from the same speech sample were played with the videotapes of the three different groups of children. Not altogether surprisingly (but very revealingly) the trainee teachers rated the speech of the African-American and Mexican-American children as less "standard" than that of the Anglo-American children, although in fact the actual quality of speech was the same for all three groups of children. Thus what the trainee teachers were reacting to was not what they heard but what they expected to hear from children from a particular kind of background. Although the trick played on the trainee teachers was rather unfair, the experiment reveals the existence of preconceived notions of speech among people who were hoping to become teachers. It is not only children whose speech is the subject of prejudice.

The ability to distinguish tiny variations in speech allows people to make superficial judgments about someone from the way he or she speaks. Just as people are often favorably or unfavorably judged on the basis of the length of their hair, the neatness of their clothes, or the state of their shoes, similarly they may be judged on the basis of their way of speaking. It has been shown in experiments that people are willing to judge their fellow citizens on the evidence of quite short samples of recorded speech. Listeners have been able to make consistent judgments about a speaker's social status, suitability for various jobs, education, race, personality, physical toughness, and the possibility of becoming a friend of the listener's. Such judgments are often inaccurate, reflecting the prejudices and stereotypes that exist in the community. The judgments are also likely to vary with the age, sex, education, race, and social background of the listener.

For example, a study in Canada showed that listeners judged speakers to be different in personality depending upon whether they were speaking English or French; the speakers were judged to be more intelligent and dependable when they were speaking English than when they were speaking French. (The listeners did not know that they were listening to the same people speaking in the two languages.) The listeners also judged the English speakers to be taller and better looking than the French speakers, thus revealing stereotypes associated with the two types of speaker in Canada. The judgments varied somewhat depending upon whether the listener was a member of the English-speaking community or of the French-speaking community, but the overall pattern of the responses was similar. In this study the speakers used two distinct languages, French and English, but similar results have been obtained when different dialects (regional and/or social) of the same language have been used.

The features of language upon which social judgments are based are often relatively small differences in pronunciation or grammar. For example, dialects of English differ according to whether the /r/ is pronounced at the end of words such as *car* and *four* or before another consonant as in *card* or *fourth*. In some communities (for example, in most of southern and midland England and in the southern United States), it is considered correct to omit the /r/ in such words. In other communities (the rest of the United States and in Scotland) it is considered correct to pronounce the /r/ in these words. Judgments about what is correct are based upon the speech of those members of the community whose way of speaking has a particular kind of prestige so that it is generally taken as the norm for educated middle-class speakers. However, there is nothing inherently better about either kind of pronunciation, as is obvious from the fact that the prestige forms are exactly reversed in New York and London, two cities with large numbers of educated, middle-class speakers. Nor is it more correct to pronounce the /r/ because it is the older form or because it is there in the spelling. In few communities is the sound corresponding to the *gh* in words such as *night* and *thought* pronounced, although it was always pronounced some seven hundred years ago and it still is in some Scottish dialects.

There is also no reason to believe that one variety of language is inherently more logical than another. In many dialects of English it is normal to use more than one indicator of negation in an utterance such as *I never touched none of them* where speakers of another dialect might say *I didn't touch any of them.* There is nothing illogical about the first form. Such multiple marking of negation was normal in English until about Shakespeare's time, though its use at the present time is restricted to certain dialects. Another example of the arbitrariness of value judgments in language can be seen in the difference between French and English as regards the marking of negation. In English multiple marking of negation, as in *I ain't done nothing,* is stigmatized. In French it is the reduction of negative marking to a single form that is stigmatized. In "correct" (that is, socially approved) French the simple negative consists of two parts, *ne* and *pas,* as in *Je ne sais pas* ("I don't know"). Many French people now use simply *pas* alone for the negative in everyday conversation, much to the disgust of purists. Nor is it illogical to say *Me and John did it* instead of *John and I did it* or to say *They big* instead of *They're big.* What is considered grammatical in the standard language is the result of a process whereby certain forms used by the dominant elite have been identified as correct in the educational system and in the media, while different forms used by other groups are labeled incorrect (ungrammatical). This is not because there is anything inherently better about either kind of form. Nor does it follow from this that use of the nonstandard forms is careless or random. Dialects of a language differ from one another in a number of ways for historical and social reasons, but all dialects are highly organized, abstract systems with their own complex rules. The reasons for valuing one dialect more highly than another are social, not linguistic, but there is no doubt that many people feel very strongly about such matters.

It is also possible for researchers to be mistaken in the interpretation of their results. In the 1960s Basil Bernstein's views on social class differences in England gained widespread attention and were influential in the United States as well as in Britain. Bernstein suggested that working-class speakers were limited to what he called a *restricted code* consisting of simple, often unfinished, sentences and limited vocabulary. In contrast, middle-class speakers could also use an *elaborated code*, which as its name suggests employed more complex constructions and vocabulary. The distinction bears a great similarity to the difference between relaxed conversation and formal or written uses of language (see next chapter) but Bernstein drew far-reaching and misleading conclusions for this difference in language use.

Bernstein's initial characterization of these codes was mainly based on recordings he made of three groups of adolescent boys. Unfortunately, these recordings provide a very slender and somewhat misleading justification for the far-reaching claims that he made. More carefully controlled studies have shown many differences from the claims Bernstein made and weakened the case for fundamental about social class differences. There is, however, one point which Bernstein made that I found supported by my own research. Bernstein claimed that the middle-class speakers used more complex adjectives and adverbs than the working-class speakers. In two separate investigations I found that the middle-class speakers used words such as *briefly*, *evidently*, and *generally* more than three times as frequently as the working-class speakers. More surprisingly, the working-class speakers seldom used the word *very*. This difference in the use of adverbs is not because the working-class speakers did not know the words but rather reflects a different style of speaking. Bernstein had argued that the middle-class speakers used language more logically. Paradoxically, I found their use of adverbs more often to be a reflection of the speaker's attitude and thus closer to the emotional use of language that Bernstein associated with the working class. Thus, even though his empirical claim was supported his interpretation turned out to be misleading. Bernstein's work (along with the attention it received) stands as a cautionary tale for those who risk making generalizations about social class differences in language. My quantitative study of speakers in Glasgow found few significant social class differences.

The importance of attitudes toward language is considerable. In many situations it is important to make a good impression when first meeting a stranger, and the way one speaks may contribute significantly to the impression created. In an interview for a job this may even be of crucial importance. As was pointed out in the previous chapter, the way children speak may affect the teacher's view of their intelligence and ability. It is particularly unfortunate if children are made to feel that their way of speaking is inferior in any way, and this can happen when the child's form of speech differs considerably from that of the teacher. The attitude of teachers toward language in the classroom is particularly important. This has been exceptionally well expressed by John Macnamara: "The teacher believes that language is to be respected and caressed for its own sake, that one needs to do penance and prepare oneself to capture the fine points of pronunciation and grammar as Sir Galahad prepared himself to seek the Holy Grail." Macnamara believes that many children are baffled by this attitude since they see language as merely a modest tool for communicating. He argues that the best way to encourage them to make use of their language learning ability is by getting the children vitally engaged in communicating.

It would be wrong to say that small differences in pronunciation and grammar are unimportant since people pay attention to such things and often attach great significance to them, but in themselves they are trivial. A rather simple metaphor may help to emphasize this point. Drinking vessels come in many shapes and sizes and are made of diverse materials and, other things being equal, we often value one more than the other. If we are thirsty, however, it is not the vessel itself but what it contains that is important.

The grammatical structure of language is like the shape of the drinking vessel and pronunciation is like the material it is made out of, but the meaning is what the cup contains. When we are thirsty we are more likely to be interested in the drink itself than in the beauty of the cup.

There are two further parallels. The first is the appropriateness for a particular situation, which is often a matter of convention. Wedgwood fine bone-china cups are often highly valued, but it is not usually considered correct to serve brandy or champagne in them. Second, what is appropriate in one situation may not be so in another. When one goes mountaineering, a plastic or metal cup may be more serviceable than a thin-stemmed wineglass. Similarly with language there is no reason to believe that any single form will be suitable for all situations, which is why so many different forms can exist within a speech community. Such diversity is to be welcomed and enjoyed rather than condemned or eradicated.

Written Language

The notion of representing a sound by a graphic symbol is itself so stupefying a leap of the imagination that what is remarkable is not so much that it happened relatively late in human history, but that it happened at all.

Jack Goody and Ian Watt *"The Consequences of Literacy"*

There is no way to determine when human beings first began to use language as we know it. The origins of language are lost in the prehistoric past and can never be recovered. Archaeological evidence is no help because bones are not the critical parts of the speech apparatus. Estimates of how long people have been using language vary from fifty to a hundred thousand years. We do know, however, that languages have been written down for widespread uses only during the past three thousand years.

The earliest writing systems used pictures to represent aspects of the world. Later these pictures became more stylized and could be used more flexibly. Later still, the symbols came to represent language rather than refer to the world directly. There are three major kinds of writing system at present. A *logographic* system has symbols that represent whole words (or at least morphemes), as does the Chinese writing system. A *syllabic* writing system has a symbol for each syllable but not for each sound. Thus the Japanese Katakana system has symbols for [pa], [ta], [ka], and so on but no separate symbols for [p], [t], and [k]. Finally, there is an *alphabetic* writing system where each symbol represents a single sound.

For some purposes it is obviously an advantage to have each symbol uniquely represent one sound so that anyone hearing a sound will know how to write it down and anyone reading a word will know how to pronounce it. This is what the International Phonetic Alphabet (IPA) was designed to accomplish. The first version of IPA was approved in 1888, and it has been used since then by linguists all over the world with varying success. But there are a number of problems. One is that some speech sounds are harder to represent in a simple way; another has been that there are not enough characters on a conventional typewriter keyboard to represent the variety of sounds in the languages of the world; a third is that phonetic transcriptions are tiring to read even for those familiar with all the symbols. There used to be a journal on phonetics printed in IPA but it has changed to normal orthography.

Most orthographies do not approach the phonetic ideal. Spanish and Italian come close but French and English are a long way from it. There are, however, compensating benefits. First, it is necessary to look at the system of English orthography. It is clear that neither the principle that one sound should be represented by one symbol nor the principle that each symbol should represent a single sound is upheld by English orthography. If we take the [i:] sound in the word *meet* we find that there are numerous ways that it can be spelled:

ee	seen
e	she
ea	meat
ie	field
ei	receive
eo	people
oe	amoeba
ae	caesarian
ey	key
ay	quay
eCe	obscene, concede, replete, obese
i	machine

Thus there are twelve ways in which the sound [i:] is represented in English. The reverse situation can be seen with the letter *s:*

[s]	cats
[z]	dogs

and the letter *c:*

[k]	cat
[s]	city

It is, however, not only single letters that are important, as was obvious in the case of [i:] where one sound is represented by more than one letter. There are also combinations of consonants:

sh [š]	ship
ch [č]	chip

Such combinations can also represent different sounds:

ch [š]	machine
ch [x]	loch
th [ð]	this
th [θ]	think
th [t]	thyme
th [th]	pothole

Just as there is a difference between sounds and phonemes, so there is a difference between letters and graphemes. Phonemes are the distinctive units of sound in a language; graphemes are the distinctive units of a writing system. In order to learn to read you must first be able to identify the letters of the alphabet but that is not enough; you have to discover how these letters are used in graphemes to represent the sounds of the language.

There have been many attempts to reform English spelling but they have all failed. George Bernard Shaw even left his considerable fortune as a reward for the development of a new alphabet for English, but it produced only an ingenious curiosity. The reason for the failure of attempts to reform English spelling is not simply a stubborn resistance to change. There are certain advantages to the present system once you have mastered it. These are not restricted to the social advantages that the economist Thorstein Veblen pointed out in *The Theory of the Leisure Class:*

> As felicitous an instance of futile classicism as can well be found, outside of the Far East, is the conventional spelling of the English language. A breach of the proprieties in spelling is extremely annoying and will discredit any writer in the eyes of all persons who are possessed of a developed sense of the true and the beautiful. English orthography satisfies all the requirements of the canons of reputability under the law of conspicuous waste. It is archaic, cumbrous, and ineffective; its acquisition consumes much time and effort; failure to acquire it is easy of detection. Therefore it is the first and readiest test of reputability in learning, and conformity to its ritual is indispensable to a blameless scholastic life.

Veblen was right that English orthography takes time and effort to master. He was also right when he pointed out that it is easy to detect errors. Teachers at all levels take great pleasure in drawing attention to these errors by annotations in red ink, but a moment's reflection is enough to make one realize how trivial many of these mistakes are. If it were not obvious what had been intended, the teacher would be unable to detect the error. Most spelling mistakes do not affect the meaning or make the passage more difficult to read. It was only after Addison and Steele in the eighteenth century taught the upwardly mobile the importance of gentility in writing that correct spelling became a fetish in England, and it has remained so ever since.

Veblen was wrong, however, in claiming that English orthography is ineffective. It is ineffective only if you need to learn how to pronounce the words from reading them, but speakers of the language already know how to pronounce them. What speakers of the language need to do is recognize the words in their written form. The different spellings of *meet, meat,* and *mete,* or of *right, write, rite,* and *wright* help us to recognize the word quickly and distinguish it from its homophones (that is, the words that sound the same).

A second advantage is that words that are morphologically related can be spelled to bring out the similarities. For example, *photograph* and *photography* are clearly related and the spelling shows this. If we spell them phonetically [fotəgræf] and [fətɒgrəfiy], the similarity is less obvious. This is also true of the examples that reflect the Great Vowel Shift (chapter 25): *divine/divinity* [dɪvaɪn]/[dɪvɪnɪtiy], *serene/serenity* [səri:n]/[sərɛnɪtiy], etc. The normal spelling brings out the relationship much more clearly.

The third, and perhaps the most important, reason is that because the normal orthography does not indicate the phonetic quality directly, the same spelling system can be used by people who speak very different dialects. Since there are many differences in pronunciation in the English spoken in the British Isles and the English spoken in the Unitied States (not to mention other parts of the world), a system of writing that was phonetically correct for one dialect would not be so for other dialects (chapter 13). For example, the dialects in which /r/ is not pronounced at the end of words or before another consonant would look very different from those in which the /r/ is pronounced. As it is, all dialects can use the same system. In fact, the writing system has not changed radically since Chaucer's time, although the pronunciation has changed considerably.

This is a fourth reason for retaining a traditional orthography; through it the writings of the past look more familiar than they would if we changed to a new spelling system that reflected contemporary pronunciation. Moreover, as the language changed, we would have to keep changing the writing system.

The existence of a writing system affects our knowledge of language. In other words, knowing a language in a literate society is very different from knowing a language in a society where writing is unknown. Partly this is because the use of written language differs in important ways from speech.

Speech is always localized in time and space. That is, an utterance must have been made at a specific time and in a particular place. The apparent exceptions are electrically recorded examples that can be replayed at a different time and in a different place. Speech is dynamic, proceeds continuously, and must be subject to on-line monitoring and analysis by the speaker and listener. If you miss something that was uttered, you cannot go back to find out what it was. You have to ask the speaker to repeat it. If you make a mistake when speaking, you cannot go back and erase it; you can only correct it by saying something else.

Speech consists of a series of continuous movements rather than a succession of discrete items. As literate speakers we tend to think of language as consisting of words and of words as consisting of sounds or letters. In speech however utterances are not segmented by pauses the way words are separated by spaces.

Speech frequently occurs in situations where the speaker and listener can see each other, so that the linguistic utterance is only part of the communication event. For this reason, there are many things that do not need to be said because they are obvious from the physical context. Moreover, the speaker makes assumptions about what the listener knows already and can adjust these assumptions based on the feedback received from the listener's responses (or lack of response). Miscommunication can be repaired immediately, either by the speaker ("self-repair") or at the request of the listener ("other repair").

The normal situation for speech is dialogic. People do not generally talk to themselves, although there are occasions when we swear or address inanimate objects and do not expect a response. In most normal speech situations, however, we expect the listener to be ready to respond in some way (chapter 21) and not simply to be a passive receiver. This is because we expect all normal members of our speech community to be capable of speaking and understanding everday language.

In contrast, written texts are generally not closely identified with the time and place of production. The exceptions include personal letters, notes, legal documents, and the like, where it is normal to give the date and place of signing if not of composition. But in many cases we have no precise notion of where and when the passage we are reading was written. This is partly because written texts can be passed on, copied, and revised. The writer may have little control over what use is made of the text once it has been committed to paper.

Written texts (in contemporary English, at least) are composed of sequences of discrete items (letters, words, sentences) and the boundaries are usually fairly clear. The rules for correct written language are deliberately taught and enforced not only in schools but by editors, supervisors, and so on.

Written texts are static and durable. They can be scanned more than once and selectively. If you miss something, you can go back and read it again. You can also skip a few pages or a chapter or two if you find it boring. How often we wish we could do the same when obliged to listen to a boring speaker!

Many written texts are produced without a specific reader in mind. Writers usually have an idea of the kind of readers they hope will read their writings but they do not usually know their readers personally. The writer accordingly can make fewer assumptions about what the reader is likely to know and there is no immediate feedback from the reader to guide the writer. The writer therefore must guard against miscommunication by trying to avoid ambiguity or anything else that might mislead the reader.

The normal situation in writing is monologic. Usually the writer works alone and so does the reader. Both writer and reader may imagine a dialogue between them but this imagined dialogue cannot change the text. The reader sometimes has to guess what the writer means; the writer always has to anticipate problems that the reader might have.

The ability to write (and to read) is less equally distributed in society than the ability to speak (and understand what is said). Writers are more conscious of explicit rules, partly because writing is something that is "taught" in school. Even where attention is paid to spoken language in school, the instruction is likely to be much more vague than that provided for writing.

As a result of these differences between spoken and written language, the linguistic features of spoken and written language differ in many ways. Some of the differences are obvious enough but others are more controversial.

Prosodic and paralinguistic features play a very important role in spoken language. In written language, punctuation and other devices such as italicization can give only a very crude indication of such features. Prosodic features include intonation (rise and fall in pitch of voice) and stress (making one syllable more prominent by loudness). Paralinguistic features include pauses, fillers such as *um* and *er,* speed, loudness, and emotional voice quality.

The notion of "sentence" is not well defined in speech. Speakers tend to utter groups of words in stretches of five to seven words at most, usually forming a coherent chunk; often but not always these chunks correspond to what we think of as clauses. Writers can use very long sequences without worrying about what can be spoken or comprehended easily, since the reader can go back and read the sentence again.

Speakers, particularly in conversational exchanges, tend to use discourse markers—for example, *well, oh, I know, I mean*—as a way of indicating orientation to what is happening in the discourse. The discourse markers have little explicit meaning but have very definite functions in discourse, particularly at transitional points. These markers are not used in written language. In the written language, equivalents are expressions such as *however, on the other hand, on the contrary,* which are used in the transition from one sentence to another.

It is often claimed that written language is more complex than spoken language. The difficulty in establishing this claim lies in the problems of defining complexity and of obtaining comparable examples. Obviously, the topic, style, and purpose of the communication will affect the nature of the language, not to mention the education of the originator. We use speech and writing for different purposes so it is not surprising that they should be stylistically different. Speech, however, is not used in a single style. We speak differently depending upon our audience, the physical situation, the nature of the speech event (for example, conversation, public lecture, or sermon); the topic, and so on. Whether written or spoken, the language will be simple or complex depending upon our purpose.

Literacy is not just a skill; it affects how people view the world and act in it. Walter Ong presents the challenge to literate adults: "Try to imagine a culture where no one has ever 'looked up' anything." Writing is a relatively recent invention in the history of human beings. Even today there are societies in various parts of the world where the language of everyday usage is not written. Such languages are no less complex or systematic than European languages that have been written for centuries. For example, the Native American languages of North America or the Aboriginal languages of Australia generally have a much more complex morphology than most European languages. There are, however, obvious differences between literate and nonliterate societies.

Probably the most important difference is in the transmission of knowledge. In a nonliterate society, generally older people will know more than young people. Knowledge resides in memory. As Amadou Hampate Ba has said: "Whenever an old man dies in Africa, a library has burned down." In a literate society, on the other hand, young people often acquire knowledge beyond what their elders know, and consequently have less reason to respect them.

In literate societies, some kinds of writing are considered *literature.* These are written works that are considered to have some artistic and (probably) moral value. In oral cultures there are also examples of language that are highly valued for the same reasons but they are not written down. Sir Maurice Bowra reports:

> In 1934 Milman Parry found a bard in Southern Serbia, a Moslem called Adro Mededovic aged about sixty, who would sing for about two hours in the morning and for another two hours in the afternoon, resting for five or ten minutes every half hour. To sing a long song took him two weeks with a week's rest in between to rest his voice. . . . The bard in this case could not read or write, and seems to have composed the poem as he went on.

This is how poems such as the *Iliad,* the *Odyssey,* and *Beowulf* were composed. It is only when they came to be written down that their form became fixed. Until then the poems existed only as performances, and there were probably differences of form, of emphasis, of order, and maybe even of events from one performance to another. Yet these are highly sophisticated works of art. What we think of as literary skills are not confined to those who can read and write. Even after poetry and other works began to be written down, most people could not read it. In England until Chaucer's time, most people would hear poems read aloud rather than read them. It was only with the introduction of printing by William Caxton in the fifteenth century that the availability of printed books made reading possible for a wider public. Until then manuscripts were too precious to circulate widely.

It is important to recall how unimportant reading and writing were to most people until relatively recently, because literacy has assumed such an exalted place in our evaluation of others, particularly school children. As Neil Postman has observed, "It is an outrage that children who do not read well, or at all, are treated as if they were stupid." Intelligence is not dependent upon the ability to read and write. If it were then we would have to conclude that most people in the past, including Homer and the "author" of *Beowulf,* were stupid, a conclusion that is unacceptable.

It is true, nevertheless, that literacy is important in technologically advanced societies. There is no illiterate science. Science depends upon measurements and records of measurements. For this and other reasons, it is useful for everyone to be able to read and write. The problem for the educational system is that nobody knows exactly how children learn to read English. As we have seen earlier in this chapter, the relationship between written English and spoken English is indirect and complex. Someone once compared the reading teacher to the rain dancer. The rain dancer goes through certain routines and hopes that rain will come, since in the past this ritual seems to have had positive effects. Similarly, it was suggested, reading teachers go through certain procedures because this is what they did in the past and most of the children succeeded in learning to read. The problem arises with those children who fail to learn. Is it the children's fault or is it the teacher's?

Whatever the answer to that question, one factor that is clearly important in Britain and in the United States is family background. In numerous studies it has been shown that children from poorer families are more likely to encounter difficulties in learning to read than children from better-off families. The usual explanation is that the latter children are more likely to have seen their parents reading and writing, to have been read to, and to have been encouraged to read before they went to school than their less fortunate peers.

It is, of course, not the case that all children from less prosperous backgrounds have difficulty in learning to read, but too many do. It is bad enough if the teachers consider such children less intelligent; it is much worse if the children come to consider themselves incapable of learning. The greatest deception is to set up a task at which the candidate will almost certainly fail and then say: "Well, you had your chance to succeed." The greatest challenge for a democratic society is to find a way of ensuring that the playing field is level and that all children have a reasonable chance of succeeding.

One also hopes that they will come to enjoy reading because there is so much pleasure, knowledge, and comfort to be gained from reading. As Erasmus remarked, "When I get a little money, I buy books; and if there is any left, I buy food and clothes." For the fortunate that is not a bad order of priorities. Or as an ordinary working man I interviewed in Glasgow said, "It's been brought home to me that you've got to be feeding a kid more than one way when they're young." But force-feeding is not the answer. As Dr. Johnson observed, "A man ought to read just as inclination leads him; for what he reads as a task will do him little good." As with all forms of language use, reading is an active process, and the more we bring to it, the more we are likely to get out of it. In Lichtenberg's pithy aphorism, "A book is like a mirror. If an ass looks in you cannot expect an apostle to look out." Reading is one of those activities that the more we do, the better it gets.

16

Register

All words have the "taste" of a profession, a genre, a tendency, a party, a particular work, a particular person, a generation, an age group, the day and hour. Each word tastes of the context and contexts in which it has lived its socially charged life. . . .

Mikhail Bakhtin, *The Dialogic Imagination*

It is easy to underestimate how great an achievement learning to speak a language actually is. As we have seen in earlier chapters, human languages are wondrously complex and delicately balanced systems, and it is remarkable that we succeed so well in this task, literally without knowing what we are doing. It is also easy to overestimate what has been achieved. When traveling in a foreign country, we may ask someone, *Do you speak English?* What we really want to know is whether that individual will be able to understand what I want and also be able to tell me so that I can also understand the answer. This is very different from "speaking English" if by that we imply knowing the totality of the English language. Strictly speaking, nobody "speaks English" (or any other language). Instead we know and use that part of the language which is necessary and useful for our activities and interests. In addition to using a form of the language (regional and social dialect) that connects us to a particular section of the community, we also learn the kinds of language necessary for our work and play. The term used for the latter kind of language differences is *register*.

One of the passages I present to my students in California is the following:

The field is set normally for an off-spinner with two slips, a gulley, mid-off, mid-on, silly mid-on, two short legs, one slightly squarer than the other, and a long leg up saving the one. Brown, bowling round the wicket, runs up, bowls, well up to Smith, almost a yorker. Smith prods forward, gets a thickish edge and the ball trickles down the leg side. No run.

Usually one of the students will identify the passage as referring to cricket but seldom will any one of them be able to summarize what has happened. I point out to them that this is not because the words for the most part are unfamiliar. Admittedly, they cannot be expected to know what a *yorker* is, but they are familiar with the words *short, leg,* and *square.* However, their knowledge of these words in

85

their most common sense will not enable them to understand the phrase *two short legs, one slightly squarer than the other* unless they know the names for fielding positions in cricket. A similar problem faces most British readers with the terms *shortstop, left field, double play,* and *knuckleball* unless they have seen a baseball game.

A rather different kind of example is:

> The deep surface is in relation with the Mylohyoideus, Hyoglossus, Styloglossus, Stylohyoideus, and posterior belly of the Digastricus; in contact with it are the mylohyoid nerve and the mylohyoid and submental vessels.

Most of my students correctly identify this as coming from an anatomy textbook but they usually guess incorrectly that it refers to the stomach (probably because of *belly* and *Digastricus*) though it describes some of the muscles in the throat that are important for speech. This kind of language is obviously not part of the everyday usage of most people but it is one of the registers of English.

The next example comes from David Maurer's book *Whiz Mob:*

> Well, I fanned this guy with the scratch, and that's what I'm looking for. The tip was thinning out fast, and I was reefing the kick.

Maurer's book is about the language used by pickpockets. *Scratch* is money and *fanned* means that he lightly frisked the man to find out where he kept his wallet. The scene is the racetrack and the *tip* is the crowd. Obviously, it is easier to pick someone's pocket when there is a large crowd and people are pressed close to each other, so the fact that it was thinning out fast was a reason for urgency. *Reefing the kick,* according to Maurer, refers to the way in which the pickpocket puts his fingers into the man's pocket and pulls up the lining just like reefing a sail, so that the wallet seems just to float out of the pocket. (I have never tried it, so I cannot vouch for its success.) Like the cricket example, this passage shows how ordinary words can take on other meanings. The difference in this case is that the thieves' slang is intended to be obscure to outsiders. This is one of the purposes of slang in general, but thieves and others engaged in socially unacceptable practices often develop forms of speech that are intended to prevent overhearers from understanding what was said.

The next example came from a column by Alfred Sheinwold in the *Los Angeles Times:*

> "She opened a stiff, biffed the return and locked me in the cat."
>
> Translated into everyday English, this would read: "Her opening lead was a singleton, and her partner returned the suit, allowing her to ruff. She then made a lead that dummy had to win, and there was no way for me to get out of the dummy."

Sheinwold's column is about bridge. The first sentence is his example of a rare form of bridge players' slang. However, his translation into "everyday English" will be no clearer to those who do not know how to play the game.

Here are a few more examples of different registers:

> Stretched intervals appear to sound more active and expressive than flat intervals. (music)

This disadvantage of averages can be somewhat alleviated through the reporting of summaries of the dispersion of responses. (statistics)

I use the term ethnomethodology to refer to various policies, methods, results, risks, and lunacies with which to locate and accomplish the study of the rational properties of practical actions as contingent ongoing accomplishments of organized artful practices of everyday life. (sociology)

Frequent use of dissolves, uneven panning, and ambiguous time ellipses make it difficult to follow what is happening. (cinema)

With the exception of a relatively small core that is common to all speakers of the language, most of our language belongs to one register or another. Often the registers of academic disciplines contain so many technical terms that they appear to be gobbledegook to those outside the discipline. Although excessive use of technical jargon can often lead to bad writing (and perhaps conceal to some extent the poverty of the ideas), precisely defined technical terms are an essential part of most disciplines. It is too easy to make fun of other people's jargon, especially when it seems that a cumbrous polysyllabic term has been used in place of a shorter everyday word. Only scholars working within the field know to what extent the more esoteric terms are justified. Scholars have a duty not to make their writing more opaque than necessary and some are more successful at this than others.

Each register not only has its own vocabulary but also its appropriate forms for all the other features of the language. For example, the drill sergeant on the parade ground, the preacher in the pulpit, the stage hypnotist, and the cattle auctioneer will not only be using different kinds of expressions, they will also be using different kinds of voices (intonation, volume, speed, and so on). These are as much a part of the register as the words particular to each.

Registers are the one part of language development that is likely to continue throughout an individual's lifetime. Some registers are clearly age-linked. Peter and Iona Opie in *The Lore and Language of Schoolchildren* give an extensive account of the kind of expressions used by children at various ages for games, truce terms (see chapter 34), teasing, challenging, and so on. By the time they are adolescents they will probably have stopped using most of these expressions, and by the time they are adults they will probably have forgotten most of them.

Adolescents and undergraduates often have forms of language that are labeled *slang*. Slang is difficult to define. It consists of expressions used as a kind of ingroup language by some speakers to identify themselves with other speakers and to distance themselves from other speakers who do not use these forms. In this respect, slang is no different from dialect or register, but slang expressions tend to be ephemeral. By the time a slang expression reaches the wider public through the mass media, it is likely to have been abandoned by the group that originally used it. There is nothing more pathetic than hearing middle-aged people using outdated slang expressions which they think will show how current and youthful their language is. Like the pickpocket's register, the slang expressions of undergraduates often refer to activities that may meet with social disapproval: drinking, taking drugs, sexual intercourse. A recent study of undergraduate slang in California produced the following expressions:

For approval: rad, awesome, jammin', cool, hip, ragin', stylin'
For disapproval: sucks, boater, dumb, lame, drag, blah
For being drunk or on drugs: trashed, bombed, plowed, blitzed, wasted, puttied, hammered, fried, stooped
For vomiting: ralph, blow chunks, technicolor yawn, prayin' blow major chow

Some of the expressions are clearly intended to be funny and others perhaps to be offensive. The main point, however, is that they are unlikely to be current in the speech of the adults the students come in contact with. Slang is often disparaged, but Whitman considered it "the lawless geminal element . . . behind all poetry."

Knowing particular registers is the key to success in many ways. It is often easy to impress others by your knowledge of technical terms or expressions, and one of the functions of education is to equip learners with the vocabulary they will need in dealing with the complexity of the physical and social world. Unfortunately, exposure to the forms of words does not always result in a true understanding of their significance. It has been said that people in modern technological societies are more ignorant than those in smaller-scale societies because there are more things that they half-know. When we are genuinely interested in something, we learn not only the precise meanings of the words but also their limitations. As Ambrose Bierce defined it in his *Devil's Dictionary,* true education is "that which discloses to the wise and disguises from the foolish their lack of understanding." Knowing the right words is the first step; knowing how to use them is the next, and that is the topic of the next chapter.

17

Style

> A man with whom, in private conversation, I am on the friendliest terms sometimes becomes a stranger to me when I hear him speak in public.
>
> Paul Valery, *Analects*

Choice always implies meaning. Even if we choose to say nothing, our silence may be meaningful. What meaning that silence has depends not only upon the situation but also on what people expect. Among the Western Apache, for example, *— interest* it is normal to greet strangers and those who have been absent for a long time with silence. Talking begins only when the parts feel at ease with each other. In most *— This is* Western societies, the way to reach the stage of feeling comfortable is through *how I* talking. Many people feel awkward in the presence of strangers if the silence goes *feel* on too long. There is a tendency to make remarks about the weather, sports, or other uncontroversial subjects just to be friendly. Again, such feelings are culturally determined. V. S. Pritchett once described how a young man in Ireland had contributed to a lengthy and lively session merely by "breathing sociably."

Where there is no choice, the use of a form does not in itself signify a special meaning. For example, the use of the word *banana* to refer to a banana does not convey any special emphasis since there is no other word that would do. Similarly, in English the choice between an infinitive and a gerund is often restricted. For example, we must say *he wants to sing* (not **he wants singing*) and *he enjoys singing* (not **he enjoys to sing*). However, when both alternatives are possible there may also be a difference in meaning, as in *he tried to sing* (but couldn't) versus *— sound* *he tried singing* (but nobody paid any attention). In the first case he did not succeed *same to* *me.* in singing and in the second he did. This is a considerable difference of meaning. In some cases, however, it is much harder to bring out a clear meaning between two alternatives, as in *he likes to sing* versus *he likes singing.* *— Anyones singing Listening* *or singing*

Differences that do not radically affect the meaning are often called stylistic differences. The whole notion is controversial because there is no adequate theory of meaning that would allow us to distinguish between important and trivial differences of meaning. As this last statement may seem rather extreme, an example may help. The following pair of sentences at one time generated a considerable amount of discussion as to whether they were synonymous (meant the same thing) or not:

    a. Everybody in this room speaks two languages.
    b. Two languages are spoken by everybody in this room.

At the time when the discussion was most heated there was a claim in syntactic theory that the active (a) and passive (b) versions of a sentence had the same meaning. Some people pointed out that in (a) everybody might speak two languages but they need not be the same two, whereas in (b) they must be the same two. This is a considerable difference in meaning. Some other people then pointed out that both (a) and (b) were ambiguous as to whether the same two languages were spoken by everyone but that it was more likely in (b) that they were the same two and more likely in (a) that they were not just the same two languages. This is a much subtler distinction in meaning. Other examples used in this kind of discussion are:

    c. Each of the boys kissed one of the girls.
    d. One of the girls was kissed by each of the boys.

In this case the question is whether more than one girl was kissed. A more amusing pair of examples is:

    e. I teach arithmetic to the little monsters.
    f. I teach the little monsters arithmetic.

In this pair it has been claimed that in (e) I teach arithmetic but there is no implication as to the impact, whereas in (f) it is implied that the little monsters learn it.

    What these examples illustrate is the difficulty of deciding whether two expressions mean the same thing. Since languages are such economical systems, it might be thought that there must be a justification for alternatives. Even if there is, however, it need not be a difference in literal meaning. The notion is clearest in reference to physical objects that may be the same despite the different labels, for example, reference to one of the taboo subjects: *feces, excrement, stool, bowel movement, b.m., ka ka, doo doo, number two, turd, crap, shit*. A choice among such alternatives, however, is not totally free but constrained by such features of the speech event as setting (for example, doctor's office, preschool, summer camp, army barracks) and who the participants are. The choice of the "wrong" alternative will not usually lead to misunderstanding but to embarrassment.

    In other cases, the choice among alternatives may depend upon the relationship between the participants:

    a. I wonder if you would be so kind as to lower your voices a little.
    b. It's getting a little noisy in here.
    c. Would you please not talk?
    d. No talking.
    e. Silence.
    f. Shhhhhhh!
    g. Shut up!

The choice of (a) rather than (g), or conversely, will depend to some extent on the relationship between the speaker and those addressed. What would be exactly right in one case might (and probably would) be totally wrong in another.

    We have a wide range of possibilities for expressing requests. There is the direct imperative: *Leave me alone, Get me the Smith file, and Tell me all about it.* There is an explicit statement: *I'm asking you to leave the meeting.* We can soften the request in a variety of ways: *I was wondering if you'd come with me, I'd like to meet your brother, You ought to say what you mean,* and *I don't suppose you could lend me some money till the end of the month.* Questions can be used to make suggestions: *How about tidying your room today?* They can also give a gentle order: *Could you possibly type this up by this afternoon?*

It is possible to imagine a number of different relationships from the following examples of attempts to secure a lift home:

> Can you give me a lift home?
> Could you possibly drop me off on your way home?
> I wonder if I could get a lift home?
> I was wondering if I couldn't get a lift home with you.
> Are you going straight home?
> I expect the last bus will have gone by now.
> Well, I'd better get started as it's a long walk home.

From direct request to strong hint to mild hint the wording offers different opportunities for the person addressed to reject the request. The more indirect the request, the less direct the refusal needs to be.

Where the choice among the alternatives is so appropriate for the situation that it does not draw attention to itself, the question of style does not usually arise except in comparison with other situations, genres, or registers. For example, the words *domicile, residence, abode,* and *home* could all be used with reference to the same place. In everyday speech the most likely choice would be *home* and the use any of the others would immediately stand out as unusual, since they belong to different registers. When the choice of a particular form among the alternatives is striking or immediately noticeable, it is often called the *marked* form (in contrast to the neutral or unmarked form). A young man who said to a friend *Would you like to come to my abode tomorrow?* would probably be thought to have attempted a joke rather than a poetic utterance. Deliberate use of marked forms is called *foregrounding.* Foregrounding is particularly common in poetry, through devices such as rhyme, alliteration, assonance, meter, stanza form, and graphic arrangement (see chapter 33).

In everyday conversation foregrounding occurs only occasionally, as when one swears for effect or makes puns. The phenomenon of swearing is a curious one and will be examined in the next chapter. Newspapers in Britain often make use of puns in headlines. *Paradise lust* was the heading for a review of a romantic play set on a Caribbean island. An editorial on the 1992 election was headed *Who will inherit the dearth?* A columnist's complaint about distortion in reporting had the title *Learning the tricks of the tirade* and another about how much time Americans put into their jobs was entitled *Working their bucks off.* An article describing a book about very pessimistic economic forecasts was headed *The profits of doom,* and a review of a book revealing how the former chief of the FBI had kept files of incriminating evidence on almost all public figures was entitled *Hoover sucks up dirt.*

A mild form of foregrounding is the use of euphemisms, which often have the effect of drawing attention to themselves rather than the reverse. Louise Pound made a collection of American euphemisms for dying, death, and burial from which the following is only a small selection:

Is out of his misery
Suffered the last great change
Gone to meet the beyond
Turned up his toes
Stepped off the deep end
Answered the last roll call
Put to bed with a shovel

Euphemisms are also common in politics and war (see chapter 20).

Rather than foregrounding, most people in everyday exchanges are more likely to accommodate to the people they are speaking with. This can be observed, for example, when students who have been talking energetically among themselves go into a room to speak with a distinguished professor. This also happens in commercial dealings. The sales personnel will often take on the speech characteristics of their customers even when they speak very differently at home or with their friends. The reverse can also happen when we wish to distance ourselves from the person we are speaking with in order, for example, to complain or to reject a proposal.

A great many factors can affect the style of communication. The occasion and the setting may create a formal or a relaxed atmosphere. We would not expect the same kind of language in a board meeting and at a poker game. The age, sex, status, and so on, of the participants are important as well as the relationships between them. People may speak differently to their superiors, their peers, and their juniors. The presence of others who may overhear what is said can also have an impact.

There are also personal aspects. We can often tell whether a person is happy, angry, sad, depressed, enthusiastic, or resigned from the tone of voice. Physical fitness and energy level can also play a part. It is the ability to mimic these qualities that makes up much of the skill of acting.

The existence of alternative ways of saying things allows for great flexibility in human relationships. Subtle differences of a stylistic kind make it possible for speakers to communicate much more than the literal paraphrasable meaning of the utterance. This aspect of communication is useful because it gives the hearer a certain scope of freedom to notice or ignore those aspects of the message that are conveyed other than directly through the words. In turn, this allows human beings to continue talking to each other when a more direct form of communication might lead to blows or embarrassment. In this respect, as in many others, language proves to be both complex and systematic.

Sex Differences

I think the English women speak awfy nice. The little girls are very feminine just because they've a nice voice. But the same voice in an Englishman—nae really. I think the voice lets the men down but it flatters the girls.

Aberdeen housewife

M ore nonsense has been produced on the subject of sex differences than on any linguistic topic, with the possible exception of spelling. Perhaps this is appropriate. The relations between the sexes have generally been considered a fit topic for comedy. In his book *Language: Its Nature Development and Origin,* Otto Jespersen has a chapter entitled "The Woman" in which he manages to include every stereotype about women that was current at the time. It is almost unfair to quote directly but even in the 1920s Jespersen should have known better, particularly since he lived in Denmark where women have traditionally shown an independent spirit. Here are a few examples:

There can be no doubt that women exercise a great and universal influence on linguistic development through their instinctive shrinking from coarse and gross expressions and their preference for refined and (in certain spheres) veiled and indirect expressions.

Men will certainly with great justice object that there is a danger of the language becoming languid and insipid if we are always to content ourselves with women's expressions.

Women move preferably in the central field of language, avoiding everything that is out of the way or bizarre, while men will often either coin new words or expressions or take up old-fashioned ones, if by that means they are enabled, or think they are enabled, to find a more adequate or precise expression for their thoughts. Woman as a rule follows the main road of language, where man is often inclined to turn aside into a narrow footpath or even to strike out a new path for himself. . . .

Those who want to learn a foreign language will therefore always do well at the first stage to read many ladies' novels, because they will there continually meet with just those everyday words and combinations which the foreigner is above all in need of, what may be termed the indispensable small-change of a language.

Woman is linguistically quicker than man: quicker to learn, quicker to hear, and quicker to answer. A man is slower: he hesitates, he chews the cud to make sure of the taste of words, and thereby comes to discover similarities with and differences from other words, both in sound and in sense, thus preparing himself for the appropriate use of the fittest noun or adjective.

The superior readiness of speech of women is a concomitant of the fact that their vocabulary is smaller and more central than that of men.

Such stereotypes are often reinforced by works of fiction. Since little information about prosodic features or paralinguistic features is contained in the normal writing system, novelists frequently try to indicate the tone of voice by descriptive verbs and adjectives to introduce dialogue. An examination of several novels revealed an interesting difference between the expressions used to introduce men's or women's speech:

MEN	WOMEN
said firmly	said quietly
said bluntly	asked innocently
said coldly	echoed obediently
said smugly	said loyally
urged	offered humbly
burst forth	whispered
demanded agressively	asked mildly
said challengingly	agreed placidly
cried furiously	smiled complacently
exclaimed contemptuously	fumbled on
cried portentously	implored
grumbled	pleaded

The surprising part is that the two lists are totally distinct. No doubt the novelists intended to be realistic in describing two very different styles of speech but, in doing so, they also reinforce the stereotypes of men and women.

In the past twenty years the question of sex differences in language has been a growth industry as scholars have attempted to claim and to counter claims that there are or are not important differences in the ways in which males and females use language. It would, of course, be surprising if there were not. Both men and women will use the forms of language, registers, and styles appropriate to the activities in which they are engaged. To the extent that these activities differ between males and females, it is to be expected that their language will differ. This much is obvious. There is no need to look for a genetic basis for such differences. It is also obvious that those in a position of power often expect to be treated with deference by those over whom they have power. To the extent that in Western industrialized societies men have more often been in positions of power over women than the reverse, it is hardly surprising if women are sometimes found to have used deferential language. There have also been certain violent activities, such as fighting or contact sports, that until recently have been exclusively a male province, and there are forms of language appropriate to them that may have been less common among women.

Even in making such banal statements, one must qualify them by reference to

"Western industrialized societies" or by limiting them to a single section of the community. For example, it is probably true that in Britain until World War I middle-class women were less likely to swear in public than middle-class men, but working-class women were less inhibited. (G. K. Chesterton reported that in an argument with a fishwife he could not compete in obscenities with her but triumphed in the end by calling her "An adverb! A preposition! A pronoun!")

In sociolinguistic studies of complex communities such as Glasgow, New York, and Norwich, it has been shown that women in the lower middle class are likely to be closer in their speech to the women in the class immediately above them than are the men, who are likely to be closer to the men in the class immediately below them. It has been suggested that this is because lower-class speech is associated with toughness and virility and the men in the lower middle class choose to identify with this image rather than with the less "masculine" speech of the upper-class men. It may not be unimportant that in these studies the interviewers were all men.

There seems, however, to be a deep-seated desire to find essential differences between the speech of men and women that can either be attributed to some discriminatory kind of socialization or, even better, to genetic disposition. This can be seen in many references to sex differences in language development. Popular belief and scholarly opinion has generally maintained that girls are more advanced in language development than boys at the same age. Jespersen, for example, claimed that girls learned to talk earlier and more quickly than boys, and that the speech of girls is more correct than that of boys.

For about fifty years after Jespersen this view was maintained in the scholarly literature on children's development. In 1954 Professor Dorothea McCarthy published an article summarizing what was known about children's language development at that time. Her conclusion about sex differences is:

> One of the most consistent findings to emerge from the mass of data accumulated on language development in American white children seems to be a slight difference in favor of girls in nearly all aspects of language that have been studied.

What McCarthy actually found, however, was that the differences were not large enough to be statistically significant. Although psychologists are normally very careful not to make claims about differences that could be the result of chance (that is, are not statistically significant), McCarthy was so convinced that girls were more advanced in their speech that she chose to interpret the evidence the way she did. In a survey of the literature up till 1975, I found that none of the studies provided convincing evidence of consistent sex differences in language development. I concluded that the burden of proof remained with those who wished to claim otherwise. To the best of my knowledge, the situation has not changed since then.

What I did find were many examples of preconceived notions of sex differences from the assertion that girls have an innate tendency toward sedentary pursuits to claims that it is easier and more satisfying for the girl baby to imitate the mother's speech than it is for the boy baby to imitate the father's. One example will illustrate the kind of attitude:

The little girl, showing in her domestic play the over-riding absorption in personal relationships through which she will later fulfill her role of wife, mother and "expressive" leader of the family . . . learns language early in order to communicate. The kind of communication in which she is chiefly interested at this stage concerns the nurturant routines which are the stuff of family life. Sharing and talking about them as she copies and "helps" her mother about the house must enhance the mutual identification of mother and child, which in turn . . . will reinforce imitation of the mother's speech and promote further acquisition of language, at first oriented toward domestic and interpersonal affairs but later adapted to other uses as well. Her intellectual performance is relatively predictable because it is rooted in this early communication, which enables her (environment permitting) to display her inherited potential at an early age.

This is contrasted with the interests of boys:

Their preoccupation with the working of mechanical things is less interesting to most mothers and fathers are much less available.

As a result the boy's language development is slower:

His language, less fluent and personal and later to appear than the girl's, develops along more analytic lines and may, in favourable circumstances, provide the groundwork for later intellectual achievement which could not have been foreseen in his first few years.

Girls, of course, are more predictable:

The girl, meanwhile, is acquiring the intimate knowledge of human reactions which we call feminine intuition. Perhaps because human reactions are less regular than those of inanimate objects, however, she is less likely to develop the strictly logical habits of thought that intelligent boys acquire, and if gifted may well come to prefer the subtler disciplines of the humanities to the intellectual rigour of science.

I am not sure whether the writer considered himself a scientist, but if his writing is an example of intellectual rigor, then give me the subtlety of the humanities any day. What makes his statement all the more incredible is that it comes after describing a longitudinal study of children that showed no important sex differences in language development.

One of the problems with attempting to demonstrate differences in language development is that measures of linguistic proficiency, particularly for young children, are extremely crude instruments. Thus it is not surprising that samples of linguistic behavior will reveal occasional differences between subgroups of the sample. Such sex differences that have shown up on tests are much smaller than those that have been shown to relate to social background. The fact that most studies show no sex differences and that many of the findings of small differences have been contradicted in other studies should be sufficient warning against drawing conclusions about the linguistic superiority of either sex.

There are some differences between males and females that do not depend upon unreliable tests of language development. Boys are much more likely to suffer from speech disorders, such as stuttering, than girls. Adult males on average have deeper voices than adult females because the vibrating part of the vocal cords is about a third longer in men. However, there may be social influences on this physiological difference. It has been claimed that in the United States women may speak as if they were smaller than they are (that is, with higher-pitched voices) and men as if they were bigger than they are (that is, with lower-pitched voices). The "Oxford voice" common among Oxford fellows (all male) at one time was remarkably high pitched, and other social groups have adopted characteristic pitch levels that are not totally "natural."

In a quantitative study of connected speech I found that women used more personal pronouns than men, particularly the pronouns *I* and *she.* In contrast, the men used the definite article *the* and the relative pronoun *which* more often than the women. These grammatical differences are no doubt related to the fact that the women make much more frequent mention of people (particularly other women) while the men more frequently mention places by name. The women also told more stories and in their stories there was more dialogue.

It was reported that once during a debate in the French parliament when a delegate pointed out that there were differences between men and women, another delegate shouted out *Vive la difference!* It is not necessary to believe that men and women are the same to be skeptical about claims as to the differences in the way men and women speak. The desire to emphasize the differences seems to be widespread. Jespersen's chapter remains as a warning signal to all who venture into this murky area that one's prejudices may show through. Jespersen obviously believed (and no doubt so did many of his readers) that what he was saying was self-evident. However, he ends the chapter by observing that "great social changes are going on in our times which may eventually modify even the the the linguistic relations of the two sexes." Eventually, even scholars following in Jespersen's footsteps may come to see that men and women are simply people and that what they have in common is more important than *la difference,* at least as far as their use of language is concerned.

It is, however, disturbing to find in a work published in 1991 the following passage by a distinguished and respected scholar:

> [I]t is clear why, as sociolinguists have often observed, women are more disposed to adopt the legitimate language (or the legitimate pronunciation): since they are both inclined towards docility with regard to the dominant usages both by the sexual division of labour, which makes them specialize in the sphere of consumption, and by the logic of marriage, which is their main if not their only avenue of social advancement and through which they circulate upwards, women are predisposed to accept, from school onwards, the new demands of the market in symbolic goods.

It is a salutary reminder that progress is often an illusion.

The Magic of Words

An order given in battle, an instruction issued by the master of a sailing ship, a cry for help, are as powerful in modifying the course of events as any other bodily act. . . . You utter a vow or you forge a signature and you may find yourself bound for life to a monastery, a woman or a prison.

Bronislaw Malinowski, *Coral Gardens and Their Magic*

We are all familiar with fairy stories in which someone utters certain words and something wonderful (or terrible) happens. We also have heard in such stories of people who can cast spells that have a binding effect on other people. We may even have read accounts of societies in which such things are said actually to occur. We mostly think of such things as absent from our own use of language, but this is not so.

To take one of the commonest but also one of the most perilous utterances, the words *I love you* may have far-reaching consequences for both speaker and the person addressed. Although the words alone without confirming behavior might not be very effective, the behavior without the words somehow will never be convincing. Of course, the words are often uttered insincerely or casually but, if they are taken seriously, then they will have serious consequences.

There are also situations in which words have a legal force as in the marriage ceremony, a binding contract, or a court of law. In the traditional marriage ceremony bride and groom make *promises* to each other, in a contract the parties *agree* to do certain things, and in a court of law a witness *swears* to tell the truth. All these forms of language have important consequences.

Promising is the most personal. Apart from its formal use in the wedding ceremony, the idea of promising tends to weaken as we grow older. Adults may ask children to promise to do (or not to do) something and expect the promise to be kept, but they are less likely to provide the proper example. Children are often heard to complain *But you promised!* only to be told *No, I only said I might.* In children's lore there are various ways (for example, crossing your fingers without being seen) to cancel out a spoken promise.

Legal agreements or contracts are an attempt to make the language as explicit and unambiguous as possible. The fact that many court cases hinge upon the interpretation of a phrase or an expression shows how difficult it is to do this. Lawyers and others attempt to take the magic out of such documents but lay persons may restore the mystery by an unanticipated interpretation.

Swearing is the most intriguing of the magical uses of language. As Geoffrey Hughes points out, we may swear *by* something sacred, swear *that* something is the case, swear *to do* something, or swear *at* somebody or something, but nowadays people are much more likely to swear *at* than swear *by*. It was not always so.

The word *swear* itself has several distinct meanings. Here are three entries from the Oxford English Dictionary:

> *swear* < OE *swerian* (Common Germanic, cf. answer) (1) to take a sacred oath (2) to promise by oath (3) to utter a form of oath lightly or irreverently, as a mere intensive, or an expression of anger, vexation, or other strong feeling; to use the Divine or other sacred name, or some phrase implying it, profanely in affirmation or imprecation; to utter a profane oath, or use profane language habitually, more widely, to use bad language.

It is clear from the association of the first two with the third that there is an element of magic in all of them. David Crystal points out the functions of the third sense:

> The functions of swearing are complex. Most obviously, it is an outlet for frustration or pent-up emotion. . . . It has also been credited with various functions as a marker of group identity and solidarity, and as a way of expressing aggression without resort to violence. . . .
>
> Sex, excretion, and the supernatural are the main sources of swear-words. One important class of items deals with words to do with body parts and functions that society considers taboo, such as *merde* [shit], balls, and other "four-letter" words. The other class deals with the names of gods, devils, sacred places, the future life, and anyone or anything that holds a sacred place in the belief systems of the community: *God, Dear Lord, By the beard of the prophet, By the holy sacrament, Heavens, Hell.*

The earliest citation in the *OED* for swearing in this sense is circa 1430. The term *swearword* originated in the United States and the earliest citation is 1883. *Cussword* was first used by Mark Twain in 1872. (*Cuss* is, according to the *OED,* a colloquial or "vulgar" American version of *curse,* itself an Old English word of unknown origin.) Even today when swearing is much more tolerated in public both from individuals and in the media, some words still have the power to shock and offend. The word *fuck* was rarely found in print until after the 1960 trial of *Lady Chatterley's Lover* in Britain. In *Webster's Third New International Dictionary* (1962) there is no entry between *fuchsite* and *fucoid.* Perhaps given the fuss over the inclusion of forms such as *ain't,* the publishers judged the market correctly. The word *condom* was omitted from the *OED* because a reader considered it obscene, and even James Boswell in his revealing diaries would not write the word in full.

Swearwords often generate euphemisms that have the curious property of functioning as imprecations without offending. The use of the deity is disguised in *zounds* (God's wounds), *egad, gosh, golly,* and *by George.* Alternatives to *Jesus Christ* include *Jeez, Jeepers Creepers, Crickey, Jiminy Christmas,* and *for crying* *out loud.* Other euphemisms include *heck* (Hell), *dam* (damn), *shoot* (shit), and *effing* (fucking). In printed works from the eighteenth century onward, asterisks were used to disguise taboo words, as in f*** or c**t. Presumably everyone reading them knew what words these forms represented, but by having them disguised in this way it was possible to pretend that they were not actually there, another example of magical thinking. The use of omissions led to a general euphemism *blankety-blank,* now in its more modern form *bleeping.* The curious label of *four-letter words* also shows that users are familiar with the number of letters in the unmentionable words. This allows comic exploitation as in the title of the book *Golf Is a Four Letter Word,* which also plays on the belief that golfers frequently swear when their shots go astray.

One of the mysteries is why certain expressions should have this power to shock. Geoffrey Hughes points out how it is not reference to objects or activities that creates the effect:

> "Snooks is a penis of the first order, and his sidekick is a real little nipple" has no impact since penis and nipple are not terms of insult, whereas their low register synonyms *prick* and *tit* are emotionally charged terms, the more so when accompanied by *little.* The same applies to *shit* and *turd,* as opposed to *dung, ordure* and *excrement.* Here the differing impact of contrasting registers is apparent, since the Anglo-Saxon element of the language provides much more emotional force than does the Norman French or the Latin. *Copulating pandemonium!* conveys none of the emotional charge of the native equivalent *fucking hell!*

Insults and compliments are forms of speech that are similar in that both are intended to have a direct effect upon the person addressed. Insults can be ignored but compliments must be acknowledged. Because it is necessary to respond to a compliment, it can be as embarrassing as an insult. If someone compliments you on your appearance, it may not seem enough simply to say *Thank you* but it may be difficult to find another suitable response. It also happens that what appears to be a compliment may be a disguised insult.

It is possible to compliment someone in private but insulting someone generally demands an audience; otherwise, it is simply abuse. As in many kinds of interaction, power relationships are very important in insults. This includes not only the relationship between the speaker and addressee but also the nature of the audience. Insulting remarks will have a different force in the presence of peers, inferiors, or superiors. Insults can also form part of joking or teasing routines.

The two areas in which insults have received most attention recently are those terms that can be considered racist or sexist. Jingoist sentiments have produced a wide range of terms for other nationalities: *frog, hun, boche, kraut, eytie, yankee, limey, pom, nip,* and *chink.* There are also labels for other groups: *wog, dago, wop, nigger, yid, spick, honkie, gook,* and *gringo.* These are "fighting words" that when used in certain circumstances can be guaranteed to provoke a physical response.

For some sad but no doubt explicable reason, derogatory terms for women greatly outnumber those for men. Hughes lists about a hundred words that have been used, some of them for a very long time, to refer to women, most of them contemptuous even when superficially positive. Quite a number of them at one time could have referred to either a man or a woman but they have since become restricted to women: *witch, shrew, harlot, wench,* and *bitch.* In addition to terms for animals, *bird, chick,* and *cow,* there are also a disturbing number of culinary terms: *dish, tart, cookie,* and *crumpet.* It is to be hoped that in the not too distant future they will all have become as obsolete as *brim, trull,* and *slammerkin,* whose use would be unlikely to excite anyone since their connotations and even their meanings are no longer current.

If there is offense, there also has to be a method of redress. *Apologies* are another way of using language to influence situations. We expect that if we say *I'm sorry, Excuse me, I apologize,* or *Forgive me,* somehow the offense will be reduced or, better still, obliterated. Sometimes, however, apologies are rejected: *It's not enough just to say you're sorry.* Perhaps to anticipate this, we often include in the apology concern for the hearer (*I hope I didn't upset you*), admission of blame (*It was a mistake*), statement of innocence (*I didn't mean to upset you*), expression of embarrassment (*I feel terrible about it*), and promises for the future (*I won't do it again*). As with promises we hope that the words will have a special effect.

In all these uses of language, there is an assumption (not always justified) of sincerity, that speakers mean what they say. If it were not for this assumption, ordinary discourse would not be viable. The ways in which people violate this principle will be examined in the next chapter.

Rhetoric

Methinks a good metaphor is something even the police ought to keep
an eye on.

Georg Lichtenberg

The English philosopher Paul Grice claimed that in *everyday conversational* exchanges there operates a cooperative principle according to which interlocutors
try to make life easy for each other by neither exaggerating nor understating the
truth and by judging just what it is, the hearer needs to be told in order to understand the message. We often violate this principle in joking, teasing, dissembling,
apologizing, and especially in arguing. In order to convince an antagonist, we do
not feel obliged to reveal everything we know or to admit ignorance. In particular,
we are often happy to say something we hope will be misinterpreted so that we
cannot be accused of lying. This happens in many forms of writing and speaking.
It is normal in advertising, political speeches, and other polemical uses of language.
It can even happen in scholarly presentations.

Someone translated into plainer English various expressions that commonly
occur in reports of research: *It is believed that* . . . ("I think"); *It is generally believed that* . . . ("My friends think so too"); *It has long been known that* . . . ("I
didn't look up the original references"); *Three of the samples were chosen for
detailed study* ("The others made no sense"); and so on. Most people will be able
to supply examples from their own reading. This kind of writing was savagely
attacked by George Orwell, who particularly disliked the use of the passive voice,
since it leaves unstated who is responsible. There is nothing wrong with using the
passive voice where mention of the agent responsible would be redundant or irrelevant. (I have used the passive quite frequently in this book where I consider it
appropriate.) It is when the passive is used to avoid responsibility that it becomes
illegitimate. *Six hundred people were made redundant at the Smith works last week*
makes it seem as if this just happened, without human intervention. In actual fact,
some powerful, rational, warm-blooded human beings sat down and decided to fire
six hundred people. The use of the passive can give the impression of an impersonal, if not inevitable, force. A similar impression can be created by the use of
nominalizations as in *The dismissal of six hundred workers at the Smith works was
announced yesterday.* Nominalizations are nouns formed from verbs (for example,

dismissal from *dismiss*). Again the use of a word such as *dismissal* conceals the agency of the managers, supervisors, or directors who made the decision to dismiss the workers. Passives and nominalizations are very common where the intent is to soften the impact of some unpleasant information. This frequently occurred during the Gulf War of 1991 in the briefings given by U.S. military personnel.

There is a widely held belief that some of the opposition to the U.S. intervention in the Vietnam conflict was strengthened by the frank reporting of horrifying events, such as the massacre at My Lai. The U.S. military was obviously concerned not to allow a similar situation during the Gulf War. Reporters were restricted in their movements and almost totally dependent on official briefings. These statements often contained passives and nominalizations. They also included many euphemisms that provoked greater attention than a more neutral expression would have received. The most notable was *collateral damage* as a way of referring to *civilian casualties,* which is itself a euphemism for ordinary people killed or injured. Such forms of speech are ways of limiting the emotional impact of what might otherwise be upsetting information. We are so accustomed to this use of language that when we hear, for example, that the authorities used *reasonable force,* we do not associate it with pain inflicted on human beings by blows from other human beings. The ultimate obscenity in this genre was Hitler's *final solution* as a way of referring to the organized murder of millions of Jews in concentration camps.

The English *Guardian Weekly* published a list of expressions used in the British press to refer to the two sides in the Gulf War. We have *reporting guidelines,* they have *censorship;* we *take out* or *eliminate,* they *destroy* and *kill;* we *launch first strikes preemptively,* they *launch sneak missile attacks without provocation*; our planes *suffer a high rate of attrition,* their planes *are shot out of the sky.* It is probably inevitable in any conflict, whether national or individual, that one should wish to characterize one's opponent negatively, and it would have been surprising if the press had behaved differently. But it is important to be aware that use of language in this way is not intended to be accurate or impartial and we should recognize it for what it is.

It is also common to use language that is more emotional, particularly when we wish to characterize our enemies. The following passage comes from a letter to the editor of a California newspaper:

> My letter really pertains to the vultures who began to gather and circle when the first newscasts began. These vultures included, but certainly were not limited to, various folks running for public office, so-called civic leaders and last, but not least, newspersons of somewhat less than professional ethics.

The writer was referring to the reaction to an amateur videotape of what most people judged to be a brutal beating of the driver of a car by a group of policemen that had been shown on television. The reaction was strong, and critical not only of the individuals involved but of the whole police department and particularly its head. The writer was writing to defend the police department against what he thought was an unfair extrapolation from a single incident to a more general complaint. By choosing to identify the critics as *vultures* the writer suggests that they are not brave enough to challenge the department directly and that they are simply taking advantage of a situation created by others, just the vultures do not themselves kill but are ready to feed on the carrion provided by others.

At the same time, the writer of the letter referred to the beating only as *the incident.* By using a neutral term such as *incident,* the writer avoids reminding readers that the topic is an alleged example of police brutality. By referring to the critics as *vultures,* the writer attacks their credibility by questioning their motives. Neither of these points is explicitly made but the message is clear enough. However, because it is implied rather than stated openly, it is harder to refute. The most frequent place in which this kind of language is used is in advertising.

In 1986 the Safe Drinking Water and Toxic Enforcement Act was passed by voters in California as Proposition 65. When it became law, all industries and businesses were required to tell the public if they used certain chemicals identified by the state of California as capable of causing cancer, birth defects, or reproductive harm. In the same issue of the *Los Angeles Times* there appeared a number of advertisements to comply with the law. The ways in which companies provided this information differed in interesting ways. GTE California headed its advertisement in large block letters TOXIC WARNING and explained about the law. Then, under the heading WARNING in equally large block letters, it described the two relevant substances, soot that could be emitted during the testing of emergency generators and lead used in the sheathing of some aerial cables.

Another company also used large block letters for the heading but this time the message was MCDONNELL DOUGLAS CORPORATION WANTS YOU TO KNOW . . . The advertisement immediately under this heading begins:

> As a longtime leader of aerospace manufacturing, McDonnell Douglas Corporation (MDC) has always made safety and a clean environment among our top priorities. What you may not know is that MDC has an equal interest in the health and safety of you—our neighbors. We share in the pride of our community and work hard to contribute to social and environmental improvements. We strive to assure that all our employees learn and practice proper work procedures that meet or exceed both safety and environmental standards.

The advertisement then states that the company uses certain chemicals that are listed under the act but does not say which they are.

The differences between these two advertisements are striking. The GTE California advertisement is almost brutally frank, but perhaps that is because the two chemicals listed are so common that the company believes that mentioning them will not cause much alarm. The McDonnell Douglas advertisement suggests that the corporation has the interests of the public in mind and would do what it does without the legislation. The fact that it does not list the chemicals might be because it uses so many, or because they are complex, or because readers might be alarmed. To draw attention to these differences is not to imply that one is better than the other. Both comply with the law but they are designed to have different effects on readers.

A third advertisement contains a statement that illustrates a frequent feature of advertising in general:

It is TRW policy to comply with all federal and state requirements to ensure the proper use, transportation, and storage of these materials.

This is one of those statements that appears to say more than it actually does. The implicit message is that the company is behaving responsibly and deserves credit for doing so. What the statement says, however, is simply that it is company policy to obey the law. It is a normal expectation of public companies that their policies will be to obey the law. It is not something that should need to be emphasized; nor is it something that deserves special admiration or praise.

There are also examples of meaningless statistics:

Four out of five people live with some degree of back pain.

Presumably without a clear specification of *some degree* this can be assumed to be true. It might even be true of everyone if the degree of back pain could be a single twinge. A subtler example is:

Your company has a proud thirty-one-year record of dividends. For example, a 1 per cent. holder in Lonrho shares in 1961 received a dividend of £1,000. A 1 per cent. holder in 1991 received a million pounds net.

Even allowing for inflation this looks like a substantial increase. However, it is meaningless without knowing how much the 1 percent holder would have had to invest in each year. It is possible, though unlikely, that the return on the investment was actually lower in 1991.

An advertisement for tourism in Australia contained the following claim:

The skies above the Outback are so clear and dark you can see stars that aren't visible anywhere else on our planet.

The statement draws attention to the clear atmosphere, but the reason for seeing certain stars that are not visible elsewhere has to do with Australia's location in the southern hemisphere, and it assumes that the readers will not visit locations such as the arid regions of South America or southern Africa.

An advertisement from the British Nuclear Forum gives some information about nuclear power:

Most people have little or no idea that every day nuclear power provides 15 million homes with electricity and saves the emission of 135,000 tonnes of carbon dioxide, and that at the last count 180,000 people depended on it for employment.

The advertisers are probably correct that "most people" would not be able to quote these figures, though quite a few would have a general idea of the three points. The advertisement goes on to spell out this information in more detail, adding some other information. It then concludes:

The way to a better understanding of nuclear power is to become familiar with all its aspects. The British Nuclear Forum hopes this message, one of a series covering issues at the heart of nuclear power, shows our willingness to give you the facts.

Advertisements often contain references to *facts,* presumably to imply that what they are saying is true. The British Nuclear Forum shows its willingness to give the public facts but for many people the facts given are not those "at the heart of nuclear power." What many people want to know is the risk of an accident, or the cost of building, maintaining, and dismantling a nuclear power station, or how the nuclear waste is to be stored or reprocessed.

Advertisements also make use of unstated presuppositions as in this one from a car dealership:

Why do so many people choose Hankins of Alresford?

The advertisement goes on to suggest a number of possible reasons but the major point has been made in the question. If you ask *why* people are doing something, you have presupposed that they do it. The question presupposes but does not overtly claim that many people choose Hankins of Alresford.

There are many other ways in which implicit messages can be conveyed. One is by the ambiguity between "inclusive *we*" and "exclusive *we*" (see chapter 29) in which the hearer or reader may or may not be included. Another is by the use of a hypothetical statement either of the form *If we do X, then Y will/may/could follow* or by using the auxiliaries *might, could,* and so on, as in *You could win $100,000.* In either case a statement that merely expresses a possibility without making clear the probability seems to suggest a likelihood that it will actually happen.

Another favorite tactic is to use a reference to someone or something that will bring positive associations, as in an advertisement for United Airlines:

He was born in 1639. And he's still flying with us today. His name is synonymous with champagne. For it was Dom Perignon who first produced this wine full of stars. So, it is only fitting that United serves his legacy, only vintage Dom Perignon, in our International First Class Cabins.

The use of the name *Dom Perignon* in this way is what is called a condensation symbol. Similar effect can be made in the United States by mention of apple pie, the flag, and baseball, while in Britain the Queen, tea, and cricket are often used in this way. Condensation symbols can also be used to create negative effects as when an opponent is called a Hitler.

An examination of all the ways in which language can be used persuasively would take a book much larger than this one. It is essential to be on one's guard against dubious implications and to remember Metternich's warning that one of the commonest uses of language is for the concealment of thought.

Conversation

[T]here is nothing more complex, structured, and revealing of our human nature than ordinary talk, and nothing more interesting than learning to notice it and to understand it as an object of beauty.

Barbara Johnstone, *Stories, Community, and Place*

One of the cleverest ways in which we use language is in conversation. It is such a common part of our everyday ordinary experience that it is hard to realize just what an achievement it is. Someone has compared it to a dance and as in a dance it is necessary to coordinate the movements carefully to avoid getting tangled up or in each other's way. It is something that young children may not know how to do. The number of times an adult has to say to a child *Don't interrupt* is an obvious indicator of this. Like most other aspects of language, the rules for conversation differ from society to society. The account in this chapter is based mainly on American and British middle-class conversations and may not be relevant to other speech communities.

There is a general rule in British and American middle-class conversation that two people may not speak at the same time. If this happens there is overlap between the two speakers and one has to stop speaking. Avoiding overlap requires a mechanism for turn-taking. In orderly conversation the change from one speaker's turn to another is usually accomplished smoothly and very quickly. Speed is important because silences are significant. A pause of more than a split second between turns may indicate some reluctance, opposition, or even rejection of what the previous speaker has said.

In order to be ready to speak, listeners must pay careful attention to what is being said so that they know when a change of turn is possible. Sometimes it is possible to judge this by paying attention to the syntax of the utterance and anticipating when the turn might end. It is necessary to anticipate this because it will be too late when the speaker does actually pause. If there are several participants, it is the first to speak next who gains the floor. On the other hand, if someone jumps in before the speaker has actually finished, then it is an interruption and can be considered rude. The dance of conversation requires split-second timing, and the way to make it flow smoothly is to be ready with your contribution the moment that the previous speaker pauses. Speakers sometimes indicate either that they are

108 The Social Art

about to end their turn or that they wish to continue it beyond a possible stopping place. This is one of the functions of those little hesitation features *um* and *er,* which can often be irritating in a long-winded speaker but can also be very helpful in signaling that the speaker has not yet finished a turn.

A speaker can choose the next speaker, including himself or herself. One of the obvious ways in which to choose the next speaker is to ask a direct question:

MEG: How'd you put it Betty?

He wasnae ["wasn't"] really disabled was he?

BETTY: Mmm

MEG: it was shell-shock

BETTY: shell-shocked

Meg's question gives Betty the opportunity to speak. Although Betty does not immediately have an answer, she responds by saying *mmm* showing that she recognizes that it was her turn. If she had hesitated longer or said nothing, someone else might have jumped in or Meg might have continued, as in fact she does after's Betty's minimal response. Meg's question and Betty's response form a pair of utterances. Some utterances come in pairs, such as greetings:

HENRY: Good morning!

TOM: Good morning!

The point about paired utterances is not that the second speaker must reply but that a failure to respond will be interpreted as significant. Thus if Tom fails to respond to Henry's greeting, Henry may believe that Tom is in a bad mood or angry with him or something like that. Some utterances may come in rounds, as when making introductions of a newcomer to a group; a failure to introduce the newcomer to one of the group would be odd.

Sometimes a speaker may use a turn to get someone's attention before making a request:

MARY: John?

JOHN: Yes?

MARY: Can you open the door for me?

A speaker may use a preinvitation:

HENRY: Are you doing anything tonight?

SUSAN: No, why?

HENRY: I wondered if you'd like to have dinner with me?

The advantage of a preinvitation is that it gives Susan the opportunity to provide an excuse before the invitation is actually given:

HENRY: Are you doing anything tonight?

SUSAN: I've got this report to finish.

HENRY: I was hoping we might have dinner together.

Erving Goffman has written extensively about ways in which people preserve face, their own and other people's. A preinvitation allows both Henry and Susan to negotiate about a dinner invitation without either needing to feel embarrassed if Henry's invitation is turned down. Susan's response is not a direct rejection of the invitation but sets up a possible face-saving explanation for a rejection. When she hears the actual invitation, she is still free to accept by saying something like *Well, I suppose the report could wait for another day.* This is one of the ways in which participants work at making conversation smooth and successful. Even if Susan does not want to have dinner with Henry at any time, both will have been able to save face. Henry need not feel rejected and Susan need not feel committed.

We use presequences of this kind for a variety of purposes. One of the most irritating for me is a preannouncement of the kind *Guess what?,* which is often used to introduce a piece of interesting news. This sometimes tempts me into a flippant response:

J: Guess what?

R: You're going to have twins.

J: No, silly, I've got tickets for the opera.

Speakers may also request permission to speak at length usually in order to tell a story. This can be done by saying something like *Do you know what happened to me yesterday?* The listener has little alternative but to say *No, what?* and then the first speaker can go on to tell even quite a long story. In other words, the speaker is claiming the right to have a long turn. Sometimes the indication that a story is imminent also gives some warning of the kind of story it is going to be: *I had a most frightening experience yesterday, A funny thing happened to me yesterday, Do you believe in coincidences?,* and so on. This is useful information because it helps the listener to know when the point of the story has been reached. It is important to know this because the storyteller must be allowed to finish the story. (See chapter 22 for an account of storytelling.) The listener also has to give some indication of having understood the story. This can be done by making an appropriate comment such as *That's incredible!* or *How very sad!* In the case of a funny story, laughter may be the best response, but it is important not to laugh in the wrong place. One of the ways in which we show that we have understood is to tell a story with a similar point. Apparently therapists who spend their time listening to their patients' stories have to learn not respond in this way!

We also show we are listening and do not wish to interrupt by giving back-channel signals such as *yes, uh-huh, mhm,* and other very short comments. These do not constitute turns or attempts to take the floor. On the contrary, they are indications that we expect the speaker to continue. We can also signal our attention by nodding or through facial expressions. On the telephone, however, we cannot see the other person so back-channel signals become even more important. If you do not provide these the speaker is likely to get worried that the line has gone dead: *Are you still there?* is an instruction to the listener to speed up the back-channel signals.

Part of the elegance of the dance of conversation comes from the economy with which references are made to places or people. A speaker will often pause slightly after mentioning someone briefly to allow the listener to indicate recognition of the person's identity. If no signal of recognition is forthcoming the speaker may add more details until the listener responds:

MARY: I met Mrs. Simpson

[short pause]

You know, the lady with the white poodle

[short pause]

Lives on Elm Street.

PETER: Oh yes.

When Peter does not appear to recognize Mrs. Simpson by her name, Mary goes on to give further information about her till she is satisfied that Peter knows who she is going to talk about. Peter indicates this by his response *Oh yes*. It is the failure to give this kind of response earlier that leads Mary to elaborate on her original way of referring to the person she had met. In the interests of economy speakers normally use the shortest form that will enable the listener to identify who is being mentioned. Jack Smith revealed in his column in the *Los Angeles Times* how he and his wife had reached a form of communication in which there is less need to be explicit:

> While we can still carry on a fairly intelligible conversation in the presence of others, our private exchanges are conducted in a form of shorthand, like the following:
> "What's on Z?"
> "I don't know."
> "Isn't it the one you wanted to see?"
> "With what's-his-name?"
> "No, the one she's married to?"
> "You don't like him."
> "No, I don't like her."
> "She isn't in it, is she?"
> "In what?"
> "The other one."
> "Oh, no"
> As what's-his-name said, "Marriage begins as a play and ends as a game of chess."

It is important for the participants in a conversation to understand each other and to show that they have understood. This is what keeps the conversation flowing. If the listener is puzzled, then he or she is not going to be able to participate effectively. For this reason, the speaker must check carefully for any distress signs from the listener. Sometimes speakers realize they have made a mistake and correct themselves:

MARY: Lives on Elm Stree—I mean Chestnut Street.

Sometimes the listener asks for confirmation or clarification:

MARY: Lives on Elm Street.

PETER: Where?

MARY: Sorry, Chestnut Street.

Sometimes the listener will complete a remark begun by another speaker:

BETTY: I don't know how many times my two brothers went down for these
accumulators and used to get their trousers all burnt with this

BILL: acid

BETTY: acid coming out.

Betty hesitated slightly after *this* and Bill, knowing what was coming, leaps in to provide the completion of the utterance, though Betty's own completion shows that Bill's contribution was probably unnecessary. Listeners often jump in to complete a speaker's utterance when the speaker seems to be at a loss for a word or uncertain how to continue. Sometimes, however, the completion is for other purposes:

BETTY: Do you know why they built the suspension bridge over the Dee?

BILL: No.

BETTY: To let people who come =

BILL: = get to the other side [laughs]

BETTY: to let people who come from the city up to the Nigg Church.

BILL: Oh.

Betty's question belongs to a special category. It is clear that she is not asking the question out of ignorance or because she expects Bill to know the answer. Her question is merely checking up that she is not about to give some information that Bill and the others present already know. Bill's initial response allows Betty to go ahead and present her information, but Bill decides to make a joke out of it by completing her utterance in a way she does not intend. On this occasion there is no pause at *people,* but Bill times his intervention exactly (indicated by the equals signs) to complete the turn for Betty. Betty does not simply complete her turn when Bill has finished speaking but begins it again so that she can convey the information as if Bill had not intervened. Bill's reponse *Oh* is an acknowledgment that this is something he did not know.

Little words such as *oh* and *well* are very important in conversation as they help to make discourse more coherent. For example, *well* is often used when someone is about to give a response that is not a direct answer to the question, as in this example from an interview:

INTERVIEWER: What did you do after the war?

NM: Well I was married by that time.

The question was about work and the answer expected would have been about NM's job. Her use of *well* is an indication that she is not about to say directly what work she had done because in fact she had not worked after she got married. *Well* is also used sometimes before a self-correction, as in *for the next four weeks—*

well for the next two. Oh is more likely to be used when the correction is by way of amplification as in *I have a wee friend a Rotarian in Laguna Beach—oh about four-foot-two* where the addition is to indicate what *wee* means. *Oh* is also used to signal understanding:

NAN: Tell him aboot ["about"] Alan Finlay
[slight pause]
The time you was on the golf course

BILL: Oh, he comes from Kilwinning this fellow

When Bill does not immediately respond to Nan's suggestion she clarifies it by referring to the occasion, and Bill acknowledges that he now knows what she is talking about by saying *Oh*. It is interesting that speakers often include the words *well* and *oh* when quoting what other people have said, particularly to indicate a change of speaker in a dramatic narrative:

"Oh" I says "Jackie, your leg's broken."
"Oh no, Willie, it cannae ["can't"] be—it cannae be broken."

Expressions such as *oh, well, you know,* and *I mean* have been studied under the heading *discourse markers,* and they have been shown not to be the stumblings of inarticulate speakers but instead often effective means of making conversation coherent. Of course, they are not always used successfully. In the dance of conversation, as in other forms of dancing, some move more gracefully than others, but the standard is generally very high.

Narratives

Storytelling is at the core of what goes on when people talk.

Barbara Johnstone, *Stories, Community, and Place*

People tell stories for a variety of purposes: to amuse, to inform, to impress, to ask for sympathy, to illustrate a point, and so on. In particular people often enjoy telling stories about their own experiences whether recent or from their past. Telling stories, however, like many other forms of speech behavior is not as straightforward as it might seem. Stories must have a point and the point must become obvious to the hearer. Children often take quite a long time to learn how to tell a story effectively, and it is clear that some adults are better storytellers than others. There are certain features that contribute to a successful story told in a conversation.

The basic requirement for a story is that something should happen. The action is usually reported in narrative clauses. Narrative clauses are normally in the past tense and uttered in the order of the events, as in this minimal narrative:

The baby cried
The mommy picked it up

If interpreted as a narrative, there are certain inferences that the listener would make. The first is that the mommy picked up the baby. The second is probably that it was the baby's mommy that picked it up, and the third that she picked it up because it had cried. None of these inferences is actually stated but they can be inferred from the two clauses and their order. It would be a very different story if the clauses were in the reverse order:

The mommy picked it up
The baby cried

In this case there is no clear inference about who or what the mommy picked up. If it were interpreted as referring to the baby then the inference might be that the reason that the baby cried was because the mommy had picked it up. Other interpretations might be based on the idea that it was whatever the mommy picked up that caused the baby to cry. Again, none of this is overtly stated. The value of such a trivial example is that it illustrates both the importance of order in the presentation of narrative clauses and the interpretive principles that the listener brings to the storytelling.

The listener's most important role is to show that the point of the story has been grasped and for this it is essential to know when the story has ended. There are two errors that the listener can make. One is to fail to notice that the story has ended, so that the narrator has to say something like *So what do you think?* The other is to say something like *That's amazing* and have the narrator say *I haven't got to the important point yet.* I once shared a house with an Irish poet, and sometimes we would sit up late in the night after he had been drinking and he would tell me what seemed like interminable stories. I often found these stories difficult to follow but I knew that my role was to listen and to express appreciation at the end. I soon learned that at the end of a story he would bite on his pipe and nod so that I could say *That's amazing* or *How remarkable* or something of that sort. Narrators can help their listeners by giving an indication that the story has come to an end by saying something like *So that was what happened* or *I've never forgotten it* or something else that is clearly not part of the story but a sign that the listener can now say something. Remarks of this kind act like a kind coda in a musical work.

The other way in which the narrator can help the listener is by giving at the beginning some indication of what kind of story will be told: *That was one the worst experiences I had, A funny thing happened to me yesterday, I've just heard the most terrible news,* and so on. Remarks of this kind are helpful because they often guide the listener as to what kind of story will follow. This is like reading the blurb of a book or the abstract of a scholarly article to find out what it contains.

The narrator also has the responsibility of making it clear, to the extent that it is required to understand the story, who the characters are, where and when the event happened, and other background information to provide the necessary orientation for the listener. This information need not be given at the beginning but can be introduced by way of asides and digressions during the narration of the action.

More important still is that the narrator has to justify taking up the listener's time. The worst response that a narrator can receive is *So what?* or *I don't see what's remarkable/funny/strange about that.* In other words, a story has to justify itself. This can be done by the narrator giving clues as to the point of the story. *The doctor told me "Another inch and you'd've been dead"* indicates that the narrator had really been in a very dangerous situation. As in this example, this kind of embedded evaluation (or validation) of the story is most successful if it is done indirectly rather than by saying *I felt really frightened.*

A good storyteller will also try to make the story as interesting as possible, which usually involves including details that are not essential to the telling of the story but add to its interest. In particular, to make the telling more dramatic narrators often quote what the characters said. It is not necessary to believe that the narrator is remembering this dialogue accurately for it to be effective. It is often possible for the narrator to indicate attitudes and emotions by the tone of voice used in reporting someone's words.

Here is a story told to me in an interview by someone I had asked if he had ever been in a situation where he thought that he might have been killed. He told me one story about how he had almost drowned, and then he went on to tell this story:

1   another time I was in a car smash with a—
2   a friend of mine had just got a new Baby Austin with a sunshine roof
3   which fortunately was open
4   and there were five of us in this
5   and he was going out by Butlins
6   and suddenly he turned round and says
7   "See I told you we could do fifty-five"
8   and he skidded
9   and we went over on our side
10   and we slid for seventy-five feet—
11   the police measured it—
12   on our side
13   and then the car caught fire
14   and we climbed out the sunshine roof
15   I got a bit of a fright that time too.

In line 1 JM tells me that the story is about a car smash, which is the abstract. In line 15 he provides the coda to indicate that the story has come to an end. This is helpful because there might have been more to come after line 14: the car might have exploded, his friend might have tried to save something, something else might have caught fire, and so on. The background information is that his friend had got a new car with a sunshine roof. The central action is that the car crashed and went on fire but they were able to get out through the sunshine roof.

It is a simple story but the details help to make it more vivid. It was a Baby Austin, that is, a very small car. There were five of them in it so they must have been jammed in tight. "Fortunately" the roof was open otherwise it might have been difficult for them to escape. They were "going out by Butlins," that is, along a road with sharp bends. The driver turns round "suddenly," which is probably why he lost control. His quoted speech "See I told you we could do fifty-five" not only tells how fast they were going but also that the driver had been boasting about how fast they could go. Clearly he was trying to go as fast as he could. They slid "on our side," which would have made it difficult to get out of the doors. They slid for "seventy-five feet," a distance that is confirmed by the fact that "the police measured it." The details reinforce the notion that this was in fact an incident in which JM might have been killed or at least injured. He has succeeded in convincing me of the danger. It makes it a more involving account of the event than if he had merely said, *I was once in a car that turned over and went on fire but I was able to get through the roof.* I had not asked him to tell me "a story" but he knew that that was what I really wanted.

Here is another example from a man I interviewed in Dundee:

1   we were playing football on the sandbank and fishing you know
2   like you cast your line
3   just throw it out
4   and forget about it you know

5   play football and that
6   well we were just enjoying werselves ["ourselves"]
7   and we forgot all about the tide
8   and the tide comes round the sandbank you see
9   and it comes round that quick
10   and we just—I happened to hear my younger brother say
11   "Norrie, look!"—the water ken ["you know"]
12   and I turned roon ["round"] and says
13   "Oh Jesus God Bill we'd better get away and get in"
14   we stood for two or three minutes
15   we're shouting for help and that you know but
16   I says "Oh what will we dae ["do"]?"
17   because once the water comes round the bank
18   it comes round that quick you see
19   well we decided to walk right across the water you see
20   and that's what we did
21   I gathered up my younger brother
22   he was only that size
23   and put him on my shoulder ken
24   my other brother he was just about my size
25   and the other mate he got his younger brother on his shoulder
26   and we walked across the water
27   it was up to about there you know
28   and any further and the sea would have been in there you see
29   well if we'd been there maybe another five or ten minutes
30   the water comes in helluva quick mind.

This story illustrates two other characteristics of narratives. In line 12 the narrator says "I turned roon and says." This change of tense from past to present is very common in storytelling and often occurs at critical points in the story. It occurs again in line 15, "we're shouting for help," where it reinforces the notion of panic. The other feature is the use of gestures in line 22, "he was only that size," and line 27, "it was up to about there you know," where the height first of his brother and then of the water was indicated by the speaker. Note also the use of the pronoun *he* in line 24, "my other brother he was just about my size," and line 25, "and the other mate he got his younger brother on his shoulder." This redundant use of the pronoun is very common in storytelling, and probably, like many other apparently superfluous items such as *you know* and *you see,* it helps to make it easier for the listener to follow the story. The narrator also says *round* in lines 8, 17, and 18 and *roon* in line 12. This kind of variation is common in speech, though it not always so clearly marked. Because we are so accustomed to the uniformity of forms in the written language, we often do not notice how much variation there is in speech. It is particularly obvious in dialects such as Scots where there is a choice between forms such as *about* and *aboot, do* and *dae,* and so on, but it occurs in all varieties of ordinary conversational language.

This story also illustrates the use of dialogue in storytelling. By reporting what someone (often including the narrator) said as in lines 11, 13, and 16, the narrator creates a more vivid and dramatic version of the story. When his younger brother says "Norrie, look!" uttered with appropriate intonation we do not need to be told that something exciting has happened. Norrie's response "Oh Jesus God" reinforces the sense of urgency in the situation. Again, when the narrator says "Oh what will we dae?" he dramatizes his anxiety rather than simply reporting or describing it. This is a very economical way of creating atmosphere and a sense of authenticity, even though we have no evidence that these were the actual words used in the situation.

Here is a more complex narrative in which a Dundee woman, Bella K., tells how she met Dirk, her husband-to-be, at the railway station after eight years of separation. He was a Dutch sailor and she had become pregnant by him early in World War II. Now he was coming back and she went to meet him at the station:

1   the day that I went down to the station to meet him
2   when he was coming back
3   I thought
4   I'll meet him at the station
5   because after all these years in front of your mother and that you know you wanted to
6   the station was your privacy
7   and there I went down
8   and no he wasnae on that train
9   and went down on the next train
10   no he wasnae on that one the one about eleven o'clock in the afternoon—in the morning
11   and in the late morning the train come in
12   there was a lot of pushing and shoving and people coming off the trains
13   and I'm looking up the platform
14   couldnae see him
15   em I was looking for a Dutch uniform
16   couldnae see him
17   and then the next thing was this navy blue suit spoke to me you know
18   he says "Is that you Bella?"
19   I never saw his face
20   all I saw—I only saw a navy blue suit
21   and he took me in his arms
22   and I could smell Sunlight Soap that strong washing soap you know
23   and it didnae smell like him
24   I don't know if you know
25   but you—your smell attracts you to people as well
26   and—and—and it didnae smell like him this strong Sunlight Soap
27   and as the years passed
28   what was love?
29   just soap?
30   I don't know

What might seem at first glance to be an artless story is actually a very well-constructed narrative. An important aspect of storytelling is the creation of suspense. Bella does this by a series of negatives "he wasnae on that train," "he wasnae on that one," "couldnae see him," "I never saw his face." If you think of a story as telling what happened, why would anyone want to tell you what did not happen? The negatives help to create a sense of concern and doubt on the part of the listener. Will Bella succeed in meeting her future husband at the station or will there be some other outcome? The negatives create suspense for the listener but they also reflect Bella's anxieties: Will Dirk actually come? Will she recognize him? Will he still want to marry her? Will she still want to marry him? When she goes there the first two times, he is not on the train. Has he changed his mind and decided not to come? On the third occasion, he has in fact arrived although she does not see him. When she finally gets to meet him again, she does not see his face and it does not smell like him. After eight years she can still remember how he used to smell. Bella had waited a long time to find out whether this was love.

Narrators also often use expressive noises to illustrate what happened. An Ayrshire coal miner told me about "a skirmish" he had had down the pit:

1	and I kent ["knew"]
2	there were a move on
3	so I shifted
4	I said
5	"I'll go and have my piece ["sandwich"]
6	and leave that time to settle"
7	so I sat down with my piece
8	and all of a sudden you hear this "Pssssst"
9	and the air knocked your bunnet aff ["cap off"] you
10	it was a hard helmet
11	you'd on
12	it just blew it aff oh aye ["yes"].

Note the contrast between the homely term *bunnet* and the more precise description *hard helmet*. The narrator first refers to the event in an understated way, *the air knocked your bunnet aff,* as if it were as harmless as your cap being blown off in a strong wind, but then makes it clear that it was a much more dangerous situation since the hard helmet is worn for protection and, if even that was blown off, it must have been quite an explosion. The art of storytelling includes the ability to convey the atmosphere of danger or excitement indirectly rather than through an explicit statement.

Education does not necessarily make people better storytellers. Many scholars investigating oral narratives have found that the best stories have come from those who are not generally recognized by society for their linguistic proficiency. Robert Louis Stevenson discovered this on his voyage to the United States: "I am sometimes tempted to think that the less literary class always show better in narration; they have so much more patience with detail, are so much less hurried to reach the points, and preserve so much juster a proportion among the facts." As with so much of language development, storytelling is another example where what is learned naturally seems to be more remarkable than what is taught.

Learning a Second Language

Life is too short to learn German.

Thomas Love Peacock, *Gryll Grange*

For some reason, many people seem to find the very notion of bilingualism threatening. Yet bilingualism (or more commonly multilingualism) is the norm for most nation-states. There are fewer than two hundred nation-states and perhaps six thousand languages. Only about ten of the nation-states can be said to be predominantly monolingual (for example, Portugal, Iceland, Japan, North Korea, South Korea, Bangladesh, and the Dominican Republic). Even in countries where the overwhelming majority speak one language, as in the United States and Britain, there may be substantial numbers of people who speak other languages. In 1976 the number of people in the United States from a non-English language background was determined to be 28 million, and it is estimated that by the year 2000 this figure will have risen to 39.5 million. However, rather than being seen as an asset, the presence of speakers of other languages is resented by many Americans. In recent years this anxiety has taken the form of "English-only" proposals designed to make English the official language of the United States and to ban the use of other languages in public institutions. This is a reaction to, among other things, the Bilingual Education Act of 1968, which for the first time in decades provided public support for instruction in a language other than English. At the same time, American educational institutions devote extensive resources to instruction in "foreign" languages, with little evidence of widespread success.

A recent study of foreign language teaching in the United States uncovered two contradictory views about foreign language learning that are widely held: (a) reasonable fluency and comprehension in a foreign language can be attained in a few months of limited classroom study; (b) Americans can never really become fluent in speaking a foreign language. Of course, if you believe (a) then (b) will soon follow. As the old joke goes, What do you call someone who can speak three languages? Trilingual. Someone who can speak two languages? Bilingual. Someone who can speak one language? An American. Many Americans, of course, learn a foreign language very well, but the self-defeating notion of foreign language requirements in American schools, colleges, and universities has had the effect of discouraging rather than encouraging language learning. Too many students have received credit for "seat time" rather than for proficiency in the language. Professor William Schaefer of UCLA comments on his own experience of language requirements:

> What inevitably happens with a course requirement is that the course becomes the end in itself, the students being subjected to what is little more than a *der-die-das* dip at the fountain. I passed my high school requirement in Latin (two years), my college undergraduate requirement in Spanish (fifteen hours), and my Ph. D. requirements in French (translating, badly, from an unprepared text) and German (translating from a prepared text, a task at which I succeeded after two attempts only because my examiner was even more inept in English than I was in German). And although on paper I am *muy* multilingual, four foreign languages, the transcript is fraudulent. It was all a game; no meaningful level of proficiency was stipulated, or anticipated, or attained.

The failure of language requirements is not surprising. There is considerable disagreement among scholars as to the optimum conditions for teaching a foreign language, but most would agree that the motivation of the learner is extremely important and that learning in small groups is advantageous. Neither of these conditions is provided by requiring attendance in large classes. The depressing point about such requirements is that they waste precious resources and discourage those learners who believe that failure is their fault. Requirements of this kind can also be disheartening for teachers, since they are not judged on their success in teaching the language but on their ability to have the students satisfy the requirement.

There are signs that market forces may at last change this policy because of the increasing financial rewards brought by knowing a second language. As more and more jobs provide opportunities for those who know a second language, efficient means of supplying that need will be developed. If American business needs employees who know a foreign language, the solution is obvious: provide incentives to both teachers and learners and supply the appropriate working conditions, namely small classes. Why so many thoughtful people believed for so long that regulation and regimentation would work better in the American educational system than in the marketplace will, however, remain a mystery.

Perhaps as a result of their own experience, many Americans are somewhat suspicious of those who can speak two languages fluently. For years there was even a belief that balanced bilinguals must be inferior to monolinguals because of the brain's limited storage capacity. It turns out that there is no evidence that bilingualism itself causes any cognitive deficit. On the contrary, research over the past thirty years has supported the view that bilinguals may be more creative and flexible in their use of language than monolinguals. Naturally, this view does not appeal much to monolinguals who believe that there ought to be some compensation for feeling at a loss when they travel abroad or go to the opera.

The age at which an individual learns a second language may affect the manner in which it is learned and the proficiency that is achieved. While there is considerable disagreement among scholars about differences between children and adults in their ability to learn a second language, the one point on which everyone agrees is that children find pronunciation easier to learn than adults do. Although some adults can learn to speak a second language without a "foreign accent," most adults do not. Children up to the age of about twelve, however, usually learn quite quickly to sound like native speakers of the language. The reasons for this difference between children and adults are a matter of some dispute but one theory is that it is linked to the maturation of the brain, which reaches its maximum size about the age of twelve. It is also possible that psychological factors play a role. Since the way you speak is a badge of identity, a foreign accent is a way of signaling that you were not brought up from an early age in the country. This may help the hearer to make a better estimate of what the speaker is likely to know. As Stuart Gilbert observed, only spies want to speak a foreign language perfectly.

Other differences between children and adults in learning a second language are harder to isolate because their learning situations are seldom the same. Generally, children have more time and energy to devote to language learning than adults and they are usually more subject to open ridicule from their peers if they make mistakes. Adults, on the other hand, often are more accustomed to gaining information from written materials and thus can make better use of texts, grammar books, and dictionaries. This may be a mixed blessing, as it is sometimes hard to apply the knowledge gained in reading to speaking and understanding what is said. In spite of differences, there is plenty of evidence that both children and adults can become very proficient in a second language, and the question that then arises is why everyone can learn one language but so many people encounter difficulties in learning a second one.

One major factor is motivation. Since learning a second language is hard work (at least for adults), it is necessary to put in much effort and time. It is easy to get discouraged, especially by the difficulty of what may seem like very small details. For example, foreign learners of English will have problems with the use of the articles, third-person singular present-tense-*s,* and the difference between gerunds and infinitives. On the other hand, English speakers learning French will encounter problems with gender, and those learning Spanish may have difficulty with pronouns. Adult learners of all three languages will have problems with prepositions. These kinds of problems are predictable from the structure of the languages to be learned.

Another factor is the difference between the learner's first language (L1) and the second language (L2) he or she is attempting to master. The carryover of forms from the L1 to the L2 is known as *interference.* For example, Spanish speakers learning English sometimes produce utterances that are incorrect in English, although the equivalents would be correct in their own language:

> He arrived *to* Mendoza.
> I want *that* you tell me.
> She gave money to the *poors.*

Interference can affect any aspect of language, but the most frequent and obvious form of interference is in pronunciation, in which the use of the type of sounds appropriate for the L1 results in a foreign accent in the L2.

Interference is predictable to a certain extent from a comparison of the two languages through a process of contrastive analysis. Contrastive analysis can also reveal problems speakers of L1 are likely to face in learning L2 not so much because of interference but because they need to learn a distinction that does not exist in their first language. For example, the English speaker learning Spanish has to learn to distinguish two forms of the verb *to be: estar* and *ser*. On the other hand, the Spanish speaker learning English may have problems distinguishing between *do* and *make* because in Spanish there is only one verb, *hacer*. A slightly more complicated example is shown by the following comparison of prepositions in English and Spanish:

Está *en* la mesa.	It is *on* the table.
Está *en* en cuarto.	It is *in* the room.
Está *en* casa.	It is *at* home.
Lo metió *en* el cajón.	I put it *into* the box.
Lo compró *en* quince pesos.	I bought it *for* fifteen pesos.
Pensó *en* salir.	He thought *of/about* leaving.
Entró *en* la sala.	She entered the room.

It can be seen that there are several ways in which Spanish *en* can be rendered in English. There are even more equivalents of English *by* in Spanish:

The book was written *by* Alarcon.	*por*
Lincoln is remembered *by* all.	*de*
Learn this *by* tomorrow.	*para*
He still hadn't arrived *by* two o'clock.	*a*
Let's go *by* boat.	*en*
by crying you won't get anywhere.	*con*
Eight divided *by* four is two.	*entre*
I go *by* the book.	*según*
He was sitting *by* me.	*junto a*
He lives right *by* my house.	*al lado de*

One way to discover the problems learners have is to look at the mistakes they make. This process has been used informally by language teachers for a very long time but it is sometimes dignified with the label *error analysis*. The advantage of error analysis is that it provides some indication of what features of the language it is reasonable to expect learners to use at a particular stage in their learning of the language. More important, it helps to guard against unreasonable expectations. Learners may get discouraged if they feel that they are not making progress, and this can happen if they are regularly corrected on a point they are unlikely to get right at that stage. Moreover, error analysis has shown that, just as in first language learning, some errors are actually an indication of progress toward the correct form.

Studies of the kinds of mistakes made by adult learners of English have shown that most of them are not the result of interference from the learner's first language. Instead most of the adult learners, regardless of their native language, seem to go through certain stages in a similar order, not unlike young children learning English as their first language. Like children, adult foreign learners also do not master one aspect of the language before going on another but move progressively closer to the language of native speakers.

One of the major differences between first- and second-language learning is that in the latter case the learning situation appears to be much more important. Children learn their first language under a wide variety of conditions and, while the actual conditions may affect the speed of learning and the kind of language learned, it is clear that exposure to the language and normal opportunities to use it are the essential ingredients of an adequate first-language learning environment. In the case of adults learning a second language, it is equally clear that exposure to the language and the opportunity to use it are not sufficient in themselves to ensure mastery of the language. It is not uncommon for adult immigrants after years in the country of their adoption to have little proficiency in the language spoken there. Similarly, many students in second-language classes emerge after several years of instruction with little ability to use the language.

The degree of proficiency an individual reaches will therefore depend upon a number of factors. Some people will be indistinguishable from native speakers, others will speak fluently with many features that reveal that they are not native speakers, while still others will run into problems in communication of varying degrees of severity. In no case, however, should knowledge of a second language be anything but an asset. There are no linguistic reasons for discouraging bilingualism.

The Evolution of Language

Language is fitted to an ape brain plan.

Terence Deacon, *The Symbolic Species*

The discussion of the origin of language has come a long way since 1866 when the Société de Linguistique in Paris banned the publication of any more articles on the topic on the grounds that there was insufficient evidence to support any theory. The topic more or less languished for the next century until it was paradoxically reinvigorated by Noam Chomsky's famous rejection of the notion that language could have developed through the processes of natural selection. This stimulated scholars in a number of fields to search for evidence that would contradict Chomsky's view. These efforts, in turn, spurred those linguists who agreed with Chomsky to find arguments to refute the claims of scholars who supported an evolutionary view of language.

The problems with the evolution of language are compounded by uncertainty about when to date the emergence of *homo sapiens,* the ancestor of present-day human beings. Perhaps as long as four million years ago creatures who were presumably our ancestors began to walk upright, probably for reasons to do with the search for food. This development had far-reaching consequences, both physiological and social. In physiological terms it led to the flattening of the chest, lowering of the larynx, and better control over breathing. At the same time, for reasons that are still not clearly understood, the upright posture probably contributed to a change in body size, and perhaps also to an increase in brain size. It also allowed the hands to be free for a variety of purposes, including throwing missiles at prey targets, which increased the opportunities for hunting. Thus, the change to an upright posture had long-range effects on human evolution.

It is far from clear, however, when this change to an upright posture led to the development of vocal communication. There is no doubt that many nonhuman primates use vocal signals to communicate with each other. Over the past half century a great deal has been found out about animal communication through observation in the field and through laboratory experiments. It is clear that even very small animals use forms of communication that often bear some similarity to human forms of communication. Vervet monkeys have been reported to utter three different alarm calls in response to spotting a leopard, an eagle, or a snake. These monkeys also appear to use "grunts" in their social interaction. Some primates can not only recognize the distress call of their own offspring but also identify the mother of an unrelated young primate calling in distress. However, these signals are very far from constituting anything close to human language.

The move to upright posture led to (or was the result of) greater mobility. These creatures were able to roam more widely in their search for food but this also meant that they lived in a much less compact society. Whatever form of communication that was used when they lived in close contact together in a well-defined part of the forest became less functional when the members of the group were likely to be dispersed more widely in their search for food. It is also likely that they would be exposed to greater dangers from a wider range of predators. There would be an obvious need for greater accuracy in communication. With hindsight it is easy to see that this improved form of communication must have been vocal, though we have no idea how complex it would have been in earliest forms.

Another critical change from our primate ancestors is that humans are born prematurely, unable to move freely or fend for themselves. During its period of immaturity all of an infant's basic needs must be met by others. At an early stage in human evolution there would have been a greater need for a relatively safe environment in which to nurture the helpless infants longer than is the case with young primates, who are quickly able to move easily at a younger age. The organization of such a location would require cooperation that would be facilitated by an effective system of communication.

Nobody would claim that any known system of animal communication comes close to the complexity of human language. The debate is simply about the contribution of a system of primate communication to the development of human language. Views about the significance of animal communication to the evolution of language divide sharply according to the affiliation of the investigators. Linguists have tended to draw attention to certain features of human language that have not been found in examples of how nonhuman animals communicate. Ethologists, on the other hand, have examined how animals communicate with each other and noted various parallels with the ways in which humans communicate. Another way of putting it is that linguists have focused mainly on the structural aspects of the communication system, while ethologists have looked at how that system is used.

The relevance of any form of animal communication to the evolution of language continues to be unclear. There is a major problem in imagining, far less explaining, how human language could have evolved from any known system of animal communication. One crux lies in what has been called *duality of patterning*. This is the fact that human languages employ two systems. One system produces meaningful utterances such that *the boy loves the girl* is different from *the girl loves the boy* or *nip* is different from *pin*. The other system has nothing to do with meaning but simply states the conditions for meaningful combinations. On this level there is no way to create an utterance such as **the the boy girl loves* or a word such as **npi or *ipn*, which are not possible combinations in English. Their impossibility is not simply because they are meaningless but because the syntactic and phonotactic rules of the language do not allow them. There is no evidence that any systems of animal communication have two levels of organization similar to those in human language. However, if we believe that human language is the result of an evolutionary process, there must have been a time when purely meaningful signals were split into meaningless parts that could be recombined into new meaningful signals. Nobody has come up with a convincing explanation of how this happened.

The current disagreement is between those who believe that this development could have evolved through a process of gradual adaptation similar to other forms of evolution and those who believe that some extraordinary or catastrophic change must have occurred to create the basis for human language. There is, however, at present no obvious way to obtain evidence that would help resolve this question. Fossil remains unfortunately do not contain most of the parts that would help.

The argument for catastrophic change has mainly been put forward by linguists who believe that language from its earliest appearance must have been structurally similar to modern languages. However, languages change relatively quickly in contrast to the slow pace of evolution. It seems more plausible to believe that language evolved in accordance with evolving cognitive abilities than that the brain changed in order to adapt to language. The universal features may have evolved because they are constrained by cognitive processing. There is no reason why the kind of impossible grammatical constructions that have been used to support claims for an innate Universal Grammar would have survived since they have no functional value.

There are many similarities here to the debate between linguists and the developmental psychologists about children's language development described in chapter 11. There is a view in animal physiology that ontogeny repeats phylogeny. The human fetus, for example, goes through a number of phases that reflect stages in the evolution of human beings. So it might be helpful to look at the evolution of language through the ways in which infants acquire language. In the early stages of language development young children begin with short utterances and proceed to longer ones. We think of this as the one-word stage, the two-word stage, and so on. But this is an adult interpretation of what the children are doing. There is no reason to believe that the children are attempting to reproduce "words." They are attempting to produce signals that will enable them to satisfy some of their needs through the cooperation of adults. These signals are a complex of sounds and intonation. In this early stage the articulation of the sounds is less clear than will be the case when the children are older, but the children succeed (usually) in communicating through rough approximations to the adult forms of words.

It seems plausible that in the first stage of developing language our ancestors similarly used global signals (probably accompanied by gestures) that referred to critical elements of their environment. These would be messages about sources of food or danger from predators. At a later stage they would begin to combine those calls into simple patterns similar to the noun verb constructions in children's language at the two-word stage. Then as their communication needs increased they began to combine calls into more complex patterns. This is what young children do. However, at some point, our ancestors in the need to develop more calls must have chosen to modify an existing call slightly. This would in time lead to the separation of form from immediate meaning so that the system we are familiar with now would have slowly evolved. This view of the development of the call system is not new but seeing it as parallel to how children develop their language has not usually been emphasized.

The major problem in attempting to understand the evolution of language is that human beings employ a form of communication that includes a complex system of abstract structures and it is hard to see how these could have evolved from simple combinations of words. Similarly, the leap in children's language from simple combinations to more complex structures is so remarkable that, as we have seen in chapter 11, some scholars have postulated that infants are born with a specific innate ability to acquire the grammar of any language. Such a claim, however, simply pushes the question back to an earlier, even more obscure time: How could this innate ability have evolved?

Evolution proceeds by natural selection or sexual selection. In the first case, organisms are faced with a need to respond to changes in the environment and those who adapt successfully are the survivors. In the second case, mates are chosen on the basis of features that give promise of producing the most robust progeny. Both processes probably contributed to the origin of human language but it is not clear how they influenced the changes in the brain that made language possible. The main disagreement is between those who believe that these changes occurred gradually like most examples of evolution and those who believe that some extraordinary development took place that made possible the new complex system of communication. However, there is no proof that earlier forms of language would have been similar in fundamental aspects to modern languages. It is more likely that earlier forms of languages evolved in tandem with changes in the brain that ultimately made possible human language as we know it today.

Those who seek precise answers to the questions of language evolution and children's language development have sometimes been tempted into magical thinking. Others who are reconciled to the idea that there are mysteries that may never be solved can simply wonder at two unexplained miracles.

Language Change

Progress is the mother of problems.

G. K. Chesterton

One of the remarkable characteristics of language is the fact that it can be transmitted so effectively from one generation to another over centuries. There are words whose meaning and pronunciation (as far as we can tell) have changed very little over two or maybe three thousand years. They have been preserved, not especially because they have been written down, though that provides some of our knowledge of their existence over the past thousand years or so. They have survived because each generation of children learns the language of the community in which they are growing up. Despite the individual nature of language learning, children grow up to speak in a way that identifies them as members of a speech community, sharing its norms. This can be seen most clearly in the survival of dialect forms (see chapter 13) that are not part of the standard language. The fact that forms which are not normally written down should survive with such persistence over long periods of time is evidence of the successful transmission of community norms. In fact, many dialect forms are conservative or relic forms; it is the standard language that has changed, for combined with stability there is also the possibility of change.

It is not surprising that languages should change. The ways in which we live, the things we use, and the kind of activities we get involved in all change, and we must be able to communicate about them. In a society in which there were few innovations over a long period of time, there would be less necessity for language to change but even then there might be some changes. For most societies linguistic change is endemic, and any aspect of language can change.

There is one factor at work in the use of language that is sometimes cited as an explanation of changes in pronunciation. This is the principle of least effort or sometimes the laziness principle. Since most human beings are sensible creatures, they do not believe in making more effort than necessary. Designers of public parks are often frustrated by this side of human nature. The landscape architect sometimes likes to design paths that wind gracefully through the park but it often happens that people create their own paths by choosing the most direct route, often cutting across corners. Human beings do this also when they speak. Speech sounds may be produced in different parts of the mouth and many of them involve the use of the tongue. Sometimes different parts of the tongue are involved in the production of two consecutive sounds. For ease of articulation, we often take the equivalent of the shortcuts taken by those crossing the park.

For example, we often just leave out a sound. This is what happens with the contracted forms *I'm* for *I am, he's* for *he is, doesn't* for *does not,* and so on. This process can also occur within words. For example, in words such as *restless, coast-guard,* and *exactly* the [t] is generally not heard and it would sound odd if articulated clearly. Some years ago there was a popular song, Donovan's "Mellow Yellow," that included as part of a kind of choral commentary the words *quite rightly* in which the [t] sounds were very clearly articulated, presumably in order to create this strange effect.

We also make sounds more similar to each other. If we contract the auxiliary in *John is driving* to *John's driving* the *s* is pronounced [z] as in [ɪz], but if we contract the auxiliary in *Jack is driving* to *Jack's driving* the 's is pronounced [s]. This is because [n] is a voiced sound like [z], but [k] is a voiceless sound like [s]. The process of changing the voiced sound [z] to the voiceless sound [s] after the voiceless consonant [k] is known as *assimilation.*

Assimilation is a very common process in speech. We do not normally notice this because we are usually more interested in what is being said rather than the smaller phonetic details but, if you listen carefully, you may hear that when someone says *This year* the first word may rhyme with *fish* rather than with *miss.* This is because the speaker is anticipating the first sound of *year* and thus produces the [s] sound further back in the mouth. Similarly, the phrase *ten minutes* may sound more like *tem minutes* as the speaker anticipates the [m] at the beginning of *minutes.* The word *handkerchief* is usually pronounced as if it were spelled *hangkerchief.* The explanation lies in the tendency in English for nasal consonants to be pronounced in the same place as an immediately following stop consonant: *camp, hand,* and *bank* (where the *n* represents the *ng* sound [ŋ] at the end of *bang,* not the [n] of *ban*). With the loss of the [d] between the [d] and [k] in normal speech, the [n] is articulated immediately before the [k] and thus is assimilated to [ŋ].

There are many examples of assimilation in the history of languages. Latin *septem* "seven" and *octo* "eight" become *sette* and *otto* in Italian. Middle English *mylne* (borrowed from Latin *molina*) has become modern English *mill.* (The word *kiln,* which retained the *n* in spelling, has regained it also in speech for many people, though some people retain the pronunciation identical to *kill.*) There is a form of assimilation known as *palatalization* that particularly affects the [k] and [g] sounds. In Early Old English the letter *c* represented the sound [k] but before and after a high front vowel this [k] changed into [č] (that is, the sound at the beginning of *choose*). So Old English *cinn* became *chin* and *ci:dan* became *chide.* The words *book* and *beech* are from the same root, but the *c* in Old English *be:c* was palatalized under the influence of the preceding front vowel. A slightly different kind of palatalization took place in Parisian French but not in Norman French, which explains why we have the word *cat* while in French it is *chat,* and the difference between *cattle* (from Norman French) and *chattel* (from Parisian French), which survives in the English legal expression *goods and chattels.*

Of course, there has to be a limit to the Principle of Least Effort. If there were not, then speech would be a series of mumbled indistinct vowels. But communication through speech does not depend solely on what the speaker does. The hearer has to be able to decode the signal and for this reason a minimal number of distinct sounds is necessary.

While it is often possible to trace back the changes that have taken place in a language, it is much harder to explain the particular direction the change has taken. For example, we know that Italian, Spanish, Portuguese, and French have all developed out of the language spoken by the Romans, commonly known as Vulgar Latin (to distinguish it from Classical Latin in which most of the surviving written works were composed). In each language the form of Vulgar Latin words has changed but not in the same way:

V. LATIN	ITAL.	SPAN.	PORT.	FRENCH	
dicto	detto	dicho	dito	dit	"said"
facto	fatto	hecho	feito	fait	"done"
pleno	pieno	lleno	cheio	plein	"full"
pluvere	piovere	llover	chover	pleuvoir	"to rain"
novo	nuovo	nuevo	novo	neuf	"nine"
foco	fuoco	fuego	fogo	feu	"fire"
oculo	occhio	ojo	olho	oeil	"eye"
palea	paglia	paja	palha	paille	"straw"
capra	capra	cabra	cabra	chèvre	"goat"
caballo	cavallo	caballo	cavalo	cheval	"horse"

Although the spellings will not tell you how these words are pronounced unless you know the rules for interpreting them, it can be seen that although in each language there are consistent changes from the Vulgar Latin forms, the changes vary from language to language. Explanations for these differences are complex and include social conditions such as the language spoken by the indigenous inhabitants or by later invaders.

Many traces of sound changes are preserved in English orthography. For example, the words *meat* and *meet* are now homophones; that is, they are pronounced exactly the same but are spelled differently, reflecting a difference in pronunciation that disappeared more than three hundred years ago. At one time *meat* was pronounced like *met* (with the vowel made longer) and *meet* was pronounced like Modern English *mate* (which was at that time pronounced more like *mat* with the vowel lengthened). Some time between the death of Chaucer in 1400 and Shakespeare's lifetime the vowel system underwent an extensive series of changes, which is known as the *Great Vowel Shift*. Roughly speaking, what happened was that the long vowels were produced with the tongue higher in the mouth so that a low vowel became a mid vowel and a mid vowel became a high vowel. Thus what was earlier pronounced [mæ:t] (like *mat* with a long vowel) became [me:t] (like *mate*), and *meet* took on its present-day pronunciation, as did *meat*. A word such as *mite* with the highest vowel could not go any higher so its vowel became a diphthong beginning with a low vowel, somewhat like its present-day pronunciation. Similar changes took place with vowels articulated in the back of the mouth. The changes affected only the long vowels and this process resulted in pairs of related words having a different vowel as in the following words:

opaque	opacity
serene	serenity
divine	divinity
cone	conic
school	scholar
abound	abundance

The stressed vowels in the words in the left column are all long vowels that were affected by the Great Vowel Shift; the corresponding stressed vowels in the words in the second column are all short and remained unaffected, thereby retaining their original sound. By using the same letter to represent what have become two distinct sounds, the spelling shows quite clearly the relationship between pairs of words such as *divine/divinity*. If the words were spelled phonetically the relationship would be less immediately obvious. The different ways in which the letters are pronounced seem to cause native speakers little trouble. (When I give my students nonsense words such as *falene/falenity,* they have no difficulty in pronouncing them "correctly," that is, like *serene/serenity.*)

Another example of an older pronunciation that has left its trace in spelling is the *gh* in words such as *night, bright,* and *light.* At one time these letters represented a sound like the final sound in Scottish *loch* or in the German composer's name *Bach.* This sound still occurs in Scottish dialects, and Scots people will often produce the sentence *It's a braw bricht moonlicht nicht the nicht* as an example of a tongue twister for English people to repeat. The words *bricht, licht,* and *nicht* are said with the short vowel [ɪ] (as in *bit*). When the *gh* [x] sound was lost, the vowel was lengthened so that, for example, *right* was pronounced the same as *write* and *rite,* and all changed as part of the Great Vowel Shift. Words such as *write, wrap, knight,* and *knot* illustrate another change that has taken place in the language. At one time the initial consonants *w-* and *k-* were pronounced but toward the end of the Middle English period the system of initial consonant clusters in English was simplified and these initial consonants ceased to be pronounced. This is an example of how sound changes can affect totally unrelated sounds.

It is also necessary to remember that dialect variation is not a recent phenomenon. During the Old English period there were at least four major dialect areas: Wessex in the south and west, Kent in the southeast, Mercia in the midlands, and Northumbria in the north. Some modern words provide evidence of this variation. There was an Old English vowel *y,* which was a front rounded vowel (that is, pronounced with the tip of the tongue high in the front of the mouth and the lips rounded) like the French vowel in *tu.* In Middle English this vowel lost its lip-rounding, but the form that it took varied in the different dialects and this variation accounts for certain modern forms. From Kentish we have *knell* (from the Old English *cnyllan*) and *merry* (from *myrge*) and from West Saxon we have *blush* (from *blyscan*), *cudgel* (from *cycgel*), and *much* (from *mycel*), but the majority of forms come from the Midland dialects, *hill* (from *hyll*), *sin* (from *synn*), *wish* (from *wyscan*), and so on. However, it is perhaps not surprising that modern English has retained the western form *shut* (from the Old English *scytan*) rather than the expected Midland form, which would have been homophonous with another well-known four-letter word.

Morphology can also change. The greatest morphological changes in English took place during the Middle English period. Old English was a highly inflected language, somewhat similar to present day German. Articles, adjectives, and nouns had suffixes that changed with case and number; verbs had suffixes to indicate person and number as well as tense. Present-day English has essentially only the -*s* suffix to indicate plurality, possession, or third-person singular present (see chapter 6) and the-*ed* suffix to indicate past tense remaining from the earlier complex system. Moreover, the use of the suffixes has become more regular. There were several suffixes to indicate plurality and possession in Old English, but now the same system applies to all nouns (with a very small number of exceptions). This process of regularization is known as *analogy* and is similar to what young children do in what is called overregularization (see chapter 6). The process of analogy can be seen in the differences in the past tense of the verb *dive*. Those who think of it as being in the same class as *like* and *type* use *dived* for the past tense, whereas those who think of it as being in the same class as *drive* and *ride* use *dove* as the past. It is not a matter of which is historically correct but which is the form used in your community. Whichever it is, the other will seem odd and perhaps even funny.

The greatest changes are in vocabulary. As the need arises, new words are created or borrowed from another language. For a variety of historical reasons, words have been borrowed into English from many diverse languages. Some examples of this will be given in the next chapter as will examples of the ways in which words have changed their meaning.

There are also social forces that affect the ways in which people speak. In a socially stratified society with the possibility of social mobility, it is natural that those who strive to move to a higher level should take on as many as they can of the superficial signs of belonging to the class to which they aspire. These are, for example, appearance, residence, life-style, and manners, including language. It has been shown in a number of empirical studies that upwardly mobile speakers often try to speak like those whose status they wish to achieve. There are two ways in which this process can introduce linguistic change. First, the higher class, wishing to maintain the distance from the social climbers, may change its form of speech to stay ahead. Second, upwardly mobile adults may overshoot the target with the result that their speech becomes "more correct" than that of the group they wish to emulate.

This phenomenon of hypercorrection can most easily be illustrated by an example that has nothing to do with linguistic change. Many people, having been told that it is incorrect to use the object form of the first-person pronoun in cases such as *It's me* or *Bigger than me,* try to avoid using *me* under any circumstances and produce utterances such as *He gave it to John and I* or *Between you and I,* which are hypercorrect (that is, wrong). All kinds of hypercorrection come from feelings of insecurity and are most likely to be found among those on the middle rungs of the social ladder. Those at the top and those at the bottom are usually less anxious about their form of speech.

Linguistic insecurity comes from the role that language plays as a badge of identity. Languages and dialects (both regional and social) have a unifying and a separatist function. They help to divide the world into "us" who speak alike and "them" who speak differently. It is this attitude that helps to explain the resistance to change in regional dialects. It is not a coincidence that conservative forms are found in areas where the people have a strong sense of local identity. In Scotland, for example, the Great Vowel Shift did not have the same effect and Scottish dialect speakers still say *moose* for *mouse* and *doon* for *down,* pronunciations that may be similar to those used two thousand years ago. The survival of the velar fricative [x] in words such as *nicht* for *night* is another example. It hardly needs to be emphasized that the Scots have a very keen sense of national identity.

The effects of linguistic change in the English language will be examined in the next chapter, and in chapter 27 we shall look at its prehistory.

The History of English

[T]he past is the compost of the future and its scholars, humble but indispensable, are the earthworms, the scarabs, the moles, who recycle the past to make the present both interesting and possible. But the past is also an epitaph susceptible of infinite anagrams, a kaleidoscope that reveals a new pattern to every new historian.

Dan Davin, *The Salamander and the Fire*

Some time between 6000 and 4000 B.C. there was spoken in the eastern part of what is now Europe a language that is thought to have been the ancestor of most (but not all) present-day European languages (see chapter 27). At a later date some of the tribes belonging to this group began to move westward. The first group relevant to the history of English are the Celts. This is not because modern English is directly descended from Celtic but because the Celts occupied most of Britain. Prior to the Celts there were Picts about whom we know little and about their language even less. The Celts spoke a language that is the ancestor of contemporary Irish, Gaelic, and Welsh. The Celts lived relatively undisturbed in Britain until the year A.D. 43 when the Romans invaded and within a few years gained control of what is now England. The north (Scotland) and west (Wales) of Britain remained Celtic, as did Ireland, and those are the areas where Celtic languages remain today, although spoken only by a minority of the populations.

The Romans ruled England for four centuries but apparently were less successful in imposing their language than in other parts of Europe, such as what are now France, Spain, Portugal, Italy and Romania. In the early part of the fifth century the Romans withdrew from Britain, leaving it defenseless. Not long after this marauding Germanic tribes invaded Britain and soon occupied most of what is now England and Scotland. They were the Angles, who gave their name to England, and the Saxons.

The Angles and Saxons brought to Britain a West Germanic language which is now known as Old English (or Anglo-Saxon). The Old English period lasted until the middle of the eleventh century. In 1066 William of Normandy invaded England to secure his claim to the throne, and his victory at the battle of Hastings, among other things, changed the language of Britain again. Old English was a Germanic language, similar in many ways to modern German. William and his court spoke Norman French, a language descended from Latin. Modern English is the result of the influence of Norman French on Old English.

During the two centuries immediately following the conquest, French was spoken at court and among the upper classes, and to some extent by the middle class. English, however, continued to be spoken by the lower classes, who were much more numerous. By the beginning of the thirteenth century the upper classes were becoming bilingual and gradually French lost ground to English. By the end of the century the country was once again predominantly English-speaking. The English that was spoken was, however, very different from Old English. The changes that had taken place can be seen by comparing these different versions of the same passage from the New Testament.

THE SOWER AND THE SEED

Matthew 13:24–30

Heofona rīçe is geworden þǣm menn gelīç þe sēow gōd sǣd on his æcere. Sōþlīçe, þā þā menn slēpon, þā cōm his fēonda sum, and ofersēow hit mid coccele onmiddan þǣm hwǣte, and fērde þanon. Sōþlīçe, þā sēo wyrt wēox, and þone wǣstm brōhte, þā ætīwde se coccel hine. Þā ēodon þæs hlāfordes þēowas and cwǣdon: "Hlāford, hū, ne sēowe þū gōd sǣd on þīnum æcere? Hwanon hæfde hē coccel?" Þā cwæþ hē: "Þæt dyde unhold mann." Þā cwēodon þā þeowas: "Wilt þū, wē gāþ and gadriaþ hīe?" Þā cwæþ hē: "Nese: þȳlæs ge þone hwǣte āwyrtwalien, þonne gē þone coccel gadriaþ. Lǣtaþ ægþer weaxan oþ rīptīman; and on þǣm rīptīman iç secge þǣm rīperum: 'Gadriaþ ǣrest þone coccel, and bindaþ sceāfmǣlum tō forbǣrenne; and gadriaþ þone hwǣte intō mīnum berne.' "   [tenth century]

Cannot understand at all!

The kyngdom of heuenes is maad lijk to a man, that sewe good seed in his feld. And whanne men slepten, his enemy cam, and sewe aboue taris in the myddil of whete, and wente awei. But whanne the erbe was growed, and made fruyt, thanne the taris apperiden. And the seruauntis of the hosebonde man camen, and seiden to hym, Lord, whether hast thou not sowun good seed in thi feeld? where of thanne hath it taris? And he seide to hem, An enemy hath do this thing. And the seruauntis seiden to him, Wolt thou that we goon, and gaderen hem? And he seide, Nay, lest perauenture ge in gaderynge taris drawen vp with hem the whete bi the roote. Suffre ge hem bothe to wexe in to repyng tyme; and in the tyme of ripe corne Y shal seie to the reperis, First gadere ge to gidere the taris, and bynde hem to gidere in kyntchis to be brent, but gadere ge whete in to my berne. [fourteenth century]

Sort of can understand (some words)

He put to besijd an nother biword saieng, the kingdoom of heven is lijk a man that soweth good seed in his feld, and whilest the men weer asleep his enmie cam and sowed darnel among the middest of his corn and went his wais, and when the blaad can vp, and the corn eared out, then the darnel appeared also. Then cam the housholders servants to him and said, "Sir, did not yow soow good seed in yor ground; from whens then hath it this darnel?"

He told them, "The enmie did this."

"Wil iou then," said the servants, "that we go and weed it out?"

"Nai," quoth he, "leest in weeding the darnel, ye pluck vp also the corn. Let booth grow togither vntil hervest, and in hervest tym I wil speek to the hervest men, 'gather first the dernel and bind it in the bundels that it might be burnt, and bring the corn in to mi garner.' "   [early sixteenth century]

a lot easier, but some words still difficult.

Another parable put he forth unto them, saying, The kingdom of heaven is likened unto a man which sowed good seed in his field: But while men slept, his enemy came and sowed tares among the wheat, and went his way. But when the blade was sprung up, and brought forth fruit, then appeared the tares also. So the servants of the householder came and said unto him, Sir, didst not thou sow good seed in thy field? from whence then hath it tares? He said unto them, An enemy hath done this. The servants said unto him, Wilt thou then that we go and gather them up? But he said, Nay: lest while ye gather up the tares, ye root up also the wheat with them. Let both grow together until the harvest: and in the time of harvest I will say to the reapers, Gather ye together first the tares, and bind them in bundles to burn them: but gather the wheat into my barn.

[Authorised Version, early seventeenth century]

Jesus told them another parable: The Kingdom of heaven is like this. A man sowed good seed in his field. One night when everyone was asleep, an enemy came and sowed weeds among the wheat and went away. When the plants grew and the heads of grain began to form, then the weeds showed up the man's servants came to him and said, "Sir, it was good seed you sowed in your field; where did the weeds come from?" "It was some enemy who did this," he answered. "Do you want us to go and pull up the weeds?" they asked him. "No," he answered, "because as you gather the weeds you might pull up some of the wheat along with them. Let the wheat and the weeds both grow together until harvest. Then I will tell the harvest workers to pull up the weeds first, tie them in bundles and burn them, and then to gather in the wheat and put it in my barn."

[The Good News Bible, mid–twentieth century]

The tenth-century version is quite opaque to modern readers but there are a few words that look familiar: *is, on, his, and, hē, wē,* and *unto.* These are indications of a relationship with present-day English and their meanings have not changed. Other words might be more familiar if spelled differently. *Mann* and *menn* would look more familiar without the double consonant but the first *menn* would be confusing because it is not the plural of *man* but the dative singular with the meaning "to the man." The bar over vowels indicates a long vowel, but this could have been indicated by doubling the vowel so that *good* and *sleepon* come closer to their modern equivalents, the latter being the past-tense plural of *sleep.* There are two letters that are no longer used in English spelling: *æ* represents a sound that is sometimes *a* and sometimes *e* in modern spelling, and *þ* is *th.* So *sæd* can be identified as *seed, æcere* as *acre,* and *þæt* as *that.* The spelling *hw* has become *wh* so that *hwæte* is not so very far from *wheat.* Other spelling correspondences might help the modern reader to identify *heofena* as *heaven, sēow* as *sow, sōþlice* as *soothly* ("truly"), *fēonda* as *fiend, wēox* as *wax* (that is, "grow"), *brōthe* as *brought, hū* as *how, þīnum* as *thine, hæfde* as *had, cwæþ* as *quoth* ("said"), *dyde* as *did, þū* as *thou, gāþ* as *go, gadriaþ* as *gather, gē* as *ye, lætaþ* as *let, ægþer* as *either, ic* as *I, secge* as *say, rīperum* as (to the) *reapers, bindaþ* as *bind,* scēaf as *sheaf,* and *berne* as *barn.* Although the words may not have exactly the same meanings nowadays (for example, *fēonda* means "enemy" rather than "fiend," *æcere* means "field" rather than "acre," *ægþer* means "both" rather than "either"), there are in fact quite a few words in this passage that have survived into the present language. Some such as *wæstm,* "fruit," and *þēowas,* "servants," have no direct descendants in modern English.

The fourteenth-century version is much more accessible. Although the spelling is somewhat different, it is much easier to recognize most of the words. Only *knytchis* ("bundles") and *brent* ("burnt") might cause problems. More importantly the syntax is more familiar. Where the Old English version has *Heofena rīce is geworden þǣm menn gelīc* (literally, "Heaven's kingdom is become to the man like") the Middle English version has prepositional phrases such as *the kyngdom of hevenes* and *lijk to a man* and the articles are familiar. Moreover, the word order is more familiar. Instead of *þā ætīewde se coccel hine* (literally, "then appeared the tare itself") we find *thanne the taris apperiden,* and *þæt dyde unhold mann* (literally, "that did evil man") becomes *An enemy bath do this thing.*

There are, however, many morphological differences from modern English. The verbs *slepten, apperiden, camen, seiden, goon,* and the like are plural forms in contrast to *cam* and *seide,* which are singular. There is also still a distinction between *thou* (singular) and *ge* (plural). The third-person plural pronoun is *hem.* Note also the verb forms *hast* and *hath.* There are also syntactic differences such as *wolt thou that we goon* (compare *do you want us to go* in the contemporary version), *whanne the erbe was growed* (not *had grown*), and *in the middle of whete* with no definite article. *Whether* is used to introduce a simple question. Note also that *hosebonde* does not mean "husband" in the modern sense but rather "householder."

The early sixteenth-century version does not seem much more similar to present-day English, but there is an important syntactic innovation. When the servants ask *Sir, did not you soow good seed in yor ground* the use of *did* in questions would not have been possible in the fourteenth century. There is no longer a distinction between the singular and plural of verbs such as *cam* but the third-person present ending remains *-th* in *soweth* and *hath.* *Hem* is now *them.* Both *ye* and *yow* (*iou*) are used but without the distinction between subject (*ge*) and object (*yow*) form that earlier existed. This passage also illustrates a sound change that has left its mark differentially on British and American English. The word for "tare" is spelled both *darnel* and *dernel.* In British English the word *clerk* rhymes with *dark* but in American English with *work.* The name *Clarke* is derived from the occupation and shows the British pronunciation. There is a corresponding difference between the Epsom Derby in England and the Kentucky Derby in the United States. In both countries the abbreviated form *varsity* retains the older pronunciation that has been lost from *university* (compare *varmint* with *vermin,* two versions of "the same word"). The passage also illustrates a more relaxed attitude toward variation in spelling *yow/īou, darnel/dernel* than is common now in formal writing.

The Authorised Version is closer still to modern English but there are quite a few differences, as can be seen by comparing it with the *Good News* version. *Which* is used as the relative pronoun for a human being where modern English uses *who.* The verb *spring* takes *was* as the auxiliary where modern English would have *had sprung.* The servants use the forms *thou* and *thy* in addressing their master and he uses *ye* in addressing them, where in the modern English version both use *you.*

The question *Wilt thou then that we go?* is *Do you want us to go?* in modern English. There are still verb forms such as *didst, hath,* and *wilt.* There is quite a difference in tone between *then appeared the tares also* and *then the weeds showed up.*

While some of the differences between the texts may be stylistic and others simply in spelling, the various versions of the parable illustrate a number of changes that have taken place in the language spoken in England over a period of about a thousand years. Whether it is right to say that it is "the same language" is another question.

Old English was a highly inflected language. There were three genders of nouns, and articles and adjectives had to agree in number. There were four cases (nominative, accusative, genitive, and dative) and the article and the adjective also had to be in the same case as the noun. Each of these distinctions was signaled by a suffix. There were also different suffixes on the verbs for first, second, and third person in the singular and for the plural. There were numerous classes of nouns and verbs with different systems of inflectional endings. There were seven classes of so-called strong verbs, which changed their main vowel to form the past tense and past participle. This system survives in a fragmentary fashion in verbs such as *drive, drove, driven* but it was much more extensive in Old English.

Old English also had a much more complex set of pronouns, including forms for two people (dual) in the first and second persons (table 26.1). With, all this morphological apparatus, word order in Old English could be much freer than it is in modern English, which has only a few inflectional suffixes left. Norman French had a much less extensive (and different) inflectional system. The role of the latter in the development of Middle English is far from clear because already by the time of the conquest there were signs that the Old English inflectional system was chang-

TABLE 26.1. Old English Pronouns

	First	Second		Third	
Singular			*Masc.*	*Fem.*	*Neut.*
Nominative	ic	þū	hē	hēo	hit
Genitive	mīn	þīn	his	hiere	his
Dative	mē	þē	him	hiere	him
Accusative	mē	þē	hine	hīe	hit
Dual					
Nominative	wit	git			
Genitive	uncer	incer			
Dative	unc	inc			
Accusative	unc	inc			
Plural					
Nominative	wē	gē	hīe		
Genitive	ūre	ēower	hiera		
Dative	ūs	ēow	him		
Accusative	ūs	ēow	hīe		

ing. Vowels in final unstressed syllables were being reduced to a single one, probably something like the second vowel in *fishes* [ə]. In Middle English the complexity of the Old English inflectional system soon becomes reduced to just two: the unstressed vowel [ə] and [s]. Along with this simplication of the inflectional system comes a loss of the agreement between nouns and articles and adjectives. Relationships must now be signaled by word order, as in modern English.

The Middle English period is generally considered to have lasted from the end of the eleventh century until the death of Chaucer in 1400. Chaucer's contemporary John Gower wrote poems in Latin, French, and English but Chaucer wrote only in English. By Chaucer's lifetime the form of English that was to develop into modern Standard English had become established. Although there were still some major changes to take place, Chaucer's English seems quite familiar, particularly if we modernize the spelling:

> Whan that Aprille with his shoures sote
> The droghte of Marche hath perced to the rote,
> And bathed every veyne in swich licour,
> Of which vertu engendred is the flour.
> > (The Canterbury Tales, lines 1–4)

> When that April with his showers sweet
> The drought of March hath pierced to the root,
> And bathed every vein in such liquor,
> Of which virtue engendered is the flower.

During the Middle English period, many words were adopted from French and many Old English words apparently dropped out of use: *leod* (people), *cempa* (warrior), *here* (army), *firen* (crime), *sibb* (peace), *lyft* (air), *wuldor* (glory), *wlite* (beauty), and *miltsian* (pity). Sometimes the Old English word survives along with the new French word but with a slightly different meaning *hearty/cordial, doom/ judgment, sheep/mutton, seethe/boil*. However, as A. C. Baugh aptly pointed out the most basic elements of the vocabulary came from Old English:

> No matter what class of society he belonged to, the Englishman *ate, drank,* and *slept,* so to speak, in English, *worked* and *played, spoke* and *sang, walked, ran, rode, leaped,* and *swam* in the same language. The *house* he lived in, with its *hall, bower, rooms, windows, doors, floor, steps, gate,* etc., remind us that his language was basically Germanic. His *meat* and *drink, bread, butter, fish, milk, cheese, salt, pepper, wine, ale,* and *beer* were inherited from pre-Conquest days, while he could not refer to his *head, arms, legs, feet, hands, eyes, ear, nose, mouth,* or any common part of his body without using English words for the purpose.

The changes in morphology that led to the reduction in the number of inflectional suffixes came about during the Middle English period. Although scholars are not agreed on the order and timing of the changes, it is clear that the loss of inflections and greater dependence on the order of words had a mutually reinforcing effect, since the loss of inflections made word order more important and the meaning conveyed by word order made the inflections redundant. Prepositions also took on some of the functions that had earlier been signaled by inflections. This can be seen in the so-called periphrastic genitive *the kingdom of God* versus the inflected genitive *God's kingdom.* In Old English there were only inflected genitives, but during the Middle English period the periphrastic genitive was used with increasing frequency. Up till the beginning of the thirteenth century, very few periphrastic genitives were used. By the beginning of the fourteenth century, periphrastic genitives were as common as inflected genitives and they became the dominant form until the fifteenth century. Thus it is not surprising that in the fourteenth-century version of the parable we find *the seruauntis of the hosebonde man* and in the sixteenth-century version *the householders servants* (note that there is no apostrophe). In present-day English the two genitives have taken on more specialized functions with the periphrastic genitive more common with inanimate nouns (for example, *the leg of the table* rather than *the table's leg*) and the reverse with animates (*John's leg* rather than *the leg of John*). There are, however, many subtleties in the use of both genitives, which signal a number of functions in addition to possession.

Changes in syntax are less frequent, partly because there are fewer syntactic constructions, but an obvious example in English is the development of the system for asking questions and forming negatives when there is no auxiliary (see chapter 5). Until the Early Modern English period the auxiliaries *do* and *did* were not used in questions and negatives. The present-day system began to emerge roughly during Shakespeare's lifetime and Shakespeare could use either form. For example, in *Macbeth* Macduff says to Malcolm *But fear not yet* and then a few lines later he says *Yet do not fear.* The doctor says of Lady Macbeth *How came she by that light?* and shortly after he asks *Do you mark that?* Banquo asks Macbeth *Why do you start?* and later in the play Macbeth asks Lennox *Saw you the weird sisters?* These examples, and they are only a few of many, show that to Shakespeare both forms were perfectly natural.

Another example is the development of the present progressive form of the verb (for example, *John is singing*). Although possible examples of its use can be found in Old English, the frequency of its occurrence has increased greatly over the centuries.

The greatest changes, however, are in vocabulary. Every day new words are being added to the language as new discoveries are made and new products created. There are two major sources of new words. One is by borrowing words from another language; the other is by creating new words, neologisms. English has borrowed words from languages all over the world: *cartoon, connossieur, dentist, patrol, restaurant, routine,* and *syndicate* from French; *poodle* and *seminar* from German; *chocolate, moose, racoon, skunk, toboggan,* and *tomato* from North American languages; *barbecue, cannibal, canoe, hurricane, potato,* and *tobacco* from Caribbean languages; *cayenne, jaguar,* and *quinine* from South American languages; *bungalow, cashmere, china, cot, jungle, loot,* and *thug* from the languages of India; *taboo* and *tattoo* from Pacific languages. In examples like these, and they are only a tiny sample, it is possible to see the reason for importing the words into the language. Before Europeans made contact with the Americas, there was no need for words such as *potato, quinine,* and *tobacco* because Europeans did not have such things and consequently did not need words for them. New inventions or practices also require new language so that we can talk about them. Sometimes the name of the person responsible is used as in *bowdlerize, boycott, mesmerize, sandwich,* and *silhouette.*

But languages do not only add new words they also lose old ones. The following words were first used in the seventeenth century but they have not survived: *anacephalize,* "sum up"; *denunciate,* "denounce"; *deruncinate,* "weed, eradicate"; *eximious,* "excellent"; *exolete,* "faded"; *suppeditate,* "supply"; and *temulent,* "drunk."

One of the most fascinating aspects of language change is how words may change their meaning. Because we are fortunate in having written records of English that go back to the eighth century, we can trace the history of many words that have survived for more than a thousand years. This can be done most easily by consulting the *New English Dictionary on Historical Principles,* more commonly known as the *Oxford English Dictionary,* or *OED* for short. This is one of the great monuments of philological scholarship. The dictionary lists words giving all their meanings and with citations of sentences in which they were used. It is thus possible to find out when a word was first used in the writings that have survived, what meaning it had then, and how its meaning has changed, if it has, over the centuries. The dictionary also gives the etymology, that is, whether it is a direct descendant of a word from an earlier stage of the language, or if it has been borrowed from another language, or if has been created out of other words. Sometimes the origin of a word is obscured by changes in the way it is pronounced so that the components are hard to recognize. A good pair of examples are the words *lord* and *lady.*

Prior to their arrival in Britain, the Angles and Saxons had formed part of the West Germanic peoples who inhabited what is now Germany and the Low Countries. The social organization was such that ordinary people required the protection of a powerful leader. (The Old English poem *The Wanderer* tells the sad story of a man who had lost his protector.) There is, however, no name for this powerful individual that is found in all the Germanic lanuages. The Angles and Saxons, soon after they arrived in Britain, used the term *hlāford,* which is the earlier form of the present-day word *lord. Hlāford,* however, is a compound word, one of whose components has become obscured. The two components are *hlāf* "bread" (now pronounced *loaf*) and *weard* "keeper or protector" (cognate with modern English *guard*). So the Anglo-Saxon lord was the keeper of the bread. Even more interestingly his wife was a *hlǣfdige* from *hlāf* and *dīg-* "to knead" (cognate with Modern English *dough*). So the Anglo-Saxon lady and lord were respectively the maker and keeper of the bread. This domestic note is absent from the corresponding terms among the continental tribes where the emphasis was on the head of a band of warriors or the leader of a drinking group.

Other indicators of past values are in the relationship between *capital, fee,* and *pecuniary,* all of which are derived from words to do with domestic herds. *Capital* is directly from Latin, but we also borrowed the word from Norman French as *cattle* and from Parisian French as *chattel* (as a word for movable goods). *Fee* is from Old English *feoh,* which meant "cattle," and *pecuniary* is from Latin *pecus,* "a herd of cattle." So we are not so very far from those societies where someone's wealth is counted in cows.

One of the characteristics that many English-speaking people pride themselves on is their sense of humor. *Humor* is directly descended from Latin *hūmō,* "water, liquid," but probably few people would be pleased to be told they had a good sense of water. *Humor* was used in the sense of "moisture" until the seventeenth century, as in John Evelyn's 1670 entry in his memoirs *At Christmas last we could hardly find humour enough in the ground to plant.* More important for its modern meaning, however, was its use to refer to the fluid or juice of an animal or plant. In medieval physiology there were said to be four fluids: blood, phlegm, choler, and melancholy (black choler). From the dominance of one of these "humors" we get the labels for certain kinds of moods or personalities: sanguine (compare French *sang,* "blood"), phlegmatic, choleric, and melancholy. As the medieval view of physiology faded, *humor* came to be used as referring to a temporary state of mind, a mood or temper. From this it came to refer mainly to whimsical or capricious moods, and finally by the end of the seventeenth century to "that quality of action, speech, or writing which excites amusement" as the *OED* puts it.

The word *complexion* (from Latin *com-,* "together," plus *plectere,* "plait, twine") orginally referred to a combination of "humors." Those who were sanguine were said to be "hot and moist," those who were choleric to be "hot and dry," and so on. *Complexion* was then used to refer to the bodily habit, constitution, or disposition of such an individual. Finally, by the middle of the sixteenth century it began to refer to the natural color, texture, and appearance of the skin, especially of the face, characteristic of one of those temperaments.

Other words preserve information about earlier cultures than the Anglo-Saxon one. The word *auspicious* comes from the Latin *auspicium,* "divination," from Latin *avis,* "bird," and *specere,* "see," from the practice of looking for omens in the entrails of a specially killed bird. The word *candidate* comes from Latin *candidatus,* "one clothed in white," from Latin *candidus,* "white," because candidates seeking political office in Rome went about in white. This going about also provides our word *ambition* from Latin *ambitio* from Latin *amb-,* "about," plus *īre,* "go." Those who have been overawed by the subject of *calculus* might be somewhat reassured to learn that it comes from a diminutive of Latin *calx,* "limestone," because calculation was done with small white stones. The modern word *budget* comes into Middle English from Old French *bougette,* which is a diminutive of Old French *bouge* from Latin *bulga,* "bag." The word *chapel* comes from Old French *chapelle* from Latin *capella,* "a little cloak," because it was the room that contained a cloak, which was the relic of a saint.

Some words have gone through many changes so that, for example, the connection between *infant* and *infantry* may not be obvious. *Infantry* comes from Old French *infanterie* from Italian *infanteria* from Italian *infante,* "child, boy, servant of a knight." As was pointed out in an earlier chapter *infant* comes from Latin *infans,* "not speaking," from Latin *in-,* "not," plus *fārī,* "to speak." In Italian the word took on the sense of "boy" and then as the knight's boy, who would be one of those on foot accompanying the knight, who was mounted on his horse.

The word *dog,* which used to refer to one particular kind of dog has replaced the more general term *hound,* which in its turn has become limited to a breed of dog. The word *knave* has taken on a negative meaning although it once meant "boy" (compare German *Knabe*). *Silly,* which once meant "innocent" and even "blessed," has taken on a pejorative sense, through the side of innocence that can be considered ignorance. *Nice,* which is from Latin *nescius,* "ignorant," meant "fastidious" in Jane Austen's time. But some words retain their original meaning in an ironic way. Many academics, when they agree to attend a *symposium,* may not be aware of its origin in the Greek *symposion* (from *syn-,* "with," plus *posis,* "a drinking"), but their behavior may suggest otherwise.

Sometimes words have entered the language from different sources giving rise to what are called *doublets,* that is, words that have a common root though the words may have taken on quite distinct meanings in English. An obvious example is the pair *shirt/skirt,* where the former is the expected development from Old English and the latter is from the northern form, influenced by Scandinavian. Many doublets come from Latin directly or through French: *fragile/frail, secure/sure, pauper/poor, count/compute, hostel/hotel.* These pairs are somewhat similar in meaning, but it is harder to believe that *catch* from Norman French is from the same word as *chase* from Parisian French. Of course, it is not only pairs of words that come from a common origin. It is often illuminating to look in a good etymological dictionary such as the *OED* or Eric Partridge's *Origins* and see how many familiar words are related: *lie, layer, lair, lager, law, ledge, ledger, log, lees, low,* and *litter* (both in the sense of a bed and of trash).

Words can also change their function as with the adverb *hopefully.* At one time the only use of *hopefully* was as an adverb of manner as, for example, in *He opened the envelope hopefully.* In recent years *hopefully* has been used as a sentence adverb as in *Hopefully, he has heard the news,* where instead of referring to "in a hopeful manner" the sense is rather "it is to be hoped that." This change of usage has provoked great hostility among those who believe that the language at the time they learned it was in a perfect state and should not change, but there are earlier examples of this kind of change, for example, the adverb *surely. Surely he knows that* does not mean that he knows it in a sure manner. It does not even mean that I am sure that he knows it, but rather that I hope he does. The frequency with which *hopefully* is used as a sentence adverb shows that there was a need for this particular usage.

The ways in which the English language has evolved and continues to change would require several volumes to describe, but it is important to remember that strictly speaking languages do not change; it is people who begin to speak differently from their predecessors. It also important to realize that not all changes are in the direction of convergence. As we saw in chapter 16, there are many differences in the kinds of language used (registers) at any one time, and some innovations have the effect of increasing this variety. Geoffrey Hughes points out that in what he calls "underground" American dialects there are many words familiar to a standard speaker that are used with other than their traditional meanings: *square, weird, pad, soul, high, acid, grass, horse, camp, trip, bird, cool, sweet, hit, heat, fruit, bread, cat, sick,* and *gross.* Some of these new uses have become more widely known, thanks mainly to the mass media, but there is always a time lag, and by the time they come to the notice of standard speakers they have probably fallen out of favor with the groups who initially used them. The process has been happening for centuries, and works such as the *OED* provide a window on to the world of the past and the concerns of earlier speakers of English, through the ways in which writers have recorded usage. It is also possible to take the process further back before the time of written records, as will be illustrated in the next chapter.

27

Indo-European

> [T]he most secure legacy of the Indo-Europeans is surely to be found in the language spoken by over two billion people in the world. It is irrelevant whether we regard ourselves as Europeans, Asians, Africans, or Americans, we cannot escape this legacy if we speak an Indo-European language. We cannot ask questions of where, when, who or how, or answer them with our most basic pronouns, we cannot count, refer to the basic parts of our bodies, describe our environment, the heavens, basic animals or relatives, or express our most fundamental actions, without making frequent recourse to an inherited system of speech that our linguistic ancestors shared 6,000 years ago.
>
> J. P. Mallory, *In Search of the Indo-Europeans*

In 1776 Sir William Jones, the founder of the Royal Asiatic Society and the chief justice of India, gave a lecture in which he drew attention to certain similarities which he had noticed between Sanskrit and European languages:

> The Sanskrit language, whatever may be its antiquity, is of wonderful structure; more perfect than the Greek, more copious than the Latin, and more exquisitely refined than either; yet bearing to both of them a stronger affinity, both in the roots of verbs and in the forms of grammar, than could have been produced by accident; so strong that no philologer could examine all the three without believing them to have sprung from some common source, which, perhaps, no longer exists. There is a similar reason, though not quite so forcible, for supposing that both the Gothic and Celtic, though blended with a different idiom, had the same origin with the Sanskrit; and the old Persian might be added to the same family.

Although Jones was not the first to notice this resemblance, his lecture is often seen as the public announcement of a long process of scholarship mainly in the first half of the nineteenth century which led to the postulation of a reconstructed ancestor for a number of languages that have been spoken in an area stretching from the British Isles and Scandinavia in the west across the whole of Europe to Siberia and a large part of the Indian subcontinent. This reconstructed language is Proto-Indo-European (PIE, for short). There are no records of PIE. It is a hypothetical language worked out on the basis of comparing examples of words from languages that have survived (or of which we have some records) with their equivalent in other Indo-European languages.

The languages that are said to be descended from this common ancestor include the following: the Germanic languages (Danish, Dutch, English, German, Icelandic, Norwegian, Swedish), the Italic languages (Latin and its descendants, French, Italian, Portuguese, Romanian, Spanish), the Celtic languages (Breton, Gaelic, Irish, Welsh), the Slavic languages (Bulgarian, Polish, Russian, Serbo-Croat, Ukranian), the Baltic languages (Latvian, Lithuanian), the Indian languages (Bengali, Gujerati, Hindi, Marathi), the Iranian languages (Kurdish, Persian, Pashto), Albanian, Armenian, and Greek, to mention only some of the most obvious examples. In addition there are important languages that are no longer spoken but of which we have some records: Tocharian and Hittite. Notice that the list given above does not include all the languages of Europe or India. Hungarian, Finnish, and Estonian belong to the Finno Ugric group, Basque is a language isolate unrelated to any other surviving language, and the languages of southern India belong to the Dravidian family.

The comparative method is to look for equivalent words (*cognates*) in each language and note which sounds correspond to each other. The numerals are a good example since their meaning is not in dispute. Some of them show great similarities, as for example, the words for *two* in a variety of Indo-European languages. The words for *hundred,* on the other hand, show a more complex relationship:

	"TWO"	"HUNDRED"
Albanian	*dy*	*qind*
Bengali	*dvi*	*sa*
Danish	*to*	*hundrede*
French	*deux*	*cent*
German	*zwei*	*hundert*
Greek	*duo*	*hekaton*
Irish	*do*	*cead*
Latin	*duo*	*centum*
Lithuanian	*du*	*simtas*
Old English	*twa*	*hund*
Persian	*do*	*sad*
Russian	*dva*	*sto*
Spanish	*dos*	*ciento*
Welsh	*dau*	*cant*

It can be seen that the words for "two" all begin with /d/ or /t/ (the German *z* represents /ts/). In some there is a /w/, a /u/; or a /v/ and the vowel varies. (Voltaire said that etymology was a science in which the consonants count for very little and the vowels for nothing at all, but that is an exaggeration.) The words that contain a /t/ rather than a /d/ all belong to the Germanic branch and this is part of the First Germanic Consonant Shift (often known as Grimm's Law after Jakob Grimm, better known for the collection of folktales that are usually now thought of as suitable only for children). As we shall see, the change from /d/ to /t/ was only one of several consonant changes that distinguish the Germanic group of languages. The reconstructed form of "two" for PIE is **dva* (the asterisk indicates that this is not a historically recorded one but a hypothetical ancestor of all the words listed).

The words for "hundred" reveal a more complex relationship. The reconstructed PIE form is **k'mtom.* In the western branches of Indo-European the initial sound has remained as /k/ in Albanian, Greek, Irish, Latin, and Welsh. In the Germanic languages, as another consequence of Grimm's Law, the /k/ has become /h/. In the Balto-Slavic languages Lithuanian and Russian and in the Indo-Iranian languages Bengali and Persian, the /k/ has become an /s/. This is one of early major splits in the Indo-European language and is known as the *centum/satem* split. The situation looks even more confusing because the later descendants of Latin, French, and Spanish, also have /s/ instead of /k/ but this is because of a later change from Latin /k/. That the sounds /k/ and /s/ should have this relationship should not come as a surprise to English speakers because we have the same kind of situation with words such as *critic, critical,* and *criticize, criticism,* where the letter *c* represents /k/ in the first two words and /s/ in the second two.

There are other differences in the words for "hundred," the most noticeable being that some of them have no /n/. Once again this should not be unfamiliar to English speakers: *What is sauce for the goose is sauce for the gander.* The word *goose* at one time was **gans* but it has achieved its present form through a series of changes that did not affect the male form. It is fundamental to the reconstruction of PIE not only that there should be correspondences between the sounds in cognate words but also that the process by which one sound replaces another should be plausible. Some of the changes are the result of processes that are explainable in articulatory terms (see chapter 25). Some changes are harder to explain in articulatory terms but are so widespread that the correspondences cannot be simply coincidental. One example is Grimm's Law, which affected the whole series of stop consonants. It was a chain shift in which the PIE "voiced aspirates" *bh, dh,* and *gh* (about which there is disagreement as to their phonetic description) became the voiced stops /b/, /d/, and /g/ in Germanic; the voiced stops /b/, /d/, and /g/ became the voiceless stops /p/, /t/, and /k/; and the voiceless stops /p/, /t/, and /k/ became the fricatives /f/, /θ/ (the initial sound in *think*), and /x/ (the sound in Scottish *loch,* like a strongly articulated /h/). As a result, the whole system of consonants has changed but the pattern remains the same.

Take, for example, the Latin word *dent-* and its English equivalent *tooth.* On the surface they appear to be totally different but the Latin sounds /d/ and /t/ maintain their PIE forms; in English, as a result of the first Germanic consonant shift, they have become /t/ and /θ/ respectively. The loss of the /n/ is by the same process that produced *goose* from **gans.* The difference of vowel disappears in the plural *teeth.* The alternation between /o/ and /e/, which also occurs in words such as *foot* versus *feet* and *blood* versus *bleed,* goes back to an important feature of PIE that survives in English only in a few instances. (The relationship between *sing* and *song* is also a PIE alternation, though a different one.) Thus, the correspondences between *dent-* and *tooth* can be seen to conform to general principles that are needed to explain other cognates in Latin and English (and in many other languages).

Of course, as we have seen in chapter 25, there are many other processes that affect linguistic change. The word *dentist* does not show the effects of Grimm's Law because it is not a native English word but was borrowed from French. The possibility of borrowing words from another language is the source of a major problem for those who wish to find out more about the speakers of PIE, their geographical location, and their way of life. A second problem is that a word may not have the same meaning in different languages.

For example, the form *bhāgos* has been reconstructed as the PIE word for a tree, in English *beech,* and this is the meaning of Latin *fagus* and Old Norse *bok.* In Russian, however, *buzina* means "elder," while in Albanian *bunge* and in Doric Greek *phagos* mean "oak." The importance of this word for identifying the home of the Indo-Europeans is that beech trees were traditionally found only west of a line from Königsberg on the Baltic to Odessa on the Black Sea. If *bhāgos* was an early PIE word and if it meant "beech," then this would be support for the view that the original home of the Indo-Europeans was west of the "beech line." On the other hand, if *bhāgos* did not mean "beech" or if it was a term developed after the Indo-Iranian branch had split off from the rest of PIE, then it would not be evidence for the homeland.

The question of the original homeland of the speakers of PIE continues to fascinate and perplex scholars. Locations from northwest Germany to Asia Minor and central Siberia have been seriously proposed by scholars on the basis of linguistic and archaeological evidence. The major problem is that there is no direct link between the reconstructed linguistic forms and the archaeological evidence since the period is far earlier than the invention of writing. Even estimates of the date vary. It has been argued that a form of PIE was spoken as far back as 6000 B.C. but most scholars would place the period for PIE as reconstructed between 4500 and 2500 B.C. The size of the original homeland is also a matter of conjecture. Roughly speaking, the larger the area (before the advent of modern communications) the greater linguistic diversity would be expected since innovations would not travel very far or very fast. (In present-day Papua New Guinea with a population of less than four million and poor communications between communities, it has been estimated that there are 850 languages.) The traditional explanation of the diversity of the present-day languages that belong to the Indo-European family is that they became more diverse as their speakers spread out in all directions from their original homeland. This diaspora has usually been seen as a series of migrations that took the original PIE speakers from some relatively small region till they occupied almost the whole of Europe, part of Siberia, Iran, and more than half of the Indian subcontinent.

At the time when these migrations began, there were a number of other languages spoken in what is now Europe. There are languages such as Basque, Etruscan, and Iberian that must have been spoken in Spain and Italy before the expansion of PIE. Etruscan and Iberian are now extinct, but Basque survives as a rare example of a European language unrelated to any other known language. There is also the family of languages known as the Finno-Ugric group, which includes Finnish, Estonian, and Hungarian. They were probably spoken in an area stretching from the northeast Baltic across Russia to east of the Urals. (Hungarian arrived in its present location during the Middle Ages.)

In his attempt to reconcile the linguistic and archaeological evidence, J. P. Mallory argues that "Proto—Indo-European probably evolved out of the languages spoken by the hunter-fishing communities in the Pontic-Caspian region." He argues that the Indo-Europeans benefited from the introduction of stockbreeding, the domestication of the horse, and the subsequent development of wheeled vehicles. This greater mobility perhaps gave them an advantage over their neighbors who were primarily agriculturalists. It is also possible that the Indo-Europeans had the kind of social organization that helped to make them successful. The Indo-Europeans, according to Mallory, then began to move into Asia and the Balkans. Then there is the westward movement of the Celts and the Italic speakers. It seems likely that the Celts arrived in western Europe about 500 B.C. occupying France, the Iberian peninsula, and the British Isles. Later the Germanic speakers moved into the northwest, finally crossing over to the British Isles, driving the Celts to the periphery, where the Celtic languages survive today: Wales, Ireland, northwest Scotland, and Brittany.

The chronology, the locations, the migrations, the process of linguistic change and diversification are all matters of dispute. Yet there is agreement that there must have been a society with enough unity to constitute a single speech community with no more than the amount of linguistic heterogeneity that we find in large political units today. On the basis of common vocabulary it is even possible to make some reasonable guesses as to what that society was like.

They had words for winter and summer, for ice and snow, and for hot and cold. They were familiar with mountains and flat lands, rivers and lakes, if not seas. The names of a number of trees are fairly well attested, including birch, willow, and the more dubious beech. They seem to have known about otters, beavers, wolves, bears, hares, mice, and hedgehogs. Among birds there are the eagle, crane, goose, and duck. Fish are more controversial. The PIE word *loksos* is the ancestor of *lox* but there is disagreement as to whether it referred to the salmon or to the salmon trout. If it were salmon, then then this would link the homeland of the Indo-Europeans with the Baltic Sea. There are also PIE words for snake, honeybee, and wasp.

Mallory suggests that a reasonable conclusion would be

> a landscape which included some trees and certainly enough to provide forest environments for a number of wild animals. A river-bank or lake-side orientation is discerned from some of the animals and birds, although in terms of prehistoric settlement this is hardly surprising. That a number of trees such as birch and willow are so closely linked with temperate climates does suggest a region of at least seasonally cold temperatures.

The Indo-Europeans certainly had cattle and sheep, as well as horses and dogs, but also nits and lice. They made butter and possibly cheese, made use of wool, and had yokes which they used in plowing. They had bows and arrows, and also boats. They had gold and copper, and possibly silver, but not iron. They had terms for the nuclear family and also for relatives by marriage on the husband's side but not on the wife's. They considered the right-hand side lucky (compare modern English *dexterous* from the Latin for "right") but reference to the left was taboo- (compare modern English *sinister* from the Latin for "left").

Indo-European languages, particularly English and Spanish, are spoken in many parts of the world, far from the original homeland. The existence of written records going back nearly three thousand years has made possible the kind of historical investigation just described, but Indo-European languages make up only a small fraction of the world's languages. Some idea of the diversity will be shown in the next chapter.

28

Languages of the World

Ethnocentrism is that state of mind in which the ways of one's own group seem natural and right for all human beings everywhere.

Roger Brown and Eric Lenneberg,
"A Study in Language and Cognition"

It is rather frustrating that there is no accepted figure on the number of languages in the world. Partly this is because there is no linguistic way of distinguishing between a language and a dialect. Certainly, there is no direct correlation between language and nation. There are about 170 nation-states and about six thousand languages, but 95 percent of the world's population makes use of a total of fewer than one hundred languages. It follows from this that some languages have a very small number of speakers. In Papua New Guinea, for example, there are about 850 languages in a population of 3.3 million, which is one reason why Tok Pisin has become widespread as a lingua franca (see chapter 32). In the central northwest Amazon region there are twenty languages in a population that has been estimated at from five thousand to ten thousand.

It is not only the number of languages that is surprising; the variety of means they use is also remarkable. At the same time, all human languages have a number of characteristics in common and Chomsky has raised the question of linguistic universals. As was described in chapter 11, he has argued that the ability of any normal child to learn any human language merely by exposure to it leads to two conclusions. One is that children must be born with a special ability to learn language, the Language Acquisition Device (LAD). The second point is that all human languages must be similar to the extent that they can be learned by any child. These universal characteristics are what Chomsky has labeled Universal Grammar (UG).

It is perhaps easiest to illustrate Chomsky's notion of a linguistic universal by pointing out the kinds of features that do not occur in human languages. For example, there are no natural languages in which a question is formed by simply reversing the order of the words in a statement. For example.

The old man is eating a red apple

In no language in the world could such a statement be made into a question in this way:

Apple red a eating is man old the?

Nor is it possible in any human language to make it a question by permuting the order of every pair of words:

Old the is man a eating apple red?

The examples seem absurd but they represent very simple mathematical operations, and it would be much easier to program a computer to carry out these operations than it is to make computers deal with natural language. There are many reasons why languages do not use mathematical operations, but a simple fact is enough to explain the absence of these two operations. The syntax of languages is not based on words but on constituents (chapter 7) and there is no simple mathematical way to identify constituent structure. It is also not clear how children come to know that language is organized in terms of constituents, since the words themselves do not usually signal this information unambiguously. To oversimplify, this is the kind of knowledge that Chomsky claims is innate, forming part of the LAD.

While the nature and extent of linguistic universals is still a matter for investigation with claims and counterclaims, it is also true that languages that are not closely related often manifest very different ways of signaling information. It is not possible in a book of this kind (or length) to do more than give a few illustrations of this variety. The following pages provide a very brief description of the major language families and a few examples of aspects of linguistic structure that are different from those found in English. The examples have been chosen in the hope that they will be comprehensible rather than because they are the most typical or the most intriguing. I know from experience with my students that their eyes tend to pass very rapidly over examples in languages they do not know, but I hope that these examples will not dismay more persistent readers.

Although we can never know how many languages have disappeared without a trace, it is safe to claim that at one time there must have been fewer languages because, as we know from the history of Indo-European (see chapter 27), a single language can split up into a number of separate languages. There are currently about 170 Indo-European languages, belonging to the Albanian, Armenian, Baltic, Celtic, Germanic, Greek, Italic, Indic, Iranian, and Slavic branches. There are at least ten other major groupings of languages.

The other major group of languages in Europe is the Finno-Ugric branch of the Uralic family. Like the early Indo-Europeans, the ancestors of the Finno-Ugric peoples lived in Europe about six thousand years ago, probably in what is now central Russia. They migrated in several directions: to Finland in the northwest, to northern Siberia in the northeast, and finally westward to present-day Hungary.

Finnish is notable for a number of characteristics, one of which is the case system. In English, with the exception of the inflected genitive (*John's book*), most syntactic relations involving nouns are indicated by prepositions. In Finnish, many of these are indicated by inflectional suffixes. In these examples the translations are merely to give some indications of the relations, but many of the cases can be used in a number of functions (as can the English genitive, which does not only indicate possession).

Nominative	talot	"the houses"
Genitive	talojen	"belonging to the houses"
Partitive	taloja	"(part) of the houses"
Inessive	taloissa	"in the houses"
Elative	taloista	"from inside the houses"
Illative	taloihin	"into the houses"
Adessive	taloilla	"at or on the houses"
Ablative	taloilta	"from the houses"
Allative	taloille	"to the houses"
Essive	taloina	"condition of the houses"
Translative	taloiksi	"converted into houses"
Abessive	taloitta	"without houses"
Comitative	taloine	"together with houses"
Instructive	taloin	"by means of houses"

Unrelated to any other language in Europe is Basque, spoken mainly in northwestern Spain but also in the southwestern part of France. There are about seven hundred thousand Basque speakers. Another non-Indo-European language in Europe is Georgian, which is a member of the Southern Caucasian group of languages. There are about forty Caucasian languages but, with the exception of Georgian, which is spoken by four million people, most of them have a relatively small number of speakers.

Just south of the Caucasus lies Turkey. Turkish belongs to the Altaic group of languages, spoken from Turkey in the west to Mongolia and China in the east. Turkish is an *agglutinative* language, that is, it forms complex expressions as single words by the addition of suffixes. For example, the word for "man" is *adam,* "to the man" is *adama,* "the men" is *adamlar,* and "to the men" is *adamlara.* Turkish also has *vowel harmony,* which means that the vowel in the suffix depends on the vowel in the stem. For example, *el* is "hand," *ele* "to the hand," *eller* "hands," and *ellere* "to the hands." The plural suffix *lar* after *adam* is *ler* after *el,* and the suffix for "to" is *e* after *el* and *a* after *adam.* It is not only the vowels *e* and *a* that are involved but the principle is the same. For example, the possessive equivalent to "my" is *im* or *um* depending upon the vowel in the stem of the word: *elim,* "my hand"; *kolum,* "my arm"; *ellerim,* "my hands"; and *kollarum,* "my arms."

Just south of Turkey we find the Semitic languages. The most important of these is Arabic, spoken by over a hundred million people. To this group also belong Hebrew, Amharic, and other languages of Ethiopia. Semitic languages have a morphological system that depends on a three consonant root that can be modified by different vowels. For example, the root KTB in Arabic refers to different aspects of "writing":

kitab	"book"
kutub	"books"
kataba	"he wrote"
yaktubu	"he writes"
takataba	"to keep up a correspondence"
katib	"writer"
kutubi	"bookseller"

maktub	"letter"
maktab	"office"
miktab	"typewriter"

What all these forms have in common are the three sounds [k], [t], and [b], in that order.

There are nearly 2,000 languages in Africa. The largest group is the Niger-Congo family, which contains about 900 languages. In the west there are languages such as Mende, Malinke, Bambara, Kpelle, Fulani, Yoruba, Ibo, Twi, and Fante. The largest subgroup is Bantu, spoken mostly south of a line extending from Cameroon in the west to Kenya in the east. The Bantu languages include Lingala, Ganda, Bemba, Shona, Zulu, and Xhosa, but the most widely spoken is Swahili. Bantu languages are agglutinative languages with a complex set of noun classes, which can be illustrated from Swahili:

kikapu   kikubwa   kile   kitatosha
(basket   big   that   "it"-will-be enough)

That big basket will be enough

vikapu   vikubwa   vile   vitatosha
(basket   big   those   "they"-will-be enough)

Those big baskets will be enough

The word for basket belongs to the *ki/vi* class, which means that it takes *ki* in the singular and *vi* in the plural, not only as a marker on the noun but also on the adjective, the demonstrative, and the verb. The *ki/vi* class contains only inanimate objects. Human beings are in the *m/wa* class:

mtoto   mzuri   mmoja   atatosha
(boy   good   one   "he"-will-be enough)

One good boy will be enough

watoto   wazuri   watatu   watatosha
(boy   good   three   "they"-will-be enough)

Three good boys will be enough

The tense marker is included in the verb. In the preceding examples, *ta* is "future"; the "past" morpheme is *li*:

watoto   wazuri   watatu   walitosha
(boy   good   three   "they"-were-enough)

Three good boys were enough

If there is a pronoun object it is also included in the verb after the tense marker:

atawalipa
a   ta   wa   lipa
(he   "future"   them   pay)

He will pay them

aliwalipa_{li}
a   wa   ilpa
he   "past"   them   pay)

He paid them

In Africa are also found the so-called click languages (Hottentot, belonging to the Khoisan family, and the Bantu languages Zulu and Xhosa), in which some consonant sounds are produced by sucking air into the mouth to produce certain clicking sounds, one of which is like the noise sometimes used to communicate with horses. Another is the *tsk tsk* sound used by many English speakers to indicate disapproval. The click languages are unique among the world's languages in using sounds of this type as phonemes, but they function just like other consonants. Because of the difficulty of producing sequences of these sounds, Zulu-speaking children practice saying tongue twisters with numerous clicks.

There are about a thousand Native American languages in the Americas, though some of them are spoken by a very small number of people and others have already become extinct. There are numerous families of languages, one of the largest being Algonquian, which includes Ojibwa, Cree, Blackfoot, Fox, and Delaware. The Native American language with the largest number of speakers in the United States is Navajo, which belongs to the Athabascan family. The Siouan languages include Dakota and Crow. Among the Iroquoian languages are Cherokee, Seneca, and Mohawk. The Uto-Aztecan languages include Papago, Pima, Hopi, Ute, and Shoshone in the southwest United States, and Nahuatl in Mexico. Mayan languages spoken in Mexico and Guatemala include Quiche, Tzeltal, Tzotzil, and Yucatec. Further south, Quechua is the most widely spoken, in Peru, Bolivia, and Ecuador, followed by Aymara, while there are large numbers of Guarani speakers in Paraguay.

One of characteristics of many Native American languages is the use of verbal suffixes, which indicate the reliability or probability of the information conveyed by the verb. These suffixes have come to be known as *evidentials*. Here are some examples from Makah, a Nootkan language spoken in northwest Washington State. (I have simplified the spelling; the colon and question mark respectively indicate a long vowel and a glottal stop.)

wiki:caxaw	"It's bad weather" (I know from my own experience)
wiki:caxak?u	"It was bad weather" (I experienced it)
wiki:caxakpi:d	"It looks like bad weather" (That's the conclusion I draw)
wiki:caxakgac?i	"It sounds like bad weather" (I hear rumblings in the distance)
wiki:caxakwa:d	"I'm told there's bad weather" (Someone told me)
wiki:caxakitwa:d	"I'm told it was bad weather" (Someone told me)

As the translations indicate, it is possible to give the same information in English. The difference is that in Makah you must chose one of the suffixes and you cannot simply say "It was bad weather," leaving it vague as to whether you know this from your own experience or have heard about it from someone else. Clearly, life would be much harder for politicians and advertisers if they were obliged always to provide an indication of the reliability of their claims.

In the Pacific are found the Austronesian (Malayo-Polynesian) languages, of which there are about a thousand. The main subgroups are Indonesian, which includes Malay, Javanese, and Tagalog; Micronesian, including Gilbertese, Ponopean, and Trukese; Melanesian, with Fijian and Motu; and Polynesian, which includes Maori, Samoan, Tahitian, and Hawaiian. In Australia there were about 250 languages, including Walbiri, Dyirbal, and Aranda. Japanese, Korean, Vietnamese, and Eskimo are relatively isolated languages not belonging to larger families, though it has been claimed that Japanese and Korean are related and that they may be part of the Altaic family.

A feature that is found in many of these languages (but also in Basque and in Mayan languages) is *ergativity*. Ergativity is a term used to refer to a system of case-marking on nouns where the subject of an intransitive verb has the same marking as the object of an intransitive verb. This is in contrast to so-called nominative/accusative systems in which the subjects of both transitive and intransitive verbs are marked the same and the objects are marked differently. Since nouns are not case-marked in English it is necessary to illustrate this with pronouns:

> he kissed her
> she fainted

In a nominative/accusative language such as English, *he* as the subject of the transitive verb *kiss* and *she* as the subject of the intransitive verb *faint* are both in the subject form, while *her* as the object of the transitive verb is in the object form. In an ergative language the same form would be used for *she* and *her,* as can be seen in this example from Samoan:

(a) na   fasi   le   teine   e   le   tama
    (past   hit   the   girl   erg   the   boy)

    the boy hit the girl

(b) na   fasi   le   tama   e   le   teine
    (past   hit   the   boy   erg   the   girl)

    the girl hit the boy

(c) na   moe   le   teine
    (past   sleep the   girl)

    the girl slept

(d) na   moe   le   tama
    (past   sleep the   boy)

    the boy slept

In the English translation "the girl" is the object in (a) and the subject in (c); "the boy" is the object in (b) and the subject in (d). In Samoan *le teine* ("the girl") and *le tama* ("the boy") are unmarked in (c) and (d) while in (a) *le tama* and (b) *le teine* which are the subjects in the English translation take the ergative marker *e*. In some ways the ergative is like the English passive *the girl was hit by the boy* and *the boy was hit by the girl* in which *by* (like the egative marker *e*) indicates the person doing the hitting, but the parallel is not exact and the functions are rather different.

In Asia the largest family is the Sino-Tibetan group, which includes Chinese, Burmese, and Tibetan. It has been estimated that approximately a quarter of the world's population speaks some form of Chinese. The most widely spoken variety and the most important politically is Mandarin, but there are four other major varieties, which are different enough for them not to be mutually intelligible. However, the use of a logographic writing system makes communication in writing possible between speakers of different varieties. Chinese is also a *tone language* in which words are distinguished by differences in pitch. Here are examples of the four different pitches in Bejing Mandarin:

[i]	high level tone	"cloth"
[i]	high rising tone	"to suspect"
[i]	falling-rising tone	"chair"
[i]	high falling tone	"meaning"

Tone languages are rare in Europe (Estonian is an example) but are common in many other parts of the world. Other tone languages in Asia include Vietnamese and Thai. Thai also is one of the languages that has a classifier system in which classes of nouns require a different form with numerals. (In the following examples I have omitted the tone markings.)

dek saam khon	"three children"
phuuji saam khon	"three women"
kaj saam tua	"three chickens"
samut saam lem	"three notebooks"

The classifier *khon* is used for human beings, *tua* for animals, and *lem* for books, carts, and sharp pointed instruments. Other classifiers are *muan* for cigars and cigarettes, *lan* for houses and buildings, *lam* for boats and floating objects, and *baj* for leaves, cups, bottles, boxes, buckets, and baskets.

The broad linguistic descriptions given in this chapter may apply only to the most prominent representatives of the language family. Languages within a single family can differ as much from each other as they do from languages in other language families. The process of linguistic change can lead members of a language family in very different directions. The geographical proximity of a language from a different language family can affect this process of change. For example, Zulu and Xhosa, which are both Bantu languages, developed click phonemes through their close contact with speakers of Khoisan languages.

It is impossible to give more than a few illustrations of the diversity of the world's languages without using more technical terms than is appropriate in a book of this kind. Inevitably, however, the question arises as to the significance of linguistic differences. This is the question that will be addressed in the next chapter.

Language and Thought

> The translatability of words or texts between two languages is not a
> matter of mere readjustment of verbal symbols. It must always be based
> on a unification of cultural context. Even when two cultures have much
> in common, real understanding and the establishment of a community
> of linguistic implements is always a matter of difficult, laborious and
> delicate adjustment.
>
> Bronislaw Malinowski, *Coral Gardens and Their Magic*

One of the most frequently cited passages on the relationship between language
and thought is the following by the pioneering American linguist Edward
Sapir:

> Human beings do not live in the objective world alone, nor in the world of social
> activity as ordinarily understood, but very much at the mercy of the particular
> language which has become the medium of expression for their society. It is quite
> an illusion to imagine that one adjusts to reality essentially without the use of
> language and that language is merely an incidental means for solving specific
> problems of communication and reflection. The fact of the matter is that the "real
> world" is to a large extent unconsciously built up on the language habits of the
> group. No two languages are ever sufficiently similar to be considered as repre-
> senting the same social reality.

Sapir and his pupil Benjamin Lee Whorf investigated various aspects of the relationship between thought and language and developed what is sometimes called
the Linguistic Relativity Theory and sometimes the Sapir/Whorf Hypothesis. The
claim, as the quotation from Sapir suggests, is that the way people perceive objects
and conceive of the world around them is affected or even determined by the
language that they speak. This theory or hypothesis has been the subject of much
debate. The main point at issue is the question whether thinking is rigidly determined by language or strongly or weakly affected by it. This in turn revolves around
the question of which aspects of language could influence thought.

The first is obviously vocabulary. It is extremely difficult to imagine much
abstract thinking going on without the words for the concepts. (It is necessary to
emphasize abstract thinking because certain kinds of problem solving need not
involve language.) A clear example is in medicine. When doctors diagnose a par-

ticular ailment in a patient, what they are doing is giving that condition a label. A nineteenth-century doctor could not have diagnosed muscular dystrophy, legionnaire's disease, or AIDS, and might have given many conditions very different labels than modern doctors. An even clearer example is in mental health. The conditions of schizophrenia, nervous breakdown, anorexia, and paranoia could not have been identified in these ways before the present century, although the conditions probably occurred. In connection with the last example, someone has pointed out that it is remarkable that we have a word for people who believe they are being persecuted when others around them do not think this is true, but we have no word for those who are in fact persecuting others without being aware of doing so. If it is true that the latter condition is as common as the former, this would be a good example of how the existence or lack of a word can affect our thinking.

It is not necessary, however, to consider such elaborate examples. Words have been borrowed into the English language from a variety of other languages. We can be sure that English-speaking people did not talk about potatoes, tobacco, chocolate, tattoos, and taboos before they had the words to do so. We have seen in chapter 16 how some speakers of a language know words and expressions that may be unfamiliar to others. In this respect it is likely that, say, a Russian-speaking physicist and an English-speaking physicist might find it easier to communicate with each other about some aspect of physics than either would have in trying to discuss the same phenomenon with a fellow countryman who knew nothing about physics. In this sense, it is not so important which language you speak but what you know and can speak about in your own language.

The commonly cited example of the arbitrariness of language is in color terms. It has been estimated that the human eye can discriminate seven and half million divisions of the color spectrum. No language has anything like this number of words. Some languages have relatively few basic color words and others have more. For example, in Tiv there are basic color words for black, white, and red, and that is all. In English the basic color words are *black, white, red, green, yellow, blue, brown, purple, pink, orange,* and *grey.* There is also a predictability to the kinds of colors that a language will have words for. If there are only two words, then the distinction is between light and dark. If there is a third word, it will be for red. Then come words for green and yellow, followed by words for blue and brown. Attempts to discover whether people who have fewer color words in their language perceive colors differently have not proved conclusive. Once again, differences within a language are likely to be more important than those between languages. Artists, decorators, and gardeners, for example, are likely to make discriminations in shades of pink or blue that ordinary people might miss, at least until the differences were pointed out. However, this last point draws attention to the most significant aspect of vocabulary: we can all learn new words when we need them or we can invent substitutes like *It's a kind of greenish blue with a touch of yellow.* If the influence of language on thought is judged in terms of vocabulary, it is most likely to be important in the ways in which words can be used for rhetorical purposes (as we saw in chapter 20).

Whorf, however, argued that it is not vocabulary alone that is important. He claimed that the speakers of a language are unconsciously influenced by the syntactic categories of the language. Whorf argued that there was a connection between the attitude to time in Western society and the ways in which European languages such as English, French, and German indicate temporal differences. He contrasted this with the structure of the Hopi language and the attitude of the Hopi to temporal events. For example, he pointed out that words such as *lightning, wave,* and *puff of smoke* are nouns in English, whereas the equivalents in Hopi are verbs. Whorf drew attention to differences between Hopi and Western behavior that he claimed were related to these linguistic differences. It is difficult to be quite sure how deterministic Whorf believed these influences to be, since he died before he could put his tentative claims into a definitive form, but his general position is clear:

> We are inclined to think of language simply as a technique of expression, and not to realize that language first of all is a classification and arrangement of the stream of sensory experience which results in a certain world-order, a certain segment of the world that is easily expressible by the type of symbolic means that language employs. In other words, language does in a cruder but also in a broader and more versatile way the same thing that science does.

Expressed in such general terms, most people would agree with this view. Many other versions of the same position could be cited from different disciplines, as for example, this statement by the sociologist C. Wright Mills:

> Language, socially built and maintained, embodies implicit exhortations and social evaluations. By acquiring the categories of a language, we acquire the "ways" of a group, and along with the language, the value-implicates of those "ways." Our behavior and perception, our logic and thought, come within the control ambit of a system of language. Along with language, we acquire a set of social norms and values.

The crucial question, however, is whether different "languages" affect the ways in which we behave or whether it is what we have learned in the language (including different "registers") that is critical. In the previous chapter we saw examples of linguistic features such as evidentials, classifiers, and ergativity that are not found in English, for example. Does this mean that the speakers of languages in which these features are found think differently from speakers of English? Obviously, this is a difficult (if not impossible) question to answer since the evidence has to be presented in some language. In other words, it often comes down to a question of translation.

Is it ever possible to achieve successful translation from one language into another? Clearly, a number of factors are important. One is the complexity of the message. Simple messages like the sign for *Exit* are relatively easy to convert into *Ausgang, Salida,* and *Sortie.* At the other extreme is the question of translating poetry. Another factor is the extent to which the speakers of the two languages share experience. It may be harder to describe the rigors of winter or the joys of spring to those who have always lived in a tropical climate. A related factor is the existence of technical terms in a language. It will not be easy to explain the advantages of digital recording over analog to those who are not familiar with some of the vocabulary of acoustics. But this is the problem that arose in connection with the notion of register in English (chapter 16) and is not solely a problem for translating from one language into another. Finally, there is the question of what counts as success in translation. In the instructions on how to assemble a piece of furniture or machinery, clarity is all important. In translating a work of literature, it is not just the basic meaning that is important but also the tone, rhythm, and associations of the words. It is also difficult to translate rhymes and other literary effects that depend upon sound sequences.

In fact all linguistic communication depends upon "translation." There is no direct communication through language. In the case of spoken language, the speaker provides certain clues on the basis of which the hearer creates an interpretation of what the speaker intended. Neither the speaker nor the hearer can know how successful communication has been except by interpreting each other's responses. Another kind of translation occurs, for example, when Anne is reporting to Bob what Charles said. Anne might say *Charles said. "I'm going to write a letter about it,"* where she purports to repeat Charles's words and might even mimic his tone of voice. Alternatively, Anne might have used reported speech, *Charles said he was going to write a letter about it,* or she might paraphrase Charles's remark as *Charles threatened/volunteered/agreed to write a letter about it.* Which form Anne uses may depend upon why Charles said it in the first place or why she is telling Bob or a great many other reasons. We take these things for granted in everyday conversation, but some of them become more salient when we are translating from one language into another.

The most obvious problem is the possibility of cultural differences. As Whorf pointed out, metaphors that are common in one language (for example, time as distance in European languages) may be absent in another (for example, Hopi). There may also be differences in the features that *must* be marked in one language (such as plural, gender, tense) but need not be in another. The next two chapters will be devoted to an examination of ways in which languages may differ in the obligatory choices they require their speakers to make. Whether these choices also force them to think differently is a much harder question.

To sum up, we do not know enough about how people think in any language to know what effect a particular language might have on that process. We are all molded, influenced, and limited by many forces, one of which is the language we use. It is possibly true, as Ludwig Wittgenstein claimed, that "the limits of my language are the limits of my world" but, as he would have been the first to admit, it all depends on how you interpret "my language." The interpretations range from the knowledge stored in my head (my idiolect), through my dialect (educated British English) and wider language (English) to the notion of human speech in general. Perhaps one day the long-awaited Martians will arrive and set us right about this. Until that day there is likely to be no clear answer.

30

Pronouns

> Talk is socially organized, not merely in terms of who speaks to whom in what language, but as a little system of mutually ratified and ritually governed face-to-face action, a social encounter.
>
> Erving Goffman

Whatever the influence language has on the way that we think, there is no doubt that a language may sometimes require the people who speak that language to pay particular attention to certain aspects of human interaction. There are features that are obligatory in one language but not in another. A clear example is the use of second-person address terms. In French, for example, the comment *You are ill* can be expressed either as *Tu es malade* or as *Vous êtes malade.* In purely grammatical terms *tu es* is the second-person singular pronoun with a singular form of the verb *être* ("to be") and *vous êtes* is the second-person plural pronoun with the plural form of the verb *être.* However, both are addressed to one person as can be seen from the adjective *malade,* which is singular. If the reference had been to more than one person the utterance would have been *Vous êtes malades.* In French there is a choice between using *tu* and *vous* when addressing one person. The rules governing this choice are complex and depend upon the relationship between the speaker and addressee. Choice of pronoun depends upon such matters as the age, position, and intimacy of the speakers; both may use the same pronoun in addressing each other or one may use *tu* but expect to be addressed with *vous* in return, and conversely. However, the crucial point is that the choice must be made. It is impossible to avoid making a choice if a second-person singular pronoun form is being used.

In present-day English, on the other hand, no such choice is necessary, though until about Shakespeare's time it was possible to use the difference between *thou* and *you* for this purpose. The Duke of Venice uses *thou* in addressing Shylock, who responds with *you.* The question that is hard to investigate, far less answer, is, Does this difference in pronoun use between English and French affect the way in which English-speaking and French-speaking people think?

The need to make a choice in second-person address forms is not limited to French. In Russian there is a similar distinction between *ty* and *vy* and the rules for the choice are perhaps even more complicated. In Spanish (*tu/Usted*), Italian (*tu/Lei*), and German (*du/Sie*), there is a distinction between the singular second-person pronoun and a third-person singular pronoun used as a term of respect, and also a distinction in the plural (*vosotros/Ustedes*), (*voi/Loro*), and (*ihr/Sie*). In all these languages the first form is likely to be chosen in addressing children, social inferiors, and people with whom you are intimate, while the second form will probably be chosen in addressing elders, social superiors, and strangers.

In Japanese the situation is even more complex. There are different forms of the first-person singular pronoun depending upon the situation:

watakushi	ordinary, rather formal
watashi	ordinary, female speaker
atashi	female speaker, informal
boku	male speaker, informal
washi	aged male speaker, informal
chin	emperor
ore	male speaker, casual, inimate
atai	young girls of lower class

The need to take social relationships into consideration before using a second-person address form may or may not affect the ways in which people think, but it certainly affects their behavior. The closest parallel for most English-speaking communities is the choice of address terms such as *Dr. Peterson, Professor Peterson, Mr. Peterson, Peterson,* or *Henry.* The same individual can be addressed in all of these ways as well as such terms as *doctor, professor, sir,* or *you.* The rules for choosing one of the ways of addressing people vary from community to community, and some visitors to California might be surprised to find themselves addressed by first name by, for example, doctor's receptionists and policemen.

There are other differences in pronoun systems between languages. For example, the pronoun *we* in English does not make it clear whether the speaker means to include the addressee or not. It is obvious when a speaker requests permission in an utterance such as *May we come in?* that the pronoun does not include the person of whom the request is made. In a suggestion such as *We could go out for dinner,* the speaker could either mean that he and another person but not the addressee could go out for dinner or it could be intended to include the person addressed. The difference is between the exclusive *we,* which does not include the addressee, and the inclusive *we,* which does. In some languages this distinction is clearly marked and a choice must be made. For example, in the Papua New Guinea creole Tok Pisin, this distinction is signaled by the difference between *yumi* (inclusive *we*) and *mipela* (exclusive *we*). In English there is only one place where there is a difference. In a plea to the addressee for release, *Let us go,* which is clearly the exclusive *we,* the pronoun cannot be contracted as in *Let's go,* which is usually inclusive.

In some languages a different form of the verb must be used depending on whether the subject of the main verb is included in the plural form, as in these examples from the South Australian language Pitjantjatjara:

nyuntu   mukuringanyi   nganana   ankuntjitkitja?
(you   want   us   to go)

Do you want us all (including you) to go?

nyuntu   mukuringanyi   nganana   ankuntjaku?

Do you want us (excluding you) to go?

paluru   mukuringanyi   nganana   ankuntjitkitja:
(he   wants   us   to go)

He wants us all (including him) to go

paluru   mukuringanyi   nganana   ankuntjaku?

He wants us (excluding him) to go

In these examples the form of the first-person plural pronoun is the same *nganana* regardless of whether the speaker is included or not. The difference is signaled on the verb with the suffix *jitkitja* if the subject of the main verb is included and the suffix *jaku* if the subject is excluded. This feature of marking a difference in subjects has come to be known as *switch-reference* and is a way of avoiding the kind of ambiguity that occurs in English. In *John said that he would do it,* only the context will enable the hearer to know whether *he* = *John* or not. In a switch-reference language, there would be no doubt. Linguists who consider examples of language isolated from their context have tended to exaggerate the importance of ambiguity. In the actual use of language hearers are more likely to complain about vagueness of reference because few utterances are ambiguous in context. Nowhere is the difference between the linguist's clinical approach to language as specimens under the microscope and the ordinary speaker's use of language greater than in their attitude to pronouns.

For ordinary people the use of pronouns need not always correspond to their dictionary meaning. The doctor making his rounds of a hospital ward may say to a patient *And how are we today?* where the *we* is neither inclusive nor exclusive but equivalent to *you.* Similarly, in books (including this one) you will find expressions such as *as we have seen* where the *we* mainly refers to the reader, though it is also true that the writer has seen. I once overheard a woman explaining to someone else why she had had to take her elderly father to the dentist: *Because he had broken his false teeth and we've only got the one set.* My first image was of them passing the teeth across the table during a meal, but the speaker was presumably using *we* with the sense of *he.* The second-person pronoun *you* can also be used in an impersonal way, equivalent to *one.* A Scottish coal miner I interviewed told me how if he had done anything wrong his mother would tell his father *and I think just for peace my faither would just gie [give] you a licking or two.* Switching pronouns like this without changing the reference to the person is quite common in speech. Someone else told me about his childhood: *When I was a kid you played around the beach an awful lot and in the summer one was in a swimsuit oh seemingly all summer.* The pronouns *I, you,* and *one* all refer to the speaker, though the latter two could also refer to his peers.

Another respect in which pronoun systems may differ is in the gender of third-person pronouns. In English it is necessary to choose between *he, she,* and *it* in the singular, but not in the plural where there is only the one form *they.* In French there is also a distinction in the plural between *ils* (masculine) and *elles* (feminine) and also in Spanish between *ellos* (masculine) and *ellas* (feminine). One consequence of this is that in French and Spanish there is no gender-neutral pronoun.

In English until recently it has been the practice in formal written styles to use *he* as the gender neutral pronoun as in examples such as:

> If anyone has lost a pen, will he please come to the office?
> When the child first goes to school he may feel anxious.
> You should ask the doctor for his advice.

It used to be claimed that the use of *he* in such examples does not imply that the person is male, but recently there have been arguments that this usage is sexist. One way to avoid the rather clumsy locution *he* or *she* is to use the plural as in *When children first go to school they may feel anxious.* This usage actually makes more sense than the original example in the singular because what we are talking about is children in general, not a particular child. The example with the doctor is more difficult because it implies that doctors are always men, but it would mean something else if made plural. Writers of public notices and advertisements nowadays usually try to avoid any phrasing that suggests that only men are intended. It is possible that the use of *he* as a gender neutral pronoun has contributed to the stereotypes about occupations and their appropriateness for men and women. If so, this would be an example that supported the Sapir/Whorf Hypothesis. Other aspects of gender will be examined in the next chapter.

31

Gender

> In German a young lady has no sex, while a turnip has. Think what
> overwrought reverence that shows for the turnip, and what callous dis-
> respect for the girl. See how it looks in print. I translate this from a
> conversation in one of the best of the German Sunday-school books:
> Gretchen: "Wilhelm, Where is the turnip?"
> Wilhelm: "She has gone to the kitchen."
> Gretchen: "Where is the accomplished and beautiful English maiden?"
> Wilhelm: "It has gone to the opera."
>
> Mark Twain, *"The Awful German Language"*

Most languages (but not all) have systems of noun classes that are usually known as genders. The gender of a noun affects the ways in which its relationship with other items in the utterance are marked. One is these is through agreement. For example, in French there are two genders, masculine and feminine. As might be expected, words referring to males are masculine and those referring to females are feminine. However, all nouns must be either masculine or feminine, so, for example, *livre* ("book"), *garage* ("garage"), and *cheval* ("horse") are all masculine, while *table* ("table"), *maison* ("house"), and *vache* ("cow") are all feminine. The gender of the noun affects the form of other items in the utterance:

Le cheval est très petit   "The horse is very small"
La vache est très petite   "The cow is very small"

The definite article is *le* in the masculine and *la* in the feminine, and the adjective is *petit* in the masculine and *petite* in the feminine. (The spelling difference indicates a difference in pronunciation; in the feminine the final [t] is pronounced but not in the masculine.)

Another way in which gender may affect other items is in the pronoun system. For example, someone might deny the assertions made about the size of the horse and the cow in this way:

Non, il est grand   "No, it is big"
Non, elle est grande   "No, it is big"

Where in English we can use the same pronoun *it* for both animals, in French *il* must be used for *cheval* and *elle* for *vache*. It is, of course, possible in English to use *he* or *she* for animals if we know what sex they are but it is not obligatory. This possibility gives an interesting classification of nouns in English:

He-class: boy, man, waiter
She-class: girl, woman, waitress
He/she-class: doctor, teacher, cousin
He/she/it-class: dog, horse, baby
She/it-class: ship, car

It is not usual to say that English has a five-gender system but this is what it actually is on the basis of pronoun selection. It is more common to say that English has a sex-based semantic gender system in which males are masculine, females are feminine, and all others neuter. Many languages have gender systems that are semantically based but not on sex. Swahili, for example, has seven noun classes, one of which is animate, meaning most people and animals, but there is no noun class that separates males from females. Other categories include plants, fruits, large objects, small objects, and elongated objects. The classes are only partially based on meaning; the form of the prefixes for singular and plural also affects the class an item belongs to. In Swahili the agreement system is extensive as can be seen in the following examples:

kikapu   kikubwa   kimoja   kilianguka
(basket   large   one   fell)

One large basket fell

vikapu   vikubwa   vitatu   vilianguka
(basket   large   three   fell)

Three large baskets fell

In the singular *kapu* ("basket") has the prefix *ki-*, which also occurs on the adjective *kubwa* ("large"), the numeral *moja* ("one"), and the verb *lianguka* ("fell"). In the plural the prefix is *vi-*, which occurs everywhere in place of *ki-*. In Swahili the agreement markers and the plural markers occur as prefixes, in contrast to most European languages where such markers occur as suffixes.

In Russian verbs agree in gender with the subject, but only in the past tense:

Ivan čital   "Ivan was reading"
Irina čitala   "Irene was reading"

This agreement occurs in the first and second person also:

ja čital   "I was reading" (male speaker)
ja čitala   "I was reading" (female speaker)
ty čital   "You were reading" (male addressee)
ty čitala   "You were reading" (female addressee)

Gender agreement in Russian occurs only in the singular. In Spanish, on the other hand, there are separate forms for all personal pronouns in the plural: *nosotras* ("we, masculine"), *nosotras* ("we, feminine"); *vosotros* ("you, masculine"), *vosotras* ("you, feminine"); *ellos* ("they, masculine"), *ellas* ("they, feminine").

The Spanish examples also illustrate how a gender system can be phonologically marked in a very straightforward manner. In Spanish (and also in Italian and Portugese), most nouns ending in -*o* are masculine and most nouns ending in -*a* are feminine and the agreement markers are the same:

los hermanos ricos   "the rich brothers"
las hermanas ricas   "the rich sisters"

Where the vowel *o* occurs in the phrase about the brothers, that is, in the definite article, in the noun itself, and in the following adjective, the corresponding vowel in the phrase about the sisters is *a*.

On the other hand, there are languages such as Tamil where all nouns are assigned to one of three genders on the basis of their meaning. Male humans and gods are in the masculine gender, female humans and goddesses are in the feminine gender, and everything else is in the neuter gender (including infants and children!). There are a few exceptions based mainly on mythology. The sun, moon, and other heavenly bodies are masculine because their names are those of gods.

There is little agreement about the gender of the sun and moon in the world's languages. In German *die Sonne* ("the sun") is feminine and *der Mond* ("the moon") is masculine, while in French (and other Romance languages such as Spanish and Italian) the sun (*le soleil, el sol, il sole*) is masculine and the moon (*la lune, la luna*) is feminine. In the Australian Aboriginal language Dyirbal, the moon was in the same noun class as men; the sun and stars were in the same class as women along with fire, scorpions, and other dangerous things. In recent years the gender system has been simplified to one that is based on more transparent meanings. For example, birds were at one time in the same noun class as women because they were believed to be the spirits of dead females, but they have been moved into the same class as other animals, namely the masculine. This is because the mythological associations have been lost.

In many gender systems based on the meaning of the words, there are anomalies that are probably the result of mythological associations that have been lost. There may be other associations with gender. There is a Russian superstition that if a knife is dropped there will be a male guest, and if a fork is dropped the visitor will be a woman. In Russian the word for a knife (*nož*) is masculine, while the word for a fork (*vilka*) is feminine. In some Polish dialects nouns referring to girls and unmarried women of any age are neuter, while the feminine is used for married women.

It is not obvious why complex gender systems exist, since some languages can function perfectly well without them. One thing that can safely be said is that gender systems are difficult for an adult learner. In language situations where there are large numbers of adult learners, there is a tendency for complex morphological systems, including gender, to be simplified. It is not surprising that languages such as English and Chinese do not have complicated gender systems.

It is often erroneously said that English is a language with little grammar. What people probably mean by this is that English has a very limited inflectional morphology. However, a glance at a grammatical description of the language, for example, *A Comprehensive Grammar of the English Language* by Randolph Quirk and his associates will immediately confront the reader with many examples of the subtle grammatical distinctions that we use every day and take for granted. Many of these distinctions are harder to classify because of the absence of overt morphological markers and thus they are not necessarily recognized as grammatical features by the ordinary speaker. On the other hand, there are some languages that have both limited morphology and more limited grammatical systems. The characteristics of these languages will be considered in the next chapter.

Pidgins and Creoles

Bob Close, who was accustomed to talking in pidgin to the natives of Northern Australia and New Caledonia, wanted a pole for some work on hand. Pointing and gesticulating to make his meaning still clearer, he gave his orders to Eliasi: "Bring one fellow stick long me two times, thick all same this arm belonga me!" Eliasi quietly replied: "Yes, I understand, Mister Bob. You want a pole twelve feet long and three inches across. I will get it at once."

An anecdote quoted by Jeff Siegel, in *Language Contact in a Plantation Environment,* to show that Melanesian Pidgin English was not commonly used on Fiji

Some of the most fascinating questions are probably unanswerable. One is about the origin of human language. With the exception of a small but vocal group, most people in Britain and the United States believe in the notion of evolution, even if the details are far from clear. The emergence of human language as an efficient system of vocal communication, however, presents a challenge to evolutionary theory, since there is a fundamental problem in even imagining how the kinds of calls primates use could have developed into human language. The problem lies in the segmental nature of language and particularly the segments known as phonemes. Since phonemes are meaningless in themselves, it is hard to see how they could have developed out of a system in which individual calls had separate meanings.

Another problem in trying to understand the evolution of language is the lack of fossil evidence. Unfortunately, bone structure is not the most important aspect of the vocal tract and the softer parts of the body do not survive as fossils. Attempts have been made to extrapolate the size of the vocal tract from skull fossils in order to determine when human beings first began to use language. Even if successful (and they have been challenged), these efforts would still not provide any explanation of how language evolved.

The nearest parallels to speech in the animal world are some forms of bird song. It has been discovered that in a species of song sparrow the song has three parts. The first identifies the song as being that of a sparrow; the second provides a signal common to the sparrows from a particular region; and the third part distinguishes the sparrow from other sparrows so that his mate (it is the males who sing) may find him. There are parallels here with the personal and dialect characteristics of human language. In song birds there also appears to be an innate disposition to sing, but the development of the kind of song characteristic of the species requires exposure to adult song during the critical period when the young bird is learning how to sing. This is similar to the situation of human infants. There is also evidence of lateralization of the brain in song birds that is similar to the lateralization of brain function for speech in human beings. It would, however, require considerable revision of evolutionary theory to show that human beings, as featherless bipeds, are literally descended from the birds.

In the absence of archaeological or biological evidence on the emergence of language, linguists have been interested in the case of languages that are known to have developed in historical times. These are languages that have emerged for particular purposes, such as trading between two groups whose languages are not mutually intelligible. The names given to such languages are pidgin and creole. The usual distinction is that pidgins are spoken by people who have previously learned another language as their primary means of communication, whereas creoles are spoken by some people as their first language, but this distinction is harder to establish than it might seem.

The origin of pidgin languages is a matter of some controversy. Some have argued that there was an original simplified form of Portuguese, developed during the fifteenth century when the Portuguese were "discovering" Africa, and that this became the basis of a nautical jargon used by sailors of different nationalities and modified accordingly. The widespread use in English pidgins of words such as *savvy* "known" and *picaninny* "child" with apparent Portuguese origins is often cited as supporting evidence for this view. Others have argued that pidgins arose from the kinds of simplification people make in speaking to very young children ("baby talk") or to foreigners ("foreigner talk").

Whatever their origins, pidgin languages are characterized by certain features. The following examples are from Loreto Todd's account of Cameroon Pidgin English (CPE). There is no inflectional morphology:

yu bin go	"you went"
i big pas mi	"he is bigger than me"
di dɔg i fut dɔn brok	"the dog's leg is broken"

The similarity of these forms to English—for example, *bin* and *been, pas* and *past*—is not accidental since the English words are the source, but it is important not to assume that the words have the same function or meaning in CPE.

References to different times are made through auxiliaries and adverbs rather than by tenses. The word order is SVO (subject-verb-object) and there is little subordination. Questions are asked by intonation rather than change of word order. There are only a few prepositions and they serve as equivalents for several in English:

gif di buk fɔ mi	"give the book TO me"
i dei fɔ fam	"she is AT the farm"
dem dei fɔ chɔs	"they are IN the church"
di mɔni dei fɔ tebul	"the money is ON the table"

There are no distinctions of gender, so the same pronoun may refer to males, females, or inanimate objects. Nouns are not usually marked for plurality, but if necessary the third-person pronoun is used:

> ma pikin dem   "my children"

Reduplication (repetition of the same form) is used for emphasis:

fain	"lovely"
fain fain	"really lovely"
big big	"very big"
pikin di kraikrai	"the child is always crying"

Possession is indicated by the pronoun:

Pita i haus	"Peter's house"
i haus	"his house"
dem haus	"their house"
Pita i wuman i haus	"Peter's wife's house"

Pidgin languages are also said to have very limited vocabularies. This leads to circumlocutions that may appear cumbrous or even comic to speakers of other languages. Suzanne Romaine gives the following examples from Tok Pisin, which is spoken in Papua New Guinea (the possessive in Tok Pisin is indicated by *bilong*):

TOK PISIN	ENGLISH
gras	grass
gras bilong fes	beard
gras bilong hed	hair
gras bilong pisin	feather
gras antap long ai	eyebrow
gras nogut	weed

A more complex example is *singsing long taim maus i pas* ("to sing when the mouth is closed," that is, to hum).

Many of the everyday words in Tok Pisin come from taboo expressions in English (for example, *bagarupim,* "ruin, destroy"; *bulsitim* "deceive, cheat"; *sit bilong faia,* "ashes"). It is unclear whether this is the result of deliberate disparagement of the native people by their overseers or simply followed from the normal foul-mouthed speech of the latter.

More than a hundred languages have been identified as pidgins or creoles. English-based creoles are (or have been) spoken in Hawaii, Guyana, Jamaica, the United States (Gullah), Belize, and many former British colonies in Africa, Australia, Melanesia, and Micronesia. French-based creoles include Haitian, Louisiana Creole, and Mauritian Creole. Portuguese is the basis of many creoles, among them Papiamentu and Samaraccan. Dutch-based creoles include Afrikaans. Other pidgins and creoles have been based on Spanish, German, Arabic, and various African languages. Native American languages gave rise to creoles such as Chinook jargon.

While in practice the distinctions may be less clear, the difference between a pidgin and a creole is that the former is used for restricted purposes and thus does not need the flexibility of a language that is to be used for all communicational needs. A creole, on the other hand, is just like any other language and therefore is likely to develop the kind of variety and stylistic complexity that we have seen in English. In fact, it has been argued that modern English is a kind of creole with its Germanic base modified by French influence after the Norman Conquest. It is possible that the wide-spread use of English as a second language, mainly for political and technological reasons, has been helped by certain creole characteristics, such as its limited inflectional morphology.

Linguists have been studying pidgins and creoles with increasing interest because of their value as a laboratory for studying language development. If it is true that creole languages develop out of pidgin languages when children begin to speak a pidgin as their first language, then an interesting question arises. Children learning a language such as English have the model of adult speech on which to base their grasp of the language, but children learning a pidgin as their first language will have to go beyond the model provided by adults. How do they know what the creole language will need that is not part of the pidgin language? This is not primarily a matter of vocabulary but of linguistic structure. Derek Bickerton has argued that children are born with a bioprogram that enables them to create certain basic grammatical categories that are important for a fully developed language but may not be part of the pidgin language. Bickerton's claim is different from Chomsky's in that his categories are semantically based, whereas Chomsky argues that children are born with an innate understanding of the syntactic structure of human language. Although Bickerton's and Chomsky's theories have been challenged by many scholars, they both attempt to provide answers to questions that are otherwise unanswerable. Whether it helps to say that what we cannot explain must be innate is the crux of the problem. Meanwhile, the development of creoles from pidgins remains yet another mystery in the evolution of human language.

In situations where the speakers of a creole are in frequent contact with the speakers of the dominant language on which the creole was based, there may be a tendency for some speakers to modify their speech in the direction of that language. This process is known as decreolization. Since the extent to which speakers modify their speech varies, a range of forms may occur. It is customary to think of this as a continuum ranging from the acrolect as the standard language to the basilect or the most creolized form. Intermediate varieties are known as mesolects. The kind of variety that can arise may be illustrated from Guyana:

English	I gave him	acrolect
	a geev him	
	a geev im	
	a geev ii	
	a giv him	
	a giv im	
	a giv ii	
	a did giv hii	
	a did giv ii	

a did gi ii
a di gii ii
a di gi ii
mi di gi hii
mi di gii ii
mi bin gi ii
mi bin gii ii
mi bin gii am

Guayanese Creole   mi gii am   basilect

As we go down the list we get further and further away from Standard English. While the variation is considerable, it is important to remember that in all forms of speech there is more variation than the written form would suggest. Different styles and different speeds affect the amount of assimilation, consonant deletion, and vowel reduction that occurs. The creole continuum is simply an extreme example of this kind of variation. In this, as in many other ways, creole languages are not essentially different from other languages that are used for the multifarious purposes of a complex society. It has been suggested that the two most widely spoken languages in the world, English and Chinese, both ought to be considered creoles because of their mixed origins. With languages, as with people, however, genealogy is only a historical curiosity. In the long run, it does not matter who your parents were but who you are and what you can do. What a language can do, or rather, what can be done in a language will be examined in the next chapter.

Literature

Literature is, and can be nothing other than, a kind of extension and application of certain properties of language.

Paul Valery, *Analects*

It used to be common for linguists to claim that all languages are equal or words to that effect. This was a natural reaction to the kind of elitism that asserted the superiority of Latin, Greek, French, or English for some reason or other. Like many generalizations the claim of equality contains an element of truth. All known human languages are highly complex, sophisticated, structured systems of communication. There are no primitive languages "with only a few hundred words," such as have sometimes been mistakenly attributed to tribes living in inaccessible parts of the world. All languages that are spoken by groups of people as their first language have to be able to deal with the complexity of interaction in the society in which the language is used. Many of the languages spoken by peoples whose way of life might seem very limited (or "primitive") to those in technologically advanced societies make subtle distinctions that are not found in, for example, modern European languages.

On the other hand, it is true that it would be impossible to write about quantum mechanics in many languages, since the necessary vocabulary does not exist, and impossible to write about anything in an even greater number of languages, since they do not have an accepted writing system. These are obvious restrictions on the ways in which a language can be used. When linguists claim that such languages are "equal" to the languages of modern technological societies, what they mean is that there is nothing in principle that would prevent these languages from developing these functions, and there are many examples of languages that have been adapted to meet new roles. Relevant examples are modern Hebrew, which has had to be expanded from an ancient religious language to meet the needs of an industrialized nation, and Bahasa Indonesia, which was deliberately chosen as the national language of a multilingual nation despite its origin as trade language of limited scope compared with higher status languages such as Javanese.

Generally, linguists have been reluctant to make value judgments about languages because there is no way to measure the complexity or simplicity of a language. We know from studies of first- and second-language learning that certain features of a language are relatively easy or difficult to learn, but there is no way to argue that, for example, a language such as English with comparatively little inflectional morphology is easier or more difficult for a child to learn than a language such as Finnish with its extensive system of inflections. It seems likely that simplification in one area (for example, inflectional morphology) will be balanced by complexity in another (for example, prepositions or articles). In the circumstances of present knowledge it is prudent not to make value judgments about languages. It is quite a different matter about the use of a language.

Probably in all societies some people are recognized as being more effective users of language than others. Such individuals gain respect as orators, storytellers, advocates, negotiators, entertainers, and preachers. In literate societies some kinds of writing are singled out as having a special value and included in the category of literature. It would take many volumes to describe the ways in which speakers and writers have used language more effectively than others, but there are a number of devices that have proved their worth over a long period of time. Some of them are mainly found in writing but others are common to both speech and writing.

One of the commonest devices is repetition. Repetition is a violation of one of Paul Grice's rules for conversation since more is being said than necessary. For example, when Macbeth says

> Tomorrow, and tomorrow, and tomorrow,
> Creeps in this petty pace from day to day.
> *(Macbeth* V,v)

the repetition of *tomorrow* is not redundant in the way that it would be in the everyday speech but reinforces the sense of monotony and despair. Similarly, in Samson's cry

> Oh dark, dark, dark, amid the blaze of noon
> (Milton, *Samson Agonistes*)

the repetition of *dark* helps to evoke his blindness.

It is not only words that can be repeated. The repetition of inflections can can also be effective as in this passage from Wordsworth:

> Not for these I raise
> The song of thanks and praise;
> But for those obstinate questionings
> Of sense and outward things,
> Fallings from us, vanishings,
> Blank misgivings of a creature
> Moving about in worlds not realized
> ("Ode on Intimations of immortality")

The echoing inflections of *questionings, fallings, vanishings,* and *misgivings* link them together much as the way gender agreements do in many languages. In verse the same effect can be created through rhyme. Rhyme is the partial repetition of the sounds of a word and this can have a hypnotic effect as in the opening of one of Coleridge's poems:

In Xanadu did Kubla Khan
A stately pleasure-dome decree
Where Alph, the sacred river, ran
Through caverns measureless to man
  Down to a sunless sea.
                    ("Kubla Khan")

In addition to the end rhymes *Khan/ran/man* and *decree/sea,* there are also the internal rhymes *Xan-/Khan* and *pleasure/measure.* Sometimes consonantal rhyme (or pararhyme) can be used, as by Wilfred Owen in a poem about a dead soldier in the First World War:

Think how it wakes the seeds—
Woke, once, the clays of a cold star.
Are limbs, so dear-achieved, are sides
Full-nerved—still warm—too hard to stir?
Was it for this the clay grew tall?
—O what made fatuous sunbeams toil
To break earth's sleep at all?
                    ("Futility")

In the words *seeds/sides, star/stir,* and *tall/toil,* it is the consonants that "rhyme." For some reason, consonantal rhymes seem to be less soothing or sentimental and thus appropriate for a poem about unnecessary death. Repetition of initial consonants, alliteration, is more common, as in these lines from Coleridge's *Ancient Mariner:*

The fair breeze blew, the white foam flew,
The furrow followed free;
We were the first that ever burst
  Into that silent sea.

In addition to the several words beginning with *f,* there is the alliteration in *breeze blew* and *silent sea.* In Old English poetry, alliteration was the principal linking device used as in this extract from *The Battle of Maldon;*

Stōdon stædefæste, stihte hī Byrhtnōð, bæd þæt hyssa gehwylc hogode tō wīge,
þe on Denon wolde dōm gefeohtan. Wōd þā wīges heard, wæpen ūp āhōf, bord
tō gebeorge, and wið þæs beornes stōp; ēode swā ānræd eorl tō þām ceorle: ægþer
hyra ōðrum yfeles hogode.
They stood there steadfast. Byrhtnoth encouraged them. Told each warrior to keep
his mind on the fight if he wished to gain glory against the Danes. Then the battle-
hardened warrior advanced. He held up his weapon and with his shield as protection he stepped forward against the warrior (on the other side). So the earl went
resolutely to the man.

In Old English verse there were two half-lines and there had to be at least one word in each half-line that began with the same consonant as, for example, *stōdon stædefæste/stihte* or words beginning with any vowel would serve, for example, *ēode ānræd/ eorl.*

Sometimes there can be repetition with slight variation as in Richard III's words:

Was ever woman in this humour woo'd?
Was ever woman in this humour won?
                    (*Richard III* I, ii)

The alliteration of *woo'd* and *won* draws attention to the change. Sometimes parallelism or repetition of a pattern can be effective as in Richard II's words:

This royal throne of kings, this scepter'd isle,
This earth of majesty, this seat of Mars . . .
This blessed plot, this earth, this realm, this England
                    (*Richard II* II, i)

Sometimes repetition and parallelism can be combined as in these lines from Milton's *Comus*:

With ruin upon ruin, rout on rout,
Confusion worse confounded

Repetition and rhyme can be combined to bring out contrasts as in Pope's lines:

A soul as full of worth as void of pride
Which nothing seeks to show, or needs to hide.
                    ("Epistle to James Craggs, Esq.")

Full and *void* are opposites and this implies the same contrast between *worth* and *pride*. Similarly, *show* and *hide* are opposites and this in turn emphasizes the contrast between *seeks* and *needs*. Parallelism with variation can also be used metaphorically as in an example from T. S. Eliot:

The yellow fog that rubs its back upon the window-panes
The yellow smoke that rubs its muzzle on the window-panes
                    ("The Love Song of J. Alfred Prufrock")

Another form of repetition includes reversing the order of elements as in Hamlet's words:

What's Hecuba to him or he to Hecuba
That he should weep for her?
                    (*Hamlet* II, ii)

or in this line from Shelley's *To a Skylark*:

And singing still dost soar, and soaring ever singest

or Richard II's

I wasted time, and now doth time waste me
                    (*Richard II* V, v)

A very moving example contains a repetition in form with a change of meaning as in Othello's words:

Put out the light, and then put out the light
(*Othello* V,ii)

where the first clause refers to the lamp and the second to Desdemona's life.

Repetition, including alliteration, can be found in speech as well. The following example comes from a story told to me by a woman in the Scottish town of Ayr about her first job in a carpet factory:

they were wild
the women were
they werenae ["weren't"] wild
they were workers
but they worked like men
and they swore like men

The succession of *w*'s is almost as vivid as in the example from Coleridge quoted earlier, and it ends with the parallel clauses that bring out the relationship between physically hard work and swearing. (Jespersen cannot have met any women who "worked like men"!)

In a brief account of his working life, an Ayrshire coal miner told me how the manager had asked him to take a position where he might be required to carry out a variety of tasks:

but the wee man says
"How aboot going to any bit
I send you—
an honest day's work for an honest day's pay?"
but I says
"What do you coont ["count"] an honest day's pay?" I says
"That's the vital bit" I says
"An honest day's pay to you might not be an honest day's pay to me"
so he suggested an amount
and I says
"Oh well fair enough"

By his repetitions of *an honest day's pay,* Willie Lang manages to suggest that he was confident about providing *an honest day's work* but he wanted to make sure that he got his just reward.

Speakers can also make use of repeated inflections in much the same way as Wordsworth, as can be seen in this example from a man I interviewed in Glasgow. He had gone to sea as a galley-boy at the age of fifteen in 1940, during World War II. I had asked him if he had felt afraid and he had told me how his greatest anxiety had been about being seasick. He described how he had been able to make use of a small chute that was used for emptying the ashes from the ship's coal-burning furnaces:

and I'd be standing there
scrubbing
or cleaning pots
and every now and again I'd make a beeline for this chute

and be sick there you know
but wunst I got by the first day
keeping
working
and keeping
being sick
and eating
being made to eat
I definitely got by the first day quite well

The succession of forms ending in *-ing* emphasizes the repetitive nature of what was actually happening *standing, scrubbing, cleaning, keeping working, keeping being sick, eating,* and *being made to eat.* The point of the story turns out to be the narrator's greater success in dealing with his seasickness in contrast to two others on their first trip who had not been sympathetic when he expressed his anxieties to them and was looking for support.

Another Ayrshire coal miner told me about the first time he went down the mine:

that's a thing
I don't think
I'll ever forget
I would never forget
I remember the first morning
going in the cage
and *going* down the pit
I mean the sensation of
going down
I mean you *go* away
the cage *goes* away
and I mean you just feel your breath
going away
I mean it's no ["not"] like a lift
I mean it goes down at some tune
the sensation was
after you were maybe about halfway doon ["down"]
you felt
as if you were *going* back up
that was the kind of sensation
it was you see

The repetitions of *go* create an intense sense of movement: *going in the cage, going down the pit, the sensation of going down, you go away, the cage goes away, you just feel your breath going away, it goes down at some tune,* and *you felt as if you were going back up.*

The Dundee woman who had worked in the shipyard as a welder during World War II (see chapter 22) told an oral history interviewer:

when you say to me
"Think on a color"

I think on grey
grey ashes in the grate
grey school uniform
grey is the color
grey's the color
when you havenae ["haven't"] got any money
I think on grey
grey days
grey rainy weather
grey
things are grey

Although she was by no means gloomy, she had had a hard life and her eloquence about the color grey expresses the sadder side of life.

Some uses of language can be boring, incomprehensible, offensive, soporific, depressing, or even dangerous, but there is also a great deal of pleasure to be got out of effective and imaginative uses of language. Just as some artists have demonstrated that there can be "found art," it is also possible for there to be "found poetry." My experience of listening carefully to tapes of interviews for twenty years has convinced me that there is a lot of aesthetic pleasure to be gained from ordinary speech, particularly from those who probably do not read much literature or even read much at all.

Literary criticism (like linguistics) has become a rather esoteric discipline and the surface features of language tend to receive less attention than they might and thus readers may get less guidance than they should. This is unfortunate because the only way to learn to recognize good writing is by reading appropriate examples. Maybe the critics feel that it is always obvious, but as Paolo Freire observed, "Experience teaches us that the obvious is not always clearly understood." It is not only adults who show their skills in using language effectively. Children also show an interest in language, as will be seen in the next chapter.

Children's Lore and Language

Before I got married I had six theories about bringing up children; now I have six children and no theories.

John Wilmot, Earl of Rochester, *Letters*

Having begun this exploration of language and its uses by looking at children's learning of language, it is only fitting that we should conclude it by considering how children use language. Adults tend to think of themselves as knowing more than those who are younger than they are, and generally they are correct in this belief. There are, however, things that children know that adults either do not know or have forgotten that they once knew. Evidence of children's lore and language was compiled by Iona and Peter Opie, who collected information from about five thousand children attending seventy schools in different parts of England, Scotland, and Wales. They published the results of their investigations in *The Lore and Language of Schoolchildren* (1959), and their work has provided the basis for subsequent inquiries.

One of their findings was the variety of truce terms in Great Britain (see fig. 34.1). Truce terms are the ways in which children call for "time out" in a game or a contest. The Opies found that, in addition to calling out a truce term, children in England often crossed their fingers, whereas in Scotland children put their thumbs up. The map shows that in the west of Scotland the term is *keys*, while in the rest of Scotland and much of the west of England and most of Wales the term is *barley* (presumably the same word as *parley*). In the eastern part of England the main term is either *kings and crosses* or *kings*. The crosses turn into *cruces, creases, cree*, and *exes* in other parts of the country. In the south of England the principal term is *fainites*. *Barley* and *fainites* may go back as far as the medieval period. Other words uncovered by the Opies include *bars, blobs, boosey, creams, cribs, croggies, nicks, peril, queens, scrases, screws, scribs, scrogs*, and *skinch*.

It is hardly surprising that children should have local words for such a purpose since this is one of the areas in which adults and the school authorities are irrelevant. The intent of the educational system in teaching the standard language is to replace local expressions with national ones so that communication is not affected

FIGURE 34.1 *Truce terms in Great Britain. (From Opie & Opie, 1959. By permission of Oxford University Press.)*

by local variation. However, in the kinds of activities that are not taught in school the homogenizing force is weakened. Another obvious example is playing truant. The Opies list a number of terms used in different parts of England: *bobbing, fagging off, jigging, mitching, playing the nick, sagging, skiving, twagging, wagging school.* There are even more terms in Scotland; for example, *plunking, foodging, jooking,* and *dogging.*

Very young children do not make or particularly enjoy linguistic jokes but children of primary school age often do. They like riddles, such as *What is it that the more it dries the wetter it gets?* The answer is *A towel* and it depends upon the ambiguity in the verb *dries* as to whether it is intransitive (that is, does not take a direct object), in which case it has the meaning "becomes dry" or whether it is transitive with an omitted direct object, in which case its meaning is "dries (something else)." A similar ambiguity can be found (with a little encouragement) in *Mother is cooking but father is only smoking.*

I use examples like these to bring out to my students the knowledge of linguistic structure that must be understood for the point of the joke to be grasped. Here are some examples:

> What happens to a deer when an Indian shoots at him and misses?
> He has an arrow escape.

(This illustrates the importance of word division in *an arrow* versus *a narrow,* similar to the confusion that arose historically resulting in *an apron* and *a napkin.*)

> What is the difference between a fisherman and a lazy student?
> One baits his hook, while the other hates his book.

(This illustrates the phonemic principle: /b/ and /h/ are phonemes of English because *baits* and *hates* are different words, as are *book* and *hook.*)

Another example illustrates how a single phoneme /š/ may be represented by the two letters *sh:*

> What is the difference between an angry circus owner and a Roman hairdresser?
> One is a raving showman and the other is a shaving Roman.

An example that illustrates morphological division (or rather a mistaken case) is:

> What is the most difficult key to turn?
> A donkey.

Syntactic examples include:

> When did the lobster blush?
> When it saw the salad dressing.

> Why did the window box?
> Because it saw the garden fence.

An example that depends upon intonation and stress is:

> Which is better, an old five dollar bill or a new one?

If *one* is unstressed, then it refers to "a new five-dollar bill"; but if *one* is stressed then the meaning is "a new one-dollar bill" and the answer becomes obvious.

Even the writing system can be involved:

What is the center of gravity?
V.

Finally, there are puns depending upon homonyms with very different meanings:

What is the difference between a warder and a jeweler?
One watches cells and the other sells watches.

The fact that children become interested in jokes and riddles of this kind is a sign that they are beginning to understand the ways in which the language is organized. It is only through education, however, that they will learn the labels for some of these distinctions and then they are likely to find grammar "boring."

William Labov found that black adolescent males in New York City who belonged to gangs and who scored badly on tests of reading ability were very proficient users of language for their own purposes. In fact, one of the keys to leadership in the gang was through skill in using language. One of the ways in which this skill is shown is through *sounding* or a competitive form of fanciful insults that are not intended to be taken literally but are a way of scoring points off the opponent. Many of the insults make reference to the addressee's mother:

Your mother got on sneakers!
Your mother wear high-heeled sneakers to church!
Your mother wear a jock-strap!
Your mother got polka-dot drawers!
Your mother wear the seat of her drawers on the top of her head!

Frequently there are explicit references to sexuality or to intimate parts of the body:

A: Your mother got a .45 in her left titty.
B: Your mother got a 45-degree titty.
A: Your mother got titties behind her neck.

There are also variations on the theme of suggesting that one's mother is a bitch:

A: His mother eat Dog Yummies.
B: They say your mother eat Gainesburgers.

The crucial point about these ritual insults is that they must be obviously false. Attempts at sounding that come too close to reality are likely to result in fights or quarrels. Sounding is a way of asserting dominance without resorting to violence. Verbal dueling occurs in many parts of the world, particularly among adolescent males.

An area in which younger children have their own expertise is in the games that they play. In the course of a series of interviews with ten-year-old girls in Scotland, I collected about a hundred rhymes for skipping with ropes, bouncing a ball, and "counting out." Many of the rhymes present evidence of a long oral tradition. Here is a rhyme that in its original version (somewhat different) goes back to the 1880s:

On the mountain stands a lady
who she is
I do not know
all she wants
is gold and silver
all she wants
is a nice young man
so call in my Jacqueline dear
my Margaret dear
my Maureen dear
so call in my Karen dear
in the merry month of May
as we go out to play
upon a summer's day
in the merry merry month of May

But part of the fascination in these rhymes is the way they can change. Here is another version I recorded:

On the mountain stands a castle
and the owner's Frankenstein
and his daughter
Fangie Potter
she's my only Valentine
so I call in (somebody) dear
(somebody) dear
(somebody) dear
so I call in (somebody) dear
and the rest go out to play

Sometimes the oral tradition reveals less deliberate changes in transmission as in this short rhyme:

Mrs. Do-Well
went to the well
to fetch a pail of water
to comb her hair
to wash her face
to dry it

The original version mentioned in 1916 referred to "Mademoiselle" but this was presumably not a familiar label to most children. An American version has "Madame Morale."

One of the most interesting aspects is how the names of historical figures remain even when the children have no idea who the person was. A good example of oral transmission was given to me by a girl in Dundee:

Peachy peachy pear or plum
I spy Tom Thumb
Tom Thumb is in the wood
I spy Robin Hood
Robin Hood is in the cellar
I spy Cinderella
Cinderella's at the ball
I spy Henry Hall
Henry Hall is a star
S-T-A-R

The girl who told me this rhyme did not know who Henry Hall was, hardly surprising since he had been best known as a bandleader before World War II, thirty
years before she was born. The Opies give a slightly longer version of this rhyme,
recorded from ten-year-olds in the 1950s:

Each, peach, pear, plum.
I spy Tom Thumb;
Tom Thumb in the wood,
I spy Robin Hood;
Robin Hood in the cellar,
I spy Cinderella;
Cinderella at the ball,
I spy Henry Hall;
Henry Hall at his house,
I spy Mickey Mouse;
Mickey Mouse in his cradle,
I spy Betty Grable.
Betty Grable is a star
S-T-A-R.

The Opies say that Betty Grable seems to have been "the most envied princess in
the Hollywood book of fairy tales" in the forties and early fifties. I did not record
any reference to Betty Grable but one to an earlier film actress:

Hi Ginger Rogers
how about a date
meet you round the corner
half-past eight
she can do the rhumba
she can do the splits
she can do the birl-around ["turn"-around]
and also the splits

The two most intriguing rhymes, however, contained references not only to World
War II figures but also to more contemporary heroes:

When the war is over
Hitler shall be dead
he wants to go to heaven
with a crown upon his head

> but the Lord says
> "No
> you have to go below
> cause there's only room for Elvis
> king of rock and roll"

Apart from the obvious time warp that puts Hitler and Elvis together, the syntax of this rhyme is interesting. "When the war is over" puts the time as during the war, although I recorded it in 1978. The use of *shall* in "Hitler shall be dead" is also notable because *shall* is rarely used in Scottish English in any constructions. I also recorded a variant of this rhyme in Ayr:

> Now the war is over
> Mussolini's dead
> he wants to go to heaven
> with a crown upon his head
> but the Lord says
> "No
> you have to go below
> there's only room for Tommy Steele
> and his old banjo"

This version is clearly postwar but the name *Hitler* would not fit the rhythm so Mussolini replaces him. The Opies cite a version dealing with Hitler and Churchill, but the original apparently dates from World War I and refers to the Kaiser:

> When the war is over and the Kaiser's deid
> He's no gaun tae Heaven wi' the eagle on 'is heid,
> For the Lord says No! He'll have tae go below,
> For he's all dressed up and nowhere tae go.

This was being sung sixty years before the versions I recorded, and it must have been passed on from generation to generation over this period of time, probably without the help of any adults.

One of the important functions of rhymes is for "counting out," that is, deciding who is to chase the others or to be the first to do something. Even the names for this person vary. The most common is *it,* but in the west of Scotland it is *bet,* in Dundee *out,* and in Aberdeen *the man.* The counting-out rhymes do not show as great originality or imagination as is found in some of the skipping-rope rhymes and ball-bouncing rhymes. A few of the counting-out rhymes show simple parallel structures:

> boy scout
> walk out
> girl guide
> step aside

This is a economical as a haiku. Two more complicated examples go back to the nineteenth century:

> As I went down hicky-picky lane
> I met some hicky-picky children

they asked me this
they asked me that
they asked me the colour of the Union Jack
red white or blue

Inky-pinky ponky
my daddy bought a donkey
the donkey died
my daddy cried
inky-pinky-ponky

This last example includes a common feature of counting-out rhymes, namely rhymes that are based on nonsense words. The nonsense words, however, may have been more meaningful at one time. The Opies quote an earlier version dating back to the middle of the nineteenth century:

Ink, pink, pen and ink;
A study, a stive, a stove, and a sink!

Another example of nonsense words is:

eeble obble
black bobble
eeble obble out

Sometimes actual words are used but in combinations that suggest they are being used purely for their sound and not for their significance:

ingle angle
silver bangle
ingle angle out

The extreme form of this is what is sometimes called "Chinese counting." I recorded only one version:

eenie
meenie
macaraca
rare-o
domino
alla paca
judi aca
um
tum
push

This is an interesting rhyme scheme *aabccbbdde* with the initial feminine rhymes contrasting with the final monosyllables.

The kind of rhythmic effect can also be achieved without rhyme, as in this ball-bouncing rhyme told to me by a girl in Ayr:

Please miss
my mother miss

> she told me miss
> to tell you miss
> I miss
> can't miss
> come to school tomorrow miss
> pains across my chest miss
> coughing all the night miss
> ooh miss
> ooh miss
> there it goes again miss

The repetitions of *miss* create the pattern of long and short lines that provide the rhythmic pattern to the "rhyme." The repetition of *miss* also parodies the kind of respect the teacher probably expects. Finally, since the aim in a ball-bouncing game is to catch the ball the repetition of *miss* could be seen as an incitement to fail.

The best examples I recorded have a rhythm that belongs more to music:

> Away up in Holland
> the land of the Dutch
> there lives a wee lassie
> I love very much
> her name is Susannah
> but where is she now
> up on the hill
> milking a cow

In fact, one girl in Aberdeen actually sang two rhymes for me. The first may have been a song she had learned other than as a ball-bouncing rhyme:

> When I was young
> my life begun
> the day I went to sea
> I jumped aboard a pirate ship
> and the captain said to me:
> "Ship her upwards
> downwards
> forwards
> backwards
> over the Irish Sea
> a bottle of rum
> to fill my tum
> and that's the life for me"

And the other one sounds like a very old song:

> Red roses on my wall
> when winter comes they'll fall
> when shall they bloom again
> hallelujah
> amen

The range of examples and the enthusiasm with which the children repeated them are evidence of a thriving oral culture in which sounds, meter, rhythm, and timing are important. Whether the children's talents in this respect were recognized by the school system is another question. The children may not get as much credit for their oral ability as they deserve, but they show quite convincingly that they are well on their way to the miraculous mastery of language that we all too often take for granted in adults.

Envoi: Confessio Amantis

The secret of being a bore is to tell everything.

Voltaire

In a short book such as this it is impossible to do more than give a slight idea of the pleasures that looking at language can provide. For most of my life I have enjoyed people using language well. Growing up in Scotland probably helped, though I was not aware of how much at that time. As a rebellious adolescent, resistant to any school pressures, I nevertheless on my own initiative worked my way through *War and Peace, Anna Karenina,* much of Dickens, and all of Scott's Waverley novels, in addition to a great deal of rubbish that I have no desire to recall. Reading was then and has remained a source of great pleasure.

At school I had attempted to learn French and German (in addition to compulsory Latin) in the hope of one day becoming a foreign correspondent on a national newspaper. My ineptitude (or that of my teachers) led me to abandon this ambition, but at the University of St. Andrews I enjoyed the required exposure to Old English so much that I specialized in English language, mainly Old and Middle English, and even made a feeble endeavor to master Old Norse. Mediocre success at this task left me with limited options when I graduated. On learning about a job teaching English as a foreign language at the British Institute in Lisbon, I decided that this was what I had always wanted to do. I soon found out that my studies at university had in no way fitted me to teach English. What I knew was useless; what I did not know was essential.

After five years of on-the-job learning in Lisbon, I was appointed to a more responsible (and better paid) position in Buenos Aires. It was there that I began to take the task of teaching English more seriously and started reading books on linguistics and applied linguistics. A year's graduate study at the University of North Wales, Bangor, gave me the opportunity to put a firmer foundation under this autodidactism, but at the same time what had been envisaged only as a means (the study of linguistics) became an end in itself. A serendipitous appointment in a new liberal arts college in California allowed me to gain a Ph.D. in linguistics at U.C.L.A. a few years later. Although I was teaching full-time (with the exception of a one-semester sabbatical to write the first draft of my dissertation) throughout my doctoral studies, I did not find it irksome because I enjoyed what I was doing. My only regret in linguistics is that there are so many aspects of the subject that I would have liked to find out more about than I have had time or energy to investigate.

Since completing my formal studies I have learned a great deal more through the demands of teaching undergraduates. In twenty-five years in a program with small resources I have had the opportunity to teach phonetics, phonology, syntax, semantics, historical linguistics, language acquisition, psycholinguistics, stylistics, language and culture, sociolinguistics, and many other courses. I cannot say that I was well qualified to teach all of them but I can say that I found none of them dull or uninteresting, though I cannot be sure that my students would say the same.

My research plans deliberately took me back to Scotland. Over the years I have interviewed about 250 people of different ages, and the tapes of these interviews have provided the material for various writings about language in Scotland. Some of the examples I have used in earlier chapters have come from these tapes. Although I am aware that the language of these examples may be more difficult for many readers than examples from more widely spoken varieties, I have included them for two reasons. One is that I can vouch for their authenticity because I recorded and transcribed them myself. In a discipline in which too many people (including myself at the time of my dissertation, and in a few cases in the present book) have been too ready to illustrate the use of language with invented examples, it is useful to have some less tainted evidence. The other is that I have been continually amazed by the kinds of examples I have recorded. The experience of interviewing in Scotland has greatly increased my respect for the skill with which ordinary people can use language. It is probably true of most communities, but I have used the examples I know to be genuine.

W. H. Auden may not have been wholly accurate when he said "The only good reason for doing anything is for fun," but it helps when you enjoy what you are doing. In the course of this book I have tried to present some of the aspects of language that I have found interesting in the hope that they will be interesting to others who might not otherwise have encountered them. I cannot hope to have succeeded totally, but as Samuel Butler said, "If you aim at imperfection there is some chance of your getting it; whereas there is none if you aim at perfection." There is plenty more to find out about language for those who are interested. The notes to the chapters give a few suggestions for further reading but any decent library will contain many other works. It is not a subject that is easily exhausted.

In preparing the additional chapters for this book, I spent more than a few hours in the library and at home consulting works that were often quite a challenge to read. This experience reinforced my awareness of the vast amount of information on language that is now available in a wide range of books and articles. Much of this material may not be fun to read but the topics are persistently fascinating and worth the effort it takes to explore them.

I began this book by examining two cartoons by Gary Larson about animals and their names, and it is perhaps fitting to end it with reference to one. I argued that there was no way that a dog could understand the name we give it. In another cartoon Larson shows a man telling another man that his new dog's name is Rex. Meanwhile, the dog is telling two other dogs that he is "Vexorg, Destroyer of Cats and Devourer of Chickens," while in return they introduce themselves as "Zornorph, the One Who Comes By Night to the Neighbor's Yard," and "Princess Sheewana, Barker of Great Annoyance and daughter of Queen La, Stainer of Persian Rugs." Larson's dogs provide us with a salutary reminder that we may not know as much as we think. It is something to keep in mind when making any general statement about language.

Appendix

A Note on Saussure, Bloomfield, and Chomsky

Samuel Johnson, in his *Dictionary of the English Language*, defined *scientifick* as "producing demonstrable knowledge; producing certainty." The history of the analytical study of language in the twentieth century shows a variety of attempts to examine language scientifically and they have produced a large body of demonstrable knowledge but they have not produced certainty. Nor have they resulted in any consensus about the nature of language.

Contemporary linguistics can be said to begin with the work of Ferdinand de Saussure (1857–1913). However, Saussure's influence is not due to his published work but to a series of lectures he gave at the University of Geneva in the years 1907–11. During this period Saussure was working out his ideas on the nature of language but he died before he was able to put his views into a coherent publishable form. After his death, two of Saussure's colleagues published an account of his views based mainly on notes taken by his students. This volume *Cours de linguistique générale* (*Course in General Linguistics*) sets out many ideas that have been influential in the twentieth-century study of language. Doubts have been raised about how accurately the volume reflects Saussure's actual thinking but it is this version that has been influential.

One of Saussure's aims was to make the study of language an independent discipline. One way in which he approached this was to draw a distinction between a language system (*langue*) and its use (*parole*). He illustrated the difference with a comparison to a situation that would be familiar at that time. He pointed out that we think of the 8:45 train from Geneva to Paris that left at that time yesterday as "the same" as the train that will leave at that time today, although the locomotive, the carriages, and the staff are probably different. The train is defined by its place in the timetable not by its physical make-up. He pointed out that linguistic entities are defined not by their physical characteristics, which may vary in many ways on different occasions, but by their place in the system that constitutes the *langue*. The study of *langue* does not require attention to how language is actually used (*parole*).

Another of Saussure's concerns was to free the study of language from the

195

historical orientation that had dominated linguistics in the nineteenth century. He drew a distinction between the *diachronic* study of language, which looked at the development of a language over time, and the *synchronic* approach, which looked at the state of a language at a particular time. He used the analogy of a game of chess. An onlooker observing an ongoing game of chess does not need to know how the pieces arrived at their present position to be able to understand the situation. Similarly, someone studying, say, English in the United States at the present day does not need to know anything about early stages of the language in medieval England. Although Saussure was interested in both the synchronic and diachronic aspects of language, his influence led to an emphasis on describing *langue* synchronically, that is, without reference to its historical development.

There is much more to Saussure's work than these two analogies but they illustrate a fundamental aspect of the approach to *langue* as set out in the *Course*. They both treat language as a static entity. In Saussure's view neither the trains nor the chess pieces move. It is their relationships in the timetable and on the chessboard that are important and these relationships are *structural.* The more fluid aspects of language were to be studied as *parole*, but unfortunately Saussure's views on this approach have been given less prominence. Saussure's major influence has been to reinforce the view that language should be studied as an abstract, static phenomenon.

There were several important scholars working on language in the United States in the first part of the twentieth century but here I want to concentrate on one, Leonard Bloomfield (1887–1949). In a review Bloomfield commented that Saussure's *parole* was "beyond the limits of our science." Bloomfield's scientific approach was to restrict evidence to what could be objectively established and did not depend upon intuition or subjective judgments. He claimed that "all scientifically meaningful statements are translatable into physical terms—that is, into statements about movements that can be observed and described in coordinates of space and time." This is similar to the position adopted by behaviorist psychologists. Bloomfield and his followers succeeded in developing a set of procedures through which they could identify the phonemes and morphemes of a language on formal, distributional grounds. Their methodological approach was to examine the phonetic record for information that would allow the identification of phonemes, and then proceed to examine how these phonemes were combined into morphemes. Only after these had been satisfactorily identified was it possible to proceed to examine syntax.

Since many problems arose in identifying and justifying both phonemes and morphemes, Bloomfield and his followers did not devote as much attention to syntax. However, they did establish a way of identifying hierarchical structure, known as *Immediate Constituent Analysis*, and this has been very influential. Bloomfield illustrated this with the example *Poor John ran away*. He pointed out that this sentence consists of two constituents *poor John* and *ran away*, but also that each of these constituents had two parts *poor* and *John* and *ran* and *away*. It was possible to establish these constituents by substitution procedures, for example *poor John* could be replaced by *he* and there would still be a valid sentence, or *ran away* could be replaced by *sang* with a similar result.

The study of syntax, however, did not become central to the study of language in the United States until the publication in 1957 of Noam Chomsky's *Syntactic Structures*. Among other things, Chomsky showed that some aspects of syntactic structure could be represented more clearly by the use of what he called *transformations*. One very impressive illustration of the method was his analysis of the English auxiliary verb system. A major problem for Immediate Constituent Analysis was what came to be called *discontinuous morphemes*. For example, it is simple to analyze the constituents of the verb in *John sings* into *sing* and *-s*, where the latter morpheme indicates third-person singular and present tense. However, there was a problem for Immediate Constituent Analysis in dealing with cases such as *John is singing* because *is* and *-ing* are part of the same morpheme but they are not contiguous. The same problem arises with cases such as *John has painted* where *has* and *-ed* form a single morpheme. Chomsky was able to show that a single transformational rule could account for all the discontinuous morphemes in the English auxiliary system. It is not necessary to state this rule here but it was a brilliant illustration of the use of transformations. Chomsky also showed how this approach could provide an elegant way of accounting for the use of *do* in questions and negatives.

Chomsky's aim, however, was not simply to solve the problem of discontinuous morphemes. He wished to show that there were important aspects of syntax that could not be described by Immediate Constituent Analysis. For example, he pointed out that a phrase such as *the shooting of the hunters* was ambiguous as to whether it referred to hunters shooting or someone shooting the hunters. Chomsky drew attention to many ambiguities of this kind that could be explained by assuming that there was an underlying structure that showed the difference while the identical surface form was the result of a transformation. He also suggested that active and passive sentences could be related by transformations so that the sentences *John broke the window* and *the window was broken by John* would have the same underlying form.

Chomsky illustrated his approach in *Syntactic Structures* with a fragment of a grammar of English and stated that the goal of a linguistic description should be to account for all the grammatical sentences of a language and exclude sequences that were not grammatical. Chomsky later refined his earlier sketch with some more complex analysis in *Aspects of the Theory of Syntax* in 1965. It was in this work that he introduced the distinction between *deep structure* and *surface structure*. Roughly speaking, the deep structure provided all the information needed to understand the sentence and the surface structure provided the information on how it should be said. Chomsky's distinction was soon borrowed into a number of unrelated fields such as music and art history.

In the 1960s there were a number of linguists working in the field of transformational-generative grammar, as it had come to be called. There were many proposals and counterproposals about such matters as the nature of deep structure and the role of transformations. This was an exciting and confusing period in which new ideas appeared on an almost daily basis but consensus grew increasingly unlikely. The history of this period is too complex to summarize briefly but the outcome was that Chomsky emerged as still the dominant figure in syntax despite many challenges to his position and authority.

However, at this point Chomsky's aims began to change. There was no longer any reference to describing all the sentences of a language. Instead the emphasis turned to the tacit knowledge that the speaker had (linguistic competence) that underlay the production and comprehension of speech. Then increasingly more emphasis was placed on the innate capability that children are born with that enables them to learn a language. He later came to refer to this innate ability as Universal Grammar and his focus has been increasingly on a way to characterize Universal Grammar.

In the early days of transformational grammar various textbooks were published which showed how this form of representation could be used in teaching students about the structure of their language or in helping them learn a foreign language. Nobody today would attempt to use Chomsky's later representations for purposes such as these because the analysis has become increasingly abstract and will be opaque to those who have not kept up with the latest developments. In fact, even some linguists who loyally followed Chomsky in his developing system through the 1980s have found themselves baffled by his latest proposals.

Chomsky's output and inventiveness are so great that it would be a Herculean task to attempt a summary or a review of his views and none will be undertaken here. However, there are some observations that apply to all his work. Chomsky's analyses take the sentence as the basic unit of language. There are some problems that result from this decision. The first is that the notion of a sentence is not well defined for spoken language; we write in sentences but we speak in utterances which may or may not correspond to written sentence structure. Second, many sequences of words that have been cited as ambiguous are only so in their written form. For example, the sequence *it is too hot to eat* is often said to be ambiguous between the sense that some food is too hot to eat and an observation about the weather. However, in speech the use of *it* with reference to food would only be used if it was clear to the listener (either by gesture or previous mention) what item was being mentioned. Similarly, any reference to the weather would be obvious from the prevailing temperature. The only ambiguity in speech would be in the first case whether *hot* referred to spiciness or temperature. It is only by citing the example in writing detached from any context that *it is too hot to eat* is structurally ambiguous in the ways suggested. This may appear to be a trivial example but claims about the interpretation of isolated written examples have regularly been used to justify very abstract analyses. Related to this problem is Chomsky's reliance on subjective judgments. Unlike Bloomfield, Chomsky believes that the only way to gain access to a speaker's knowledge of language is through the speaker's intuition about acceptability. Unfortunately, speakers may have little privileged knowledge about how they speak, as is often illustrated by the embarrassment people experience when hearing themselves on a tape-recording. On the other hand, academics in particular are very accustomed to making judgments about written language.

More important, Chomsky's analysis no longer deals with what most people consider language to be. Chomsky draws a distinction between two senses of the word *language*. The first is what he calls *I-language* (internalized language) which is the organization of structures in the brain that underlies the comprehension and production of language. The second is what he calls *E-language* (externalized language) which is what most people understand by the word *language*, namely a form of spoken and written communication. Chomsky believes that only I-language can be studied scientifically and his method is to construct a model based on inferences from subjective judgments about invented sentences. There is no direct evidence for the structure of this model so it is hardly surprising that its shape has changed in fundamental and unpredictable ways over the past fifty years. Some of those who study I-language are optimistic that improved methods of exploring the functioning of the brain will help to support their analysis but others are more skeptical.

While Chomsky and his followers have developed what is essentially a separate discipline, there has been a great deal of work done on the study of language by those who believe that E-language can be investigated meaningfully through less introspective methods. The Linguistic Society of America (LSA) was founded in December 1924 by twenty-nine linguists. The membership of the LSA is now close to four thousand, and most of them work on observable aspects of language. Some linguists work on endangered languages, attempting to preserve as much as possible before their last speakers disappear. Other linguists investigate language variation and change. Every aspect of language from phonetics to semantics and pragmatics has its group of specialists. Others study language development and second-language learning. The range of topics covered in this book gives some indication of the varied interests of those who study E-language and much has been discovered about its nature as a result of their efforts.

Saussure still receives attention at the present time, partly because of his influence in setting the model for structural analyses in a number of fields and partly because of recent discoveries of his actual notes. Bloomfield is of interest now mainly to those who look back on the history of linguistics. Noam Chomsky, however, shares with Sigmund Freud the record of being two of the most frequently cited individuals in a wide range of publications over the past fifty years. There are interesting parallels in the ways in which their very different kinds of work have aroused similar kinds of loyalty and opposition. Their theories about the functioning of the brain are based on similar kinds of reasoning. Whatever assessment their views will receive in the future, there is no denying that both have made a tremendous impact on twentieth-century thought.

Further Reading

Chapter 1

There are a number of helpful textbooks providing an introduction to linguistics: E. Finegan and N. Besnier, *Language: Its Structure and Use*; V. Fromkin and R. Rodman, *An Introduction to Language*; G. Yule, *The Study of Language*. Much useful and fascinating information is contained in D. Crystal, *The Cambridge Encyclopedia of Language*, and in N. E. Collinge (ed.), *An Encyclopedia of Language*. The most complete reference work is W. Bright (ed.), *International Encyclopedia of Linguistics*, in four volumes.

Chapter 2

The articles in *The Development of Language*, edited by J. B. Gleason, give a good overview of research in the area of children's language acquisition. E. Ochs, *Culture and Language Development: Language Acquisition and Language Socialization in a Samoan Village*, and B. B. Schieffelin, *The Give and Take of Everyday Life: Language Socialization of Kaluli Children*, give insightful accounts of language development in non-English-speaking communities. *The Journal of Child Language* contains articles on a wide range of topics. The notion of linguistic competence was introduced by Noam Chomsky. See his *Aspects of the Theory of Syntax* and *Knowledge of Language*.

Chapter 3

C. E. Snow and C. A. Ferguson (eds.), *Talking to Children*, and R. Scollon, *Conversations with a One-year-old*, give good accounts of children's early language development. The example of an exchange between a mother and her three-month-old daughter comes from C. E. Snow, "The Development of Conversation between Mothers and Babies." M.A.K. Halliday, *Learning How to Mean*, describes his son's early communication system. P. Ladefoged, *A Course in Phonetics*, gives a good introduction to articulatory phonetics. A. Kendon, *Conducting Interaction*, deals with nonverbal communication. Useful books on sign language are H. Lane and F. Grosjean, *Recent Perspectives on American Sign Language*, and E. S. Klima and U. Bellugi, *The Signs of Language*.

Chapter 4

A. Cruttenden, *Intonation*, and D. L. Bolinger, *Intonation and Its Parts*, deal with some of the complexities of intonation. In *Discourse Strategies*, J. J. Gumperz examines examples of miscommunication that can occur through a misunderstanding of intonation in interethnic exchanges.

Chapter 5

P. H. Matthews, *Morphology*, presents the issues raised by morphological systems in a coherent account. An older work that contains a wide range of examples from many languages is E. A. Nida, *Morphology*. R. Brown, *A First Language*, describes in great detail the order in which three children learned to use the grammatical morphemes of English.

Chapter 6

Much information on the role of brain size and language development is contained in E. H. Lenneberg, *Biological Foundations of Language*. D. Slobin (ed.). *A Cross-cultural Study of Language Acquisition*, provides a wide range of information on children learning languages other than English. A very readable account of children's language development at this stage is J. Bruner, *Child's Talk*. The French philosopher is Merleau-Ponty.

Chapter 7

Almost all work on children's syntactic development has been influenced by the theories of Noam Chomsky, but it is not easy to suggest a work that presents his views in an accessible form. This is partly because his theories have evolved over the years, and there is usually a time lag between the proposal of a new notion and its incorporation into empirical research on language development. His *Knowledge of Language* provides a comprehensive introduction to his views. Two other books that deal with children's early syntactic development are L. Bloom, *Language Development*, and M. Bowerman, *Early Syntactic Development*. A good account of deixis is given in C. J. Fillmore's *Santa Cruz Lectures on Deixis*. A comparison of blind and sighted children's early language development is given in A. Dunlea, *Vision and the Emergence of Meaning*.

Chapter 8

Children's later syntactic development is discussed in C. Chomsky, *Acquisition of Syntax in Children from 5 to 10*, and in S. Romaine, *The Language of Children and Adolescents*. An article on children's knowledge of kin terms is S. E. Haviland and E. V. Clark, "This Man's Father Is My Father's Son."

Chapter 9

The standard work is J. Lyons, *Semantics*. On children's understanding, see M. Donaldson, *Children's Minds,* and J. Tough, *The Development of Meaning*. J. Piaget, *The Language and Thought of the Child,* has many interesting observations about children's views of the world.

Chapter 10

S. Levinson, *Pragmatics*; M. Stubbs, *Discourse Analysis*; G. Brown and G. Yule, *Discourse Analysis*; and M. McCarthy, *Discourse Analysis for Teachers*, provide good introductions to the topic. Much of this work was inspired by the writings of J. L. Austin, *How to Do Things with Words*. The fundamental importance of context is examined in A. Duranti and C. Goodwin, *Rethinking Context*. The volume on *Cross-cultural Pragmatics*, edited by S. Blum-Kulka and others, deals with apologies and requests. The remark by Wittgenstein is quoted in R. Monk's biography of the philosopher, *Ludwig Wittgenstein*.

Chapter 11

Chomsky's *Knowledge of Language* sets out his basic position clearly and D. Lightfoot, *The Acquisition of Language*, gives an example of an approach following Chomsky's view. The popular success of S. Pinker, *The Language Instinct*, probably gave many people the misleading impression that the nativist view it presents was generally accepted and uncontroversial. P. W. Jusczyk, *The Discovery of Spoken Language,* N. Matasaka, *The Onset of Language*, D. K. Oller, *The Emergence of the Speech Capacity*, M. Tomasello, *Constructing a language*, and M. Tomasello and D. I. Slobin, *Beyond Nature-nurture* provide more plausible accounts of children's language development without the appeal to a specific innate knowledge of grammar. From a similar perspective, H. Diessel, *The Acquisition of Complex Sentences*, shows how children's ability to use and understand more complex syntax increases with age. Two collections of articles, B. MacWhinney, *The Emergence of Language*, and U. Goswami, *Blackwell Handbook of Childhood Cognitive Development*, contain a wide range of useful information. The remark by James McCawley is quoted in John Lawler's obituary notice in the journal *Language*. Alexander Luria's comments are from his autobiographical work *The Making of Mind*.

Chapter 12

P. Trudgill, *Sociolinguistics*, covers the field very clearly. A more technical account is provided in J. K. Chambers and P. Trudgill, *Dialectology*. A good account of the complexity of language use is given in D. Hymes, *Foundations in Sociolinguistics*.

Chapter 13

W. N. Francis, *Dialectology*, is an accessible introduction to dialectology. The quotation by Gaston Paris comes from this work. P. Trudgill, *The Dialects of England,* is a good account of English dialects written with a minimum of technical language. *The Linguistic Atlas of Scotland,* by J. Y. Mather and H.-H. Speitel, contains a treasury of Scottish dialect forms as does *The Concise Scots Dictionary,* edited by M. Robinson. The examples of syntactic differences in Alabama come from an article by C. Feagin and those in Hawick from an article by K. Brown, both contained in *The Dialects of English*, edited by P. Trudgill and J. K. Chambers. The quotation from J. E. Joseph comes from his *Eloquence and Power: The Rise of Language Standards and Standard Languages*. James Sledd's remark is from his article "Bi-dialectalism: The Linguistics of White Supremacy."

Chapter 14

The classic work in social variation is W. Labov, *The Social Stratification of English in New York City,* from which figure 14.1 is taken. The Glasgow examples are from R.K.S. Macaulay, *Language, Social Class, and Education*. A good survey of work and methods since then is L. Milroy, *Observing and Analysing Natural Language*. J. and L. Milroy discuss the importance of attitudes in their *Authority in Language*. The evidence for no social class differences at birth is given in in an article by M. Golden and B. Birns, "Social Class and

Infant Intelligence." An excellent account of the effect of children's upbringing on their language development is given in S. B. Heath, *Ways with Words.* The best work on teenagers and their language is P. Eckert, *Jocks and Burnouts.* The survey of seven-year-olds cited is reported in *From Birth to Seven* by R. Davie, N. Butler, and H. Goldstein. The study involving the trainee teachers is described in F. Williams, *Explorations of the Linguistic Attitudes of Teachers.* The Canadian study of listeners' judgments is to be found in *Attitudes and Motivation in Second-language Learning* by R. C. Gardner and W. E. Lambert. The quotation from J. Macnamara comes from his article "Attitudes and Learning a Second Language."

Bernstein's early papers are reprinted in *Class, Codes and Control.* My analysis of his work and comparable quantitative results are to be found in my *Talk That Counts.*

Chapter 15

A good introduction to the difference between oral and literate cultures is W. Ong, *Orality and Literacy.* D. Biber, *Variation across Speech and Writing,* deals with the linguistic characteristics of written and spoken language. There is much useful information in *Comprehending Oral and Written Language,* edited by R. Horowitz and S. J. Samuels. The educational problems in dealing with literacy are eloquently discussed in J. P. Gee, *Social Linguistics and Literacies.* D. Schiffrin, *Discourse Markers,* gives a comprehensive account of the use of these expressions. The quotation from Bowra is in his *Heroic Poetry.* Neil Postman's remark is in his article "The Politics of Reading."

Chapter 16

The term *register* owes much to the work of M.A.K. Halliday, *Language as a Social Semiotic.* The examples of student slang come from P. Munro (ed.), *U.C.L.A. Slang.*

Chapter 17

A description of the Apache uses of silence can be found in K. Basso, *Western Apache Language and Culture.* E. Andersen, *Speaking with Style,* shows how even young children adapt their speech to different situations. L. Pound's article on euphemisms is be found in her *Selected Writings.*

Chapter 18

As pointed out in this chapter, there have been numerous works on this topic in recent years but most of them must be approached with caution. A well-balanced account is J. Coates, *Women, Men and Language.* The examples of novelists' ways of introducing men's and women's speech come from a paper by Nan Wonderly when she was an undergraduate at Pomona College. Dorothea McCarthy's article is "Language Development in Children." Other references to the quotations in children's language development will be found in my article "The Myth of Female Superiority in Language." The passage cited at the end of the chapter comes, I regret to say, from *Language and Symbolic Power* by P. Bourdieu, p. 50. Perhaps it has lost or gained something in translation from the French original.

The best book on this topic is P. Eckert and S. McConnell-Genet, *Language and Gender.* The quantitative results are from my book *Talk That Counts.*

Chapter 19

A very readable, enjoyable, and informative account of taboo language is given by G. Hughes in his book *Swearing: A Social History of Foul Language, Oaths and Profanity in English*. The quotation from D. Crystal is taken from *The Cambridge Encyclopedia of Language*. I. L. Allen gives a good account of derogatory terms for other people in *The Language of Ethnic Conflict*.

Chapter 20

H. P. Grice sets out the cooperative principle in his article "Logic and Conversation." George Orwell's strictures are contained in his article "Politics and the English Language." A fuller treatment of the subject can be found in J. Wilson, *Politically Speaking*. A good account of metaphors is contained in G. Lakoff and M. Johnson, *Metaphors We Live by*. The quotation from Lichtenberg is taken from J. P. Stern's volume about the philosopher, *Lichtenberg*.

Chapter 21

The study of conversation has become a separate field known as conversation analysis, based mainly on the approach developed by the late Harvey Sacks, who was killed in a car accident before he could present his ideas in a definitive form. The method is shown in the article "A Simplest Systematics for the Organization of Turn-taking for Conversation" by H. Sacks, E. Schegloff, and G. Jefferson. R. E. Nofsinger, *Everyday Conversation,* is an admirably dear introduction to this topic. There is a more technical chapter in S. Levinson, *Pragmatics*. The idea of conversation as a dance comes from D. Tannen, *Talking Voices*. Some of E. Goffman's many insights can be found in *Forms of Talk*. P. Brown and S. Levinson, *Politeness,* looks at the subject from a cross-cultural perspective.

Chapter 22

The study of oral narrative has been greatly influenced by the ideas of W. Labov, set out in a chapter in his *Language in the Inner City*. B. Johnstone, *Stories, Community and Place: Narratives from Middle America,* contains many acute observations on storytelling, as does R. Bauman, *Story, Performance, and Event*. The brief narrative about the baby crying was used by Harvey Sacks to illustrate the kinds of interpretation necessary to make sense of speech.

Bella K.'s story is analyzed more fully in my book *Extremely Common Eloquence* along with many other examples of narrative skill.

Chapter 23

A good introduction to language learning is D. R. Preston, *Sociolinguistics and Second Language Acquisition*. The topic of bilingualism is fully examined by C. Hoffman in *An Introduction to Bilingualism* and S. Romaine in *Bilingualism*. The Spanish examples are taken from R. P. Stockwell, J. D. Bowen, and J. W. Martin, *The Grammatical Structures of English and Spanish*. The report on language teaching in the United States is R. D. Lambert, "Language Instruction for Undergraduates in American Higher Education."

Chapter 24

There are many recent works on the evolution of language. P. Carruthers and A. Chamberlain, *Evolution and the Human Mind,* L. Jenkins, *Biolinguistics,* and D. Lightfoot, *The Development of Language,* present the nativist side. M. H. Christiansen and S. Kirby, *Language Evolution,* and T. Deacon, *The Symbolic Species,* argue the contrary position, as do most of the scholars in a collection edited by A. Wray, *The Transition to Language* (particularly the article by M. H. Christiansen and M. R. Elleson). R. Dunbar, *Grooming, Gossip and the Evolution of Language* is a very readable book that suggests an interesting view of language evolution. There is a great deal of interesting information about animal communication in M. D. Hauser, *The Evolution of Communication,* J. Maynard Smith and D. Harper, *Animal Signals,* and W. A. Hillix and D. M. Rumbaugh, *Animal Bodies, Human Minds: Ape, Dolphin, and Parrot Language Skills.*

Chapter 25

There is a vast literature on language change but much of it is written in highly technical language. A readable work is A. Arlotto, *Introduction to Historical Linguistics.* The role of linguistic insecurity and hypercorrection is fully discussed in W. Labov, *The Social Stratification of English in New York City* and *Sociolinguistic Patterns.* A stimulating account of linguistic change in English is provided by J. Milroy, *Linguistic Variation and Change.* One of the ways in which languages may change is that they lose their speakers and become "dead" languages. The process of language death is examined in N. C. Dorian (ed.), *Investigating Obsolescence.*

Chapter 26

A standard work is A. C. Baugh, *A History of the English Language.* Many fascinating examples of change of meaning are discussed in Owen Barfield, *History in English Words.* The Anglo-Saxon, Middle English, and Early Modern English texts of the parable of the sower and the seed are taken from L. H. Frey (ed.), *Readings in Early English Language History.* The examples cited from G. Hughes come from *Words in Time.*

Chapter 27

I have based this chapter largely on the excellent summary of research in J. P. Mallory, *In Search of the Indo-Europeans: Language, Archaeology and Myth.*

Chapter 28

The eleventh edition of *Ethnologue: Languages of the World,* edited by B. Grimes, lists 6,170 languages. K. Katzner, *The Languages of the World,* gives much useful information on a wide range of languages. More detailed information is given in B. Comrie (ed.), *The World's Major Languages,* from which I have taken some of the examples. The examples of evidentials come from W. Chafe and J. Nichols (eds.), *Evidentiality.* Some of the Thai examples come from M. Haas's article "Numeral Classifiers in Thai." R. S. Tomlin, *Basic Word Order,* gives detailed information on word order in a wide variety of languages.

Chapter 29

E. Sapir, *Language,* despite its date, remains one of the best introductions to the study of language. B. L. Whorf's views are contained in the collection of articles *Language, Thought and Reality.* There is an interesting discussion of Whorf in G. Lakoff, *Women, Fire, and Dangerous Things.*

Chapter 30

I have taken some examples and guidance from P. Mühlhäuser and R. Harré, *Pronouns and People: The Linguistic Construction of Social and Personal Identity.*

Chapter 31

I have based this chapter mainly on the comprehensive survey in G. G. Corbett, *Gender: A Comprehensive Grammar of the English Language* by R. Quirk, S. Greenbaum, G. Leech, and J. Svartvik is a massive volume of 1,779 pages and deals with most aspects of English grammar, but even it cannot cover all aspects of the subject. An innovative account of verbal constructions is R.M.W. Dixon, *A New Approach to English Grammar, on Semantic Principles.*

Chapter 32

The examples in this chapter are taken from S. Romaine, *Pidgin and Creole Languages,* and L. Todd, *Modern Englishes: Pidgins and Creoles.* The bioprogram is described in D. Bickerton, *Roots of Language and Language and Species.* The evolution of language is discussed in P. Lieberman, *The Biology and Evolution of Language* and *Uniquely Human.* G. Sankoff deals with the development of Tok Pisin in *The Social Life of Language.* J. Rickford describes the Guyanese situation in *Dimensions of a Creole Continuum.*

Chapter 33

D. Tannen gives some excellent examples of rhetorical skills in *Talking Voices.* Examples of such skills in other societies are given in D. L. Brenneis and F. R. Myers (eds.), *Dangerous Words,* and in K. A. Watson-Gegeo and G. M. White, *Disentangling.*

Many other examples of the skilful use of language in everyday speech can be found in my book *Extremely Common Eloquence.*

Chapter 34

The classic account of children's lore is I. Opie and P. Opie, *The Lore and Language of Schoolchildren.* See also B. Sutton-Smith, *The Folkgames of Children.* The examples of "sounding" are from W. Labov, *Language in the Inner City.*

Chapter 35

Some of the Scottish examples come from my *Locatin Dialect in Discourse.*

Appendix

Bloomfield's major work is *Language.* Probably the most relevant of Chomsky's many works are *Syntactic Structures, Aspects of the Theory of Syntax, Knowledge of Language,* and *New Horizons in the Study of Language and Mind.* Chomsky writes very clearly but some of the arguments may be hard to follow because of the complexity of the material. Good accounts of the developments in twentieth-century American linguistics are given in P. H. Matthews, *Grammatical Theory in the United States from Bloomfield to Chomsky,* and F. J. Newmeyer, *Generative Linguistics.* A very readable account of other approaches to the study of language in the United States is given in S. O. Murray, *American Sociolinguistics.* Alternative versions of syntactic analysis are examined in W. Croft and D. A. Cruse, *Cognitive Linguistics,* and F. J. Newmeyer, *Language Form and Language Function.*

Glossary

ABSTRACT (OF A NARRATIVE): A way in which speakers will often indicate what kind of story they are about to tell (for example, *A funny thing happened to me yesterday, I got myself into trouble last week*).

ACCUSATIVE CASE: In an inflected language the form of a noun that usually marks the direct object of the verb (for example, in Latin *puellam,* "the girl," is in the accusative case in *puer amat puellam,* "the boy loves the girl," and is marked by the suffix *-m*).

ACTION VERB: A verb that describes or refers to the process of doing something. *Run, sing, hit,* and *write* are all action verbs. *Own, know,* and *understand* are not action verbs. See also **agent, stative.**

ADJECTIVE: A word that qualifies or modifies a noun (for example, *big, clever, slow*).

AGENT: One who carries out an action. *John* is the agent in *John opened the door, John gave Mary a present,* and *The idea was suggested by John.*

AGGLUTINATIVE LANGUAGE: A language in which complex words are formed by a sequence of grammatical morphemes. Turkish and Swahili are examples of agglutinating languages.

ALLITERATION: A rhetorical method by which words that begin with the same sound occur in proximity, suggesting some kind of link.

ALLOPHONE: One of the sounds (**phones**) that is used as an example of a phoneme in a particular context. In English the allophones of the phoneme /t/ include the aspirated [tʰ] in *ton,* the unaspirated [t] in *stun,* and the glottal stop that can sometimes be heard in *mountain* or *bottle.*

ALPHABETIC WRITING SYSTEM: A system of writing in which, in principle, each letter represents a single sound. In practice, most alphabetic writing systems also use combinations of letters to represent individual sounds.

ANALOGY: A process of language by which irregular grammatical forms are made more regular. For example, the past of *help* used to be *help* but it is now *helped* by analogy with other regular verbs.

ANAPHORA: A term used for the process of referring back to someone or something that has been mentioned previously. In *When I saw John I told him to hurry up,* the pronoun *him* most likely refers to *John* who has been mentioned previously. In that case *him* is an anaphoric expression.

ANAPHORIC EXPRESSION: See **anaphora.**

ANGLO-SAXON: The name sometimes used to refer to the Germanic language spoken in Britain from the fifth to the twelfth centuries. Also known as **Old English.**

ARTICLE: A function word used in many languages with nouns. In English the **definite article the** (as in *I bought the car*) is used when the speaker (or writer) expects the hearer (or reader) to know which car I bought. The **indefinite article** *a* (as in *I bought a car*) is used when there is not the same expection that the hearer or reader will know which car I bought.

ASPIRATION (ASPIRATED):   A term used to refer to the puff of air that accompanies the release of initial voiceless stop consonants in English as at the beginning of words such as *pin, ton, king.*

ASSIMILATION: The process by which one sound becomes more like another either in rapid speech or as a form of historical change. The negative prefix *in-* in *inactive* has become *im-* before [p] in *impossible* because both [m] and [p] are produced with the lips while [n] is not.

AUXILIARY VERB: A verb that is used with a main verb to carry information about mood, aspect, and voice. In *he is coming, she has arrived,* and *they were seen, is, has,* and *were* are auxiliary verbs. See also **modal.**

BACK CHANNEL SIGNAL: A signal given by the listener to show that he or she is paying attention. Back-channel signals may be simple noises, such as *mm, uhuh,* words or phrases, such as *quite, of course, I see,* or merely nods and facial expressions.

BACK VOWEL: A vowel that is produced with the back of the tongue being the highest part. The vowels in *boot, boat,* and *bought* are back vowels.

BOUND MORPHEME: A morpheme that cannot occur by itself (that is, it is not a word). Examples of bound morphemes in English are the prefixes *dis-* and *un-* and the suffixes *-ly* and *-ness.*

CATAPHORA: A term used in anticipation of future identification. In *when he came in the room, John was frowning* the pronoun *he* is used in anticipation of the identifying name *John.* The conditions under which cataphora can be used unambiguously are complex.

CHANNEL: A term sometimes used to refer to the medium of communication. Speech uses the auditory channel and writing the visual channel.

CLASSIFIER: In some languages nouns belong to certain classes that are identified by a particular morpheme. These morphemes are known as classifiers.

CLAUSE: A syntactic unit in which there is usually only one main verb. See **main clause, coordinate clause,** and **subordinate clause.**

CLICK LANGUAGES: The name given to those languages that use click sounds as part of their repertory of sounds.

CLOSED SYLLABLE: A syllable ending in a consonant, for example, *map, cat,* and *back* in contrast to those ending a vowel, for example, *see, go,* and *new,* which are **open syllables.**

CODA (TO A NARRATIVE):   The way in which a narrator may indicate the end of a story (for example, *and that was what happened, so I'll just have to try again*), and thus open the floor to other speakers.

COGNATE: A term used to describe two or more languages or words that are related historically. French, Spanish, and Italian are cognate and so are their words for "public square": *place, plaza,* and *piazza.*

CONDENSATION SYMBOL: A condensation symbol is used because of the associations, good or bad, that it is likely to arouse, for example, *Boy Scout* or *Hitler.*

CONSONANT: A speech sound that can function as the beginning or ending of a syllable but not usually as its center. In the word *cat* the first and last sounds are consonants and the middle sound is a vowel.

CONTENT WORD: A word that refers to some aspect of the world, real or imaginary, in contrast to **function words,** which have a purely grammatical function.

CONTRASTIVE ANALYSIS: A method by which two languages are compared to discover in what respects they are similar and in what respects they differ. It has been used in the preparation of materials for teaching a second language.

COOPERATIVE PRINCIPLE: The notion that in ordinary conversation interlocutors are doing their best to prevent misunderstandings arising by being truthful, accurate, and avoiding exaggeration. The principle is violated in lying, including "white lies" told to protect the hearer.

COORDINATE CLAUSE: A clause introduced by one of the coordinating conjunctions *and, but, so,* and *or.*

COUNT NOUN: A noun which has a plural (for example, *a book, three books*) in contrast to a **mass noun** (for example, *happiness*).

CREOLE LANGUAGE: A language that has developed from the combination of two separate languages.

DATIVE CASE: In an inflected language the form that is usually taken by the indirect object. In *John gave the book to Mary, Mary* would be in the dative case.

DEFINITE ARTICLE: The form *the,* which is used when the speaker expects the hearer to identify which item has been mentioned in a noun phrase.

DEICTIC EXPRESSION: An expression that takes its orientation from the point of view of the speaker, for example, *here* (near the speaker) in contrast to *there* (away from the speaker).

DEIXIS: The use of **deictic expressions.**

DEMONSTRATIVE: A deictic expression indicating proximity (*this*) or distance (*that*) from the speaker.

DERIVATIONAL MORPHEME: A morpheme that makes a new word from an existing one, for example, *un-* and *-ment* in *unemployment* from the verb *employ.*

DIALECT: The variety of language spoken by a group of people.

DIRECT OBJECT: The noun or noun phrase that is directly affected by the action of the verb. In *John kissed Mary, Mary* is the direct object of the verb *kissed.*

DISCOURSE: A connected sequence of spoken utterances or written sentences.

DISCOURSE MARKER: Expressions such as *well, oh, you know,* and *I mean* that are often used in speech but are outside the syntax of the utterance in which they appear and add little to the paraphrasable meaning of the utterance. Such expressions are very useful in guiding the participants in conversation and making possible the smooth progress of turn-taking.

DOUBLET: One of a pair of words that have a common source but have reached the language through different paths, for example, *cattle* from Norman French and *chattel* from Parisian French, both from Latin *capital.*

ERGATIVITY: A term used to describe the syntax of certain languages where the direct object of a transitive verb and the subject of an intransitive verb take the same form and the subject of a transitive verb is marked differently.

ERROR ANALYSIS: A method of discovering potential difficulties that learners of a second language might face by looking at the errors made by learners at different stages of proficiency.

EVALUATION (OF A NARRATIVE):   The information contained in a narrative that makes clear the point of the story. If the story is about a dangerous event the evaluative part should bring out either explicitly or implicitly just how dangerous the situation actually was.

EVIDENTIALS: Those features or expressions in a language that give some indication of the reliablity or accuracy of the information contained in a statement, for example, whether it is something the speaker has experienced directly or knows about at second or third hand.

EXCLUSIVE *WE*:   The use of the first-person plural pronoun to exclude the person addressed, as in a request for permission. In *May we leave now?*, the *we* presumably does not include the person whose permission is being asked. Some languages have different forms for inclusive and exclusive *we*.

FIRST GERMANIC CONSONANT SHIFT: A series of changes in the pronunciation of consonants that affected all and only the languages in the Germanic branch of Proto-Indo-European. Also known as **Grimm's Law.**

FOREIGN ACCENT: Speakers who retain phonetic features of their first language while speaking a second language are said to have a foreign accent. It is usually more difficult for adult learners of a second language to avoid speaking with a foreign accent than it is for children under the age of twelve.

FREE MORPHEME: A morpheme that can occur as a word without other morphemes.

FRICATIVE: A consonant that is produced when air is forced through a narrow passage causing audible friction as in the sound [s] in *miss*.

FRONT VOWEL: A vowel that is produced with the front of the tongue being the highest part. The vowels in *meat, mitt, met, mate,* and *mat* are all front vowels.

FUNCTION WORD: A term used to refer to words whose function is primarily grammatical, for example, articles, prepositions, and conjunctions. Used in contrast to **content word.**

GENITIVE CASE: The case that typically expresses the relationship of possession, for example, in *John's book, John* is in the genitive case. This is the **inflected genitive** because the case is indicated by the suffix *-s*. In *the cover of the book,* the relationship is indicated by the preposition *of,* which is the **periphrastic genitive.**

GENRE: A term borrowed from literary criticism to refer to different types of uses of language. Narrative, conversation, telling jokes, and preaching a sermon are all examples of different genres.

GERUND: A gerund is the *-ing* form of the verb when it is functioning as a noun and is the subject or object of another verb, for example, *singing* in *Singing is enjoyable* or *He enjoys singing.*

GLOTTAL STOP: A consonant produced by complete closure of the vocal cords in the glottis and transcribed [?]. It is often heard in American speech in the word *mountain.*

GRAMMATICAL MORPHEME: An inflectional morpheme that is used to indicate syntactic relations, for example, past tense *-ed* in *he waited* or plural *-s three cups.*

GRAPHEME: The term in writing that corresponds to **phoneme** in speech. A grapheme can be a single letter as *m, a,* and *p* in *map* or a combination of letters as *ch* in *chin* or *e.e* as in *complete* or *obscene.*

GRIMM'S LAW: See **first Germanic Consonant Shift.**

HIGH VOWEL: A vowel that is made with some part of the tongue raised toward the roof of the mouth. The vowels in *seat, sit, suit,* and *soot* are high vowels.

HOMOGRAPH: A written form that has two or more pronunciations. The *bow* of a ship is pronounced differently from the *bow* in a girl's hair.

HOMONYM: Two or more words that have the same form but are unrelated in meaning, for example, *bank* as the side of a river and as a financial institution.

HOMOPHONE: Two or more words that sound the same but are unrelated and are spelled differently, for example, *write, right, rite.*

HYPERCORRECTION: A term used to refer to the situation in which speakers by trying to be "correct" overdo things. Some speakers who have been told not to use *me* in utterances such as *It's me* try to avoid using *me* even when it is correct. *He gave it to John and I* is an example of hypercorrection.

IDIOLECT: A term used to refer to the personal dialect of an individual speaker.

IMPERATIVE: The form of the verb that is used to give explicit orders. In *Open your books* and *Don't move for a moment, open* and *don't move* are imperatives.

INCLUSIVE WE: The use of the first-person plural pronoun to include the person addressed, as in *What shall we do?* Some languages have different forms for inclusive and exclusive *we.*

INDEFINITE ARTICLE: The form *a/an,* which is used when the speaker does not expect the hearer to know which item is being mentioned in a noun phrase.

INDEXICAL EXPRESSION: An expression that is used to orient the hearer as to what in the immediate environment the speaker is talking about, for example, *that book over there.*

INDO-EUROPEAN: The family of languages descended from the hypothesized common ancestor **Proto-Indo-European (PIE).**

INFINITIVE: The form of the verb that is not inflected for tense and is usually preceded by *to.* In *John wants to sing* and *I persuaded him to leave, to sing* and *to leave* are infinitives.

INFLECTED LANGUAGE: A language in which several grammatical relationships are signaled by bound morphemes. Old English (Anglo-Saxon) was, like modern German, a highly inflected language. In modern English there are only a few inflections, such as *-s* in *John drinks.*

INFLECTED GENITIVE: See **genitive.**

INTERFERENCE: When the learner's first language causes the learner to make specific mistakes in using the second language, the result is usually described as interference.

INTERNATIONAL PHONETIC ALPHABET (IPA):   A form of transcription of speech sounds first published in 1889 and modified since then, IPA provides an unambiguous way to transcribe the sounds of any language.

INTONATION: The term used to refer to the patterns of pitch used to produce utterances. Intonation patterns are specific to each language.

INTRANSITIVE VERB: A verb that does not take an object, for example, *fall* or *arrive.*

IPA: See **international phonetic alphabet.**

IRREGULAR VERB: A verb that forms its past-tense other than by adding the regular past tense suffix *-ed. Come/came, break/broke, buy/bought,* and *cut/cut* are examples of irregular verbs.

ISOGLOSS: The geographical boundary that distinguishes two regional dialects on the basis of their use of a word, pronunciation, or other usage.

LAD: See **Language Acquisition Device.**

LANGUAGE: A more complex term than it might appear. **Language,** without any article, is used as an abbreviation for human language in contrast to forms of animal communication. A **language,** on the other hand, is used to refer to the form of human language spoken by (usually) a reasonably large group of people. Different forms of a language are often called **dialects** but there is no simple linguistic criterion by which the distinction between a dialect and a language can be established.

LANGUAGE ACQUISITION DEVICE (LAD):   The innate capacity in the brain that, according to some scholars, enables infants to acquire any human language without explicit teaching by adults. The LAD was first proposed by Noam Chomsky and the notion has had considerable influence on the study of children's early language development. Many scholars, however, do not accept the need for such a specific language learning ability and the notion remains controversial.

LENGTH: Length (duration) can be used to distinguish sounds in a language. Both vowels and consonants can be long or short.

LEXICAL TONE: In many languages, such as Chinese and Thai, words can be distinguished by the tone, rising, falling, or level with which they are uttered. This feature is known as lexical tone.

LINGUISTIC COMPETENCE: The term introduced by Noam Chomsky to refer to the knowledge of a language a speaker must have to be able to speak and understand the language. It is not accessible to observation, even by introspection, but can only be inferred from the speaker's use of the language (see **linguistic performance**) and the speaker's judgments about the correctness of utterances.

LINGUISTIC PERFORMANCE: The term introduced by Noam Chomsky to refer to the speaker's use of language. It does not refer only to speaking but also to understanding what is said. All language behavior is part of performance. Chomsky has argued that the "performance errors" that speakers make need not reflect the speaker's competence.

LINGUISTIC UNIVERSAL: A term used in reference to any property of language claimed to be found in all languages.

LINGUISTIC VARIABLE: This term is generally used for linguistic features that vary in a given speech community according to the social class, sex, age, and other social distinctions of the speakers.

LOCATIVE: The form of expression used to indicate place. In inflected languages there is often a locative case. In English, prepositions are used to indicate place.

LOGOGRAPHIC WRITING SYSTEM: A system of writing in which each symbol represents a separate concept, as in Chinese characters. The numerals (such as "6") and other mathematical symbols (such as "=") are also logographic symbols and retain their significance when used by speakers of languages whose equivalent words are not mutually intelligible.

MASS NOUN: A noun that has no plural and does not take the indefinite article, for example, *happiness.* Contrasted with **count noun.**

MODAL VERB: One of a set of verbal auxiliary verbs used to express such notions as volition, permission, and obligation. The modal verbs in English include *can, may, must, shall,* and *will.*

MORPHEME: The smallest meaningful unit in a language. The word *unemployment* consists of the morphemes *un-, employ,* and *-ment.* Some morphemes are complete words (**free morphemes**); others are parts of words (**bound morphemes**). Morphemes should not be confused with syllables. *Butter* has two syllables but is only one morpheme, whereas *cats* is only one syllable but it consists of two morphemes, *cat* and *-s.*

MORPHOLOGY: The study of the ways in which morphemes are used in a language.

NOMINALIZATION: The process of forming a noun from a verb or a clause. *The destruction of the city* is a nominalization from *Somebody destroyed the city.*

NOMINATIVE CASE: In an inflected language the case that is used for the subject of the verb.

NONFINITE VERB: A form of the verb that is not marked for tense, infinitive, or gerunds.

NONRESTRICTIVE RELATIVE CLAUSE: A relative clause that provides additional information about some thing or person that is already identified. In *Mary's sister, who is still living in Seattle, has just had a baby,* the phrase *Mary's sister* identifies the individual and the nonrestrictive relative clause *who is still living in Seattle* gives some additional background information about her.

NOUN: A word used to refer to a person, place, thing, quality, or act (for example, *man, house, sock, truth, height, arrival*).

NOUN PHRASE (NP): A syntactic unit that can function as the subject or object of a verb. It can consist of a single noun (*happiness*), a pronoun (*you*), or a phrase containing a noun (*a book, the big house, the owner of the green Mercedes*).

OBJECT: The term used to refer to the **noun phrase** directly affected by the verb, for example, *Mary* in *John kissed Mary* or *the car* in *Peter stole the car*.

OLD ENGLISH: The variety of Germanic spoken in England from the fifth to the eleventh century. Also known as **Anglo-Saxon.**

ORIENTATION (IN A NARRATIVE).: The parts of a narrative that provide the background information (who, what, where, when) necessary to understand the story.

OVERREGULARIZATION: The term given to children's application of general rules where in the adult language there are exceptions, for example, *foots* for *feet* or *breaked* for *broke*. The term was developed from an adult perspective. From a child's perspective the process is "regularization" and it is the adults who use "underregularization."

OVERLAP: The term used to describe the situation in conversation when one speaker begins to speak before another speaker has finished speaking.

PALATALIZATION: The term used to refer to a phonetic process in which the tongue moves in the direction of the palate (the roof of the mouth). The sound [š] in *ship* is palatalized in contrast to the sound [s] in *sip*. Historically, certain consonants have become palatalized when preceding or following high front vowels, which are articulated close to the palate.

PARALINGUISTIC: The term used to refer to those features of speech, such as voice quality, loudness, and tempo, that are not part of the linguistic signal but which may play a very important role in communication, particularly in the communication of affect.

PARARHYME: A literary device in which the vowels change but the consonants remain the same, for example, *side* and *sad*.

PASSIVE: The form of the verb in which the noun phrase that would be the direct object in the active mood becomes the subject and the latter may be indicated through a *by*-phrase (or omitted altogether). The passive of *the boy stole the money* is *the money was stolen by the boy* or simply *the money was stolen*.

PAST TENSE: The form of the verb normally used to indicate that the event or state happened at some time in the past, for example, *John knew* in contrast to *John knows*.

PERFECT TENSE: The form of the verb in English that is made up with some form of the auxiliary *have* and the past participle of a verb, for example, *he has left.*

PERIPHRASTIC GENITIVE: See **genitive.**

PHONE (also ALLOPHONE):   The sound that is uttered as the token of a phoneme in actual speech.

PHONEME: A member of the class of sounds that make up the basic signaling units of a language. Phonemes are the sounds that distinguish words. The words *bill, dill, fill, gill, hill, kill, mill, nil, pill, rill, sill, till,* and *will* are distinguished from each other by their initial sounds. This is part of the evidence to show that /b, d, f, g, h, k, m, n, p, r, s, t, and w/ are phonemes in English. Each language has a distinct set of phonemes.

PHONEMIC: Characteristic of phonemes. Phonemic differences are those which are capable of distinguishing the words of a language in contrast to **phonetic** differences.

PHONETIC: Phonetic descriptions are made in terms that universally describe the processes by which speech sounds are produced. Not all the phonetic details that can be heard are important for distinguishing words in a language. To know which sounds are significantly different from each other (phonemes) it is necessary to establish the ways in which the sounds are systematically used in the language. A phonetic description ought to be given in terms that could apply to any language. A phonemic description refers to characteristics of a particular language.

PHONOLOGY: The study of phonemic differences in languages.

PHONOTACTIC RULES: The rules for combining sounds into larger units. In some languages, such as Samoan, the phonotactic rules permit only consonant/vowel (CV) syllables. In English, syllables can contain as many as three consonants initially, as in *strip,* and four consonants after the vowel, as in *sixths.*

PHRASE: A group of words that functions as a unit, as in the **noun phrase** *the retiring chairman* or the **verb phrase** *thanked the committee.*

PIDGIN: A language that arises in the situation where the speakers of languages that are not mutually intelligible need to communicate with each other for practical reasons but neither set of speakers learns the other's language. A pidgin, consequently, is a language spoken by nobody as a first language. When children grow up speaking a pidgin as their first language it is generally called a **creole language.**

PIE: See **Proto—Indo-European.**

PITCH: The perception of sounds as being higher or lower. Differences in pitch are used in intonation and in some languages to distinguish words (**lexical tone**).

POLYSEMOUS: Words that have several different, though possibly related, meanings are said to be polysemous. The word *bill* in the sense of a request for payment, a bank note, and a theater announcements is polysemous.

PRAGMATICS: The study of the meaning of utterances in context.

PREPOSITION: A function word preceding a noun phrase that indicates some physical or grammatical relation. *To* in *to the house* and *of* in *the middle of the week* are prepositions. In some languages, known as **inflected languages,** these relationships are indicated by case inflections rather than by prepositions.

PRESENT PROGRESSIVE: The form of the verb used in English when referring to an action that is occurring at the present moment, for example, *John is singing* in contrast to the **simple present** form, *John sings,* in which there is no reference to any event or time. The present progressive consists of a form of the verb *be* with the suffix *-ing* added to the verb.

PRINCIPLE OF LEAST EFFORT: A term sometimes used to explain the process of linguistic change in which combinations of sounds are simplified for ease of articulation.

PRONOUN: A function word that can function as a noun phrase. First and second-person pronouns (*I, we,* and *you*) are **deictic** terms that take their reference from the speaker. Other pronouns can be used as substitutes for noun phrases that have already been mentioned.

PROSODIC FEATURES: Those features of articulation (for example, stress and intonation) that affect longer parts of the utterance than single phonetic segments.

PROTO—INDO-EUROPEAN (PIE): The hypothetical language postulated to be the ancestor of the major family of European languages. **PIE** was discovered by comparing words of similar or related meanings that were believed to be cognates and working out a plausible earlier form from which all the later forms could have developed by regular processes of phonetic change.

REFLEXIVE PRONOUN: A pronoun that refers to a noun phrase mentioned earlier in the same clause. In *Harry voted for himself,* the reflexive pronoun *himself* refers to *Harry.*

REGIONAL DIALECT: A variety of a language that is spoken in a specific region and that is distinct in some noticeable features from the varieties spoken in the surrounding areas.

REGISTER: A term used to refer to a variety of language used in connection with a particular activity or body of knowledge. Football, preaching, chemistry, music, and linguistics all have specialized vocabularies and manners of speaking that constitute their registers.

REGULAR VERB: A verb that forms its past tense by adding the suffix *-ed* to the basic form, for example, *wish/wished, rob/robbed, wait/waited.* As the examples show, this suffix may be pronounced [t], [d], or [ɒd].

RELATIVE CLAUSE: A clause that provides information about a noun phrase. In *the woman who sold me the car cheated me,* the relative clause is *who sold me the car.* Relative clauses can be **restrictive** or **nonrestrictive.**

RESTRICTIVE RELATIVE CLAUSE: A relative clause that identifies or limits the reference of the noun phrase that it modifies. In *the customers who bought the earlier version are entitled to a free upgrade,* the restrictive relative clause *who bought the earlier version* identifies which customers are entitled to a free upgrade.

RHYME: A literary device used in poetry where words that end in the same syllable but not the same word are said to rhyme. While it is often an effective feature of successful poetry, the excessive or inept use of rhyme can be tiresome as Alexander Pope complained in his "Essay on Criticism":

> Where-e'er you find "the cooling western breeze"
> In the next line, "it whispers thro' the trees";
> If crystal streams "with pleasing murmurs creep,"
> The reader's threaten'd (not in vain) with "sleep."

ROUNDED VOWEL: A vowel that is produced with the lips rounded. The vowels in *shoe, show,* and *Shaw* are rounded vowels.

SAPIR/WHORF HYPOTHESIS: The name given to the theory that speakers of distinct languages think differently and that the differences in thought are caused by differences between the languages. The name comes from Edward Sapir (1884–1939), one of the pioneers of American linguistics, and his pupil Benjamin Lee Whorf (1897–1941), who between them first formulated the theory in a form that provoked a number of empirical studies in attempts to support or refute it.

SAT SCORE: The Scholastic Aptitude Test is a test used by most U.S. colleges and universities as an indicator of the potential success of those applying for entrance to the institution. Although its usefulness has been challenged and there has been considerable controversy over its form, SAT scores have played an important role in determining the future of many young Americans over the past decades.

SEGMENTAL: Used to refer to those discrete units that can be identified in the stream of speech but mainly to the minimal units of sound (**phones**).

SEMANTICS: The study of the meaning of linguistic units and their combinations. This is probably the most controversial and least understood aspect of language. It is often claimed that semantics studies the meaning of items in isolation from any context, but many scholars now argue that this is impossible since some context must always be assumed. A major difficulty is to know where (if at all) to draw the line between semantics and **pragmatics.**

SENTENCE: This is generally taken to refer to the largest syntactic construction that is totally independent and not part of another construction. While for many linguists the notion is uncontroversial, there are others who point out that the sentence is well defined only in writing. There is no satisfactory definition of the sentence for spoken language. In this book I have used **utterance** rather than sentence as the term for large syntactic units in speech.

SHIFTER: A term sometimes used in reference to those **deictic** words that shift their reference with the speaker, for example, *I, you, here, now.*

SIBILANT: One of the class of fricatives and affricates that are produced with a high-frequency hiss: [s], [z], [š], [ž], [č], and [ǰ].

SIGN LANGUAGE: A visual, gestural linguistic system used by many people who have impaired hearing. Sign language is a fully effective language system capable of expressing the same range of messages as spoken language, though there are unique characteristics to each.

SIMPLE PRESENT TENSE: Although labeled "present," this tense does not usually refer to the present moment, "now." For that we regularly use the **present progressive** The simple present tense is used to refer to general conditions, abilities, or habitual actions. In *Jim plays the clarinet,* there is no implication that Jim is playing the clarinet now but rather that Jim can play the clarinet and perhaps often does.

SLANG: A term loosely used to describe some expressions that are used by some groups of people and not by other groups and are not part of the standard language.

SOCIAL DIALECT: A variety of a language spoken by a group of people who are identified by some social characteristic, usually social class.

SOUNDING: A competitive form of exchanging ritual insults, found mainly among African American adolescents. Also known as **woofing, signifying,** and **playing the dozens.**

SOV: Subject-object-verb, one of the commonest forms of word order found in the languages of the world.

STANDARD ENGLISH: A confusing term that is more often used polemically than with any precise reference. It is the form of English used in most printed works and in formal speech events such as news broadcasts or academic lectures. The extent to which ordinary people speak Standard English is an empirical question that has never been fully investigated.

STATIVE VERB: A verb that is not usually found in the present progressive form. For example, we do not say *he is knowing the answer* or *this bottle is containing a magic potion.* The stative verbs are the exception to the rule that the simple present tense does not refer to the present moment, now. In *Peter knows the answer,* I am asserting that Peter knows the answer at this very minute.

STOP CONSONANT: A consonant that is produced with a complete interruption of the airstream in the mouth, for example, [p], [b], [t], [d], [k], [g]. The nasal consonants [m], [n], and [gn] are also stops although the air is allowed to pass out through the nose. The only stop consonant that does not have a closure in the mouth is the **glottal stop.**

STRESS: The term used to indicate the force with which a syllable is uttered. Those syllables that are more prominent have strong stress and those that are less prominent have weak stress. In English we distinguish some verbs from nouns by stress. *CONvict* is a noun but *conVICT* is a verb.

STYLE: A controversial term that is used to refer to ways in which what is said (or written) may vary according to the circumstances in which it is produced and the people to whom it is addressed. Stylistic differences range from slight phonetic details to whole expressions and types of vocabulary.

SUBJECT: The noun phrase that (in English and many other languages) governs the form of the verb. In *the dog is howling* and *the dogs are howling* the form of the verb is determined by whether the subject (*the dog/the dogs*) is singular or plural.

SUBORDINATE CLAUSE: A clause that does not usually occur by itself but forms part of a larger unit with a main clause. In *before he tried the door, Henry knocked quite loudly,* the clause *before he tried the door* is a subordinate clause and *Henry knocked quite loudly* is the main clause. The latter could occur by itself but the former would be very odd by itself.

SUFFIX: A bound morpheme that is attached to the end of a root or stem morpheme.

SUPRASEGMENTAL: A feature that affects more than just single phonetic segments. See **prosodic features.**

SVO: Subject-verb-object, the normal order of syntactic forms in English and many other languages.

SWITCH-REFERENCE: In certain languages, the obligatory marking in subordinate clauses when a pronoun does not refer back to someone or something mentioned in the main clause.

SYLLABIC WRITING SYSTEM: A system of writing in which each symbol corresponds to a syllable, in contrast to an **alphabetic writing system** in which each symbol ideally corresponds to a single phonetic segment.

SYLLABLE: All words consist of syllables, but some have only one (monosyllables) and others several (polysyllabic) words. The most common type of syllable in the world's languages contains one consonant followed by one vowel (a CV syllable), but many languages, including English, have very complex syllables.

SYNTAX: The combination of phrases into larger units. This is probably the most abstract part of language structure because there seems to be no necessary relationship between forms of syntactic structure and the meanings that they express.

TAG QUESTION: A question formed in English by adding to a statement an auxiliary verb and a pronoun and sometimes a negative. In *Mary is getting better, isn't she?,* the tag question is *isn't she?*

TELEGRAPHIC SPEECH: A term sometimes used to describe the stage in children's language development when they omit the function words in a fashion similar to the ways in which adults used to try to save money by omitting words from a telegram, since the cost was reckoned by the number of words.

TONE LANGUAGE: A language in which individual words are distinguished by the tone with which they are uttered. Chinese and Thai are examples of tone languages.

TRANSITIVE VERB: A verb that takes a direct object, for example, *pick, kill.*

TRUCE TERM: The expression used by children when they want to interrupt a game momentarily for some reason.

TURN-TAKING: The manner in which orderly conversation takes place. In the United States and Britain speakers normally take turns in speaking rather than attempting to drown out the other person.

UNIVERSAL GRAMMAR: The features of language that are claimed to be common to all human languages and to form the basis of the **language acquisition device.**

UNROUNDED VOWEL: A vowel that is produced with the lips spread or in a neutral position. The vowels in *seat, sit, set,* and *sat* are unrounded vowels.

UTTERANCE: A stretch of speech produced at a particular time and place.

VELAR FRICATIVE: A fricative produced by raising the tongue in the direction of the place in the roof of the mouth where the [k] and [g] sounds are produced. It is rare in most varieties of English except in borrowed words such as *Bach, loch.*

VERB PHRASE: A unit of syntactic structure consisting of the verb and its complement. In *Henry gave the beggar some money,* the verb phrase is *gave the beggar some money*; in *John sang* the verb phrase is *sang.*

VOICED SOUND: A sound that is produced with the vocal cords vibrating. All the vowels in English are voiced and so are the consonants beginning the words *bin, din, gap, vine, this, zinc, man, nap.*

VOICELESS SOUND: A sound that is produced without the vocal cords vibrating. The consonants beginning the words *pin, tin, cap, fine, think, sink, ship* are voiceless.

VOWEL: A speech sound that can occur alone or as the center of a syllable. The word *owe* consists of a single vowel and the middle sound in *cat* is a vowel.

VOWEL HARMONY: A system of assimilation in some languages (for example, Turkish) in which subsequent vowels take on some of the characteristics (for example, rounding or fronting) of a vowel earlier in the same word.

VSO: Verb-subject-object is the normal order in a number of languages (for example, Irish, Hebrew).

WH-QUESTION: A question asked with one of the interrogatives *who, what, which, where, why, how.* Such questions cannot be answered by a simple *yes* or *no.*

WORD ORDER: A term used to refer to the normal order of subject, object, and verb in a language. The three most commonly found orders are **SOV, SVO,** and **VSO.**

YES/NO QUESTION: A question that can be answered by a simple *yes* or *no*.

Phonetic Symbols
for English

Consonants		Bilabial	Labiodental	Interdental	Alveolar	Alveopalatal	Velar	Glottal
Stops	voiceless	p			t	k		ʔ
	voiced	b			d		g	
Fricatives	voiceless		f	θ	s	š		h
	voiced		v	ð	z	ž		
Affricates	voiceless					č		
	voiced					ǰ		
Nasals	voiced	m			n		ŋ	
Liquids	voiced				r,l			
Glides	voiced	w				y		

Vowels		Front	Central	Back
High	Tense	i		u
	Lax	I		U
Mid	Tense	e		o
	Lax	ɛ	ə,ʌ	
Low	Tense			ɔ
	Lax	æ	a	

Examples of consonants		Examples of vowels	
/p/	the first sound in *pin*	/i/	the vowel in *seat*
/t/	the first sound in *tin*	/e/	the vowel in *tail*
/k/	the first sound in *kin*	/u/	the vowel in *food*
/4/	the first sound in *fat*	/ɔ/	the vowel in *saw*
/θ/	the first sound in *thigh*	/o/	the vowel in *go*
/s/	the first sound in *sink*	/I/	the vowel in *sit*
/š/	the middle sound in *mission*	/ɛ/	the vowel in *tell*
/h/	the first sound in *hat*	/U/	the vowel in *good*
/č/	the first sound in *cheap*	/a/	the vowel in *hot*
/m/	the final sound in *rum*	/æ/	the vowel in *hat*
/n/	the final sound in *run*	/ʌ/	the vowel in *hut*
/ŋ/	the final sound in *rung*	/ə/	the first sound in *about*
/r/	the first sound in *rip*		
/l/	the first sound in *lip*		
/w/	the first sound in *wet*		
/y/	the first sound in *yet*		
/ǰ/	the first sound in *jeep*		

References

Allen, Irving Lewis. 1983. *The Language of Ethnic Conflict: Social Organization and Lexical Culture.* New York: Columbia University Press.

Anderson, Elaine Slosberg. 1992. *Speaking with Style: The Sociolinguistic Skills of Children.* London: Routledge.

Arlotto, Anthony. 1972. *Introduction to Historical Linguistics.* Boston: Houghton Mifflin.

Austin, J. L. 1962. *How to Do Things with Words.* London: Oxford University Press.

Bakhtin, Mikhail M. 1981. *The Dialogic Imagination: Four Essays by M. M. Bakhtin.* Edited by Michael Holquist, translated by Caryl Emerson and Michael Holquist. Austin: University of Texas Press.

Barfield, Owen. 1954. *History in English Words.* New ed. London: Faber and Faber.

Basso, Keith H. 1990. *Western Apache Language and Culture.* Tucson: University of Arizona Press.

Baugh, Albert C. 1957. *A History of the English Language.* New York: Appleton-Century-Crofts.

Bauman, Richard. 1986. *Story, Performance, and Event: Contextual Studies of Oral Narrative.* Cambridge: Cambridge University Press.

Bernstein, Basil. 1971. *Class, Codes and Control.* Vol. 1. London: Routledge and Kegan Paul.

Biber, Douglas. 1988. *Variation across Speech and Writing.* Cambridge: Cambridge University Press.

Bickerton, Derek. 1981. *Roots of Language.* Ann Arbor, Mich.: Karoma.

———. 1990. *Language and Species.* Chicago: University of Chicago Press.

Bierce, Ambrose. 1957. *The Devil's Dictionary.* New York: Sagamore Press.

Bloom, Lois. 1970. *Language Development: Form and Function in Emerging Grammars.* Cambridge, Mass.: MIT Press.

Bloomfield, Leonard. 1933. *Language.* New York: Holt.

Blum-Kulka, Shoshana, Juliana House, and Gabriele Kasper, eds. 1989. *Cross-cultural Pragmatics: Requests and Apologies.* Norwood, N.J.: Ablex.

Bolinger, Dwight L. 1986. *Intonation and Its Parts: Melody in Spoken English.* Stanford, Calif.: Stanford University Press.

Bourdieu, Pierre. 1991. *Language and Symbolic Power.* Translated by Gino Raymend and Matthew Adamson. Oxford: Polity Press.

Bowerman, Melissa. 1973. *Early Syntactic Development: A Cross-linguistic Study with Special Reference to Finnish.* Cambridge: Cambridge University Press.

Bowra, C. Maurice. 1952. *Heroic Poetry.* London: Macmillan.

Brenneis, Donald L., and Fred R. Myers, eds. 1984. *Dangerous Words: Language and Politics in the Pacific.* New York: New York University Press.

Bright, William, ed. 1992. *International Encyclopedia of Linguistics.* 4 vols. New York: Oxford University Press.

Brown, Gillian, and George Yule. 1983. *Discourse Analysis.* Cambridge: Cambridge University Press.

Brown, Penelope, and Stephen C. Levinson. 1987. *Politeness: Some Universals of Language Usage.* Cambridge: Cambridge University Press.

Brown, Roger. 1973. *A First Language: The Early Stages.* Cambridge, Mass.: Harvard University Press.

Brown, Roger W., and Eric Lenneberg. 1954. "A Study in Language and Cognition." *Journal of Abnormal and Social Psychology* 49:454–62.

Bruner, Jerome. 1983. *Child's Talk: Learning to Use Language.* New York: Norton.

Carruthers, Peter, and Andrew Chamberlain, eds. 2000. *Evolution and the Human Mind: Modularity, Language, and Meta-cognition.* Cambridge: Cambridge University Press.

Chafe, Wallace, and Johanna Nichols, eds. 1986. *Evidentiality: The Linguistic Coding of Epistemology.* Norwood, N.J.: Ablex.

Chambers, J. K., and Peter Trudgill. 1980. *Dialectology.* Cambridge: Cambridge University Press.

Chomsky, Carol. 1969. *The Acquisition of Syntax in Children from 5 to 10.* Cambridge, Mass.: MIT Press.

Chomsky, Noam. 1957. *Syntactic Structures.* The Hague: Mouton.

———. 1965. *Aspects of the Theory of Syntax.* Cambridge, Mass.: MIT Press.

———. 1979. *Language and Responsibility.* Hassocks, England: Harvester.

———. 1986. *Knowledge of Language: Its Nature, Origins, and Use.* Cambridge, Mass.: MIT Press.

———. 1988. *Language and Problems of Knowledge.* Cambridge, Mass.: MIT Press.

———. 2000. *New Horizons in the Study of Language and Mind.* Cambridge: Cambridge University Press.

Christiansen, Morten H. and Simon Kirby, eds. 2003. *Language Evolution.* Oxford: Oxford University Press.

Christiansen, Morten H., and Michelle R. Elleson. 2002. "Linguistic adaptation without linguistic constraints: The role of sequential learning on language evolution." In *The transition to language,* ed. Alison Wray, 335–58. New York: Oxford University Press.

Coates, Jennifer. 1986. *Women, Men and Language.* London: Longman.

Collinge, N. E., ed. 1990. *An Encyclopedia of Language.* London: Routledge.

Comrie, Bernard, ed. 1987. *The World's Major Languages.* New York: Oxford University Press.

Corbett, Greville G. 1991. *Gender.* Cambridge: Cambridge University Press.

Croft, William, and D. Alan Cruse. 2004. *Cognitive Linguistics.* Cambridge: Cambridge University Press.

Crystal, David. 1987. *The Cambridge Encyclopedia of Language.* Cambridge: Cambridge University Press.

Cruttenden, A. 1986. *Intonation.* Cambridge: Cambridge University Press.

Davie, R., N. Butler, and H. Goldstein. 1972. *From Birth to Seven.* London: Longman.

Davin, Dan. 1987. *The Salamander and the Fire.* Oxford: Oxford University Press.

Deacon, Terrence. 1997. *The Symbolic Species: The Co-evolution of Language and the Human Brain.* London: Penguin.

Diessel, Holger. 2002. *The Acquisition of Complex Sentences.* Cambridge: Cambridge University Press.

Dixon, R. M. W. 1991. *A New Approach to English20Grammar, on Semantic Principles.* Oxford: Oxford University Press.

Donaldson, Margaret. 1978. *Children's Minds.* Glasgow: Collins.

Dorian, Nancy C., ed. 1989. *Investigating Obsolescence: Studies in Language Contraction and Death.* Cambridge: Cambridge University Press.

Dunbar, Robin. 1996. *Grooming, Gossip and the Evolution of Language.* London: Faber and Faber.

Dunlea, Anne. 1989. *Vision and the Emergence of Meaning: Blind and Sighted Children's Early Language.* Cambridge: Cambridge University Press.

Duranti, Alessandro, and Charles Goodwin, eds. 1992. *Rethinking Context: Language as an Interactive Phenomenon.* Cambridge: Cambridge University Press.

Eckert, Penelope. 1989. *Jocks and Burnouts: Social Categories and Identity in the High School.* New York: Teachers College.

Eckert, Penelope, and Sally McConnell-Genet. 2002. *Language and Gender.* Cambridge: Cambridge University Press.

Fillmore, Charles J. 1975. *Santa Cruz Lectures on Deixis.* Bloomington: Indiana University Linguistics Club.

Finegan, Edward, and Nico Besnier. 1989. *Language: Its Structure and Use.* San Diego: Harcourt Brace Jovanovich.

Francis, W. N. 1983. *Dialectology.* London: Longman.

Frey, Leonard H., ed. 1966. *Readings in Early English Language History.* New York: Odyssey Press.

Fromkin, Victoria, and Robert Rodman. 1993. *An Introduction to Language.* New York: Holt.

Gardner, Robert C., and Wallace E. Lambert. 1972. *Attitudes and Motivation in Second-language Learning.* Rowley, Mass.: Newbury House.

Gee, James Paul. 1990. *Social Linguistics and Literacies: Ideology in Discourses.* London: Falmer Press.

Gleason, Jean Berko, ed. 1989. *The Development of Language.* 2d ed. Columbus, Ohio: Merrill.

Goffman, Erving. 1981. *Forms of Talk.* Philadelphia: University of Pennsylvania Press.

Golden, Mark, and Beverly Birns. 1976. "Social Class and Infant Intelligence." In *Origins of Intelligence: Infancy and Early Childhood,* ed. Michael Lewis, 299–351. New York: Plenum.

Goody, Jack, and Ian Watt. 1972. "The Consequences of Literacy." In *Language and Social Context,* ed. Pier Paoli Giglioli, 311–57. Harmondsworth, England: Penguin.

Goswami, Usha, ed. 2002. *Blackwell Handbook of Childhood Cognitive Development.* Oxford: Blackwell.

Grice, H. P. 1975. "Logic and Conversation." In *Speech Acts,* ed. Peter Cole and Jerrold Morgan, 41–58. New York: Academic Press.

Grimes, Barbara, ed. 1988. *Ethnologue: Languages of the World.* 11th ed. Dallas: Summer Institute of Linguistics.

Gumperz, John J. 1982. *Discourse Strategies.* Cambridge: Cambridge University Press.

Haas, Mary R. 1942. "Numeral Classifiers in Thai." *Language* 18:201–5.

Halliday, Michael A. K. 1975. *Learning How to Mean.* London: Edward Arnold.

———. 1978. *Language as Social Semiotic: The Social Interpretation of Language and Meaning.* London: Edward Arnold.

Hauser, Marc D. 1996. *The Evolution of Communication.* Cambridge, Mass.: MIT Press.

Haviland, Susan E., and Eve V. Clark. 1974. "This Man's Father Is My Father's Son: A Study of the Acquisition of English Kin Terms." *Journal of Child Language* 1:23–47.

Heath, Shirley Brice. 1983. *Ways with Words: Language, Life, and Work in Communities and Classrooms.* Cambridge: Cambridge University Press.

Hillix, William A., and Duane M. Rumbaugh. 2004. *Animal Bodies, Human Minds: Ape, Dolphin, and Parrot Language Skills.* New York: Kluwer Academic.

Hoffman, Charlotte. 1991. *An Introduction to Bilingualism.* London: Longman.

Horowitz, R., and S. J. Samuels, eds. 1987. *Comprehending Oral and Written Language.* New York: Academic Press.

Hughes, Geoffrey. 1988. *Words in Time: A Social History of the English Vocabulary.* Oxford: Blackwell.

———. 1991. *Swearing: A Social History of Foul Language, Oaths and Profanity in English.* Oxford: Blackwell.

Hymes, Dell. 1974. *Foundations in Sociolinguistics: An Ethnographic Approach.* Philadelphia: University of Pennsylvania Press.

Jenkins, Lyle. 2000. *Biolinguistics: Exploring the Biology of Language.* Cambridge: Cambridge University Press.

Jespersen, Otto. 1922. *Language: Its Nature, Development and Origin.* London: Allen and Unwin.

Johnstone, Barbara. 1990. *Stories, Community, and Place: Narratives from Middle America.* Bloomington: Indiana University Press.

Jones, Sir William. 1807. *Works.* Edited by Anna Maria Jones. 13 vols. London: Stockdale.

Joseph, John Earl. 1987. *Eloquence and Power: The Rise of Language Standards and Standard Languages.* London: Frances Pinter.

Jusczyk, Peter W. 1997. *The Discovery of Spoken Language.* Cambridge, Mass.: MIT Press.

Katzner, Kenneth. 1977. *The Languages of the World.* London: Routledge and Kegan Paul.

Kendon, Adam. 1990. *Conducting Interaction: Patterns of Behaviour in Focused Encounters.* Cambridge: Cambridge University Press.

Klima, Edward S., and Ursula Bellugi. 1979. *The Signs of Language.* Cambridge, Mass.: MIT Press.

Labov, William. 1966. *The Social Stratification of English in New York City.* Washington, D.C.: Center for Applied Linguistics.

———. 1972a. *Language in the Inner City.* Philadelphia: University of Pennsylvania Press.

———. 1972b. *Sociolinguistic Patterns.* Philadelphia: University of Pennsylvania Press.

Ladefoged, Peter. 1975. *A Course in Phonetics.* New York: Harcourt Brace.

Lakoff, George. 1987. *Women, Fire, and Dangerous Things: What Categories Reveal about the Mind.* Chicago: University of Chicago Press.

Lakoff, George, and Mark Johnson. 1980. *Metaphors We Live By.* Chicago: University of Chicago Press.

Lambert, Richard D. 1990.*Language Instruction for Undergraduates in American Higher Education.* Washington, D.C.: National Foreign Language Center.

Lane, Harlan, and Francois Grosjean, eds. 1980. *Recent Perspectives on American Sign Language.* Hillsdale, N.J.: Erlbaum.

Lawler, John. 2003. "James D.McCawley." *Language* 79:614–625.

Lenneberg, Eric H. 1967. *Biological Foundations of Language.* New York: Wiley.

Levinson, Stephen C. 1983. *Pragmatics.* Cambridge: Cambridge University Press.

Lieberman, Philip. 1984. *The Biology and Evolution of Language.* New York: Wiley.

———. 1991. *Uniquely Human: The Evolution of Speech, Thought, and Selfless Behavior.* Cambridge, Mass.: Harvard University Press.

Lightfoot, David. 1999. *The Development of Language: Acquisition, Change, and Evolution.* Oxford: Blackwell.

Luria, Alexander R. 1979. *The Making of Mind: A Personal Account of Soviet Psychology.* Cambridge, Mass.: Harvard University Press.

Lyons, John. 1977. *Semantics.* Cambridge: Cambridge University Press.

Macaulay, Ronald K. S. 1977. *Language, Social Class, and Education: A Glasgow Study.* Edinburgh: Edinburgh University Press.

———. 1978. "The Myth of Female Superiority in Language." *Journal of Child Language* 5:353–63.

———. 1980. *Generally Speaking: How Children Learn Language.* Rowley, Mass.: Newbury House.

———. 1991. *Locating Dialect in Discourse: The Language of Honest Men and Bonnie Lasses in Ayr.* New York: Oxford University Press.

———. 2005a. *Extremely Common Eloquence: Constructing Scottish Identity through Narrative.* Amsterdam: Rodopi.

———. 2005b. *Talk that Counts: Age, Gender, and Social Class Differences in Discourse.* New York: Oxford University Press.

Macnamara, John. "Attitudes and Learning a Second Language." 1973. In *Language Attitudes: Current Trends and Prospects,* ed. Roger W. Shuy and Ralph W. Fasold, 36–40. Washington, D.C.: Georgetown University Press.

MacWhinney, Brian, ed. 1999. *The Emergence of Language.* Mahwah, N.J.: Erlbaum.

Malinowski, Bronislaw. 1933. *Coral Gardens and their Magic.* 2 vols. London: Allen and Unwin.

Mallory, J. P. 1989. *In Search of the Indo-Europeans: Language, Archaeology and Myth.* London: Thames and Hudson.

Masataka, Nobuo. 2003. *The Onset of Language.* Cambridge: Cambridge University Press.

Mather, James Y., and Hans-Henning Speitel. 1975–86. *The Linguistic Atlas of Scotland.* 3 vols. London: Croom Helm.

———. 1991. *Morphology.* 2d ed. Cambridge: Cambridge University Press.

Matthews, Peter H. 1993. *Grammatical Theory in the United States from Bloomfield to Chomsky.* Cambridge: Cambridge University Press.

Maurer, David W. 1955. *Whiz Mob: A Correlation of the Technical Argot of Pick-pockets with Their Behavior Pattern.* Gainesville, Fla.: American Dialect Society.

Maynard Smith, John, and David Harper. 2003. *Animal Signals.* Oxford: Oxford University Press.

McCarthy, Dorothea. 1954. "Language Development in Children." In *Manual of Child Psychology,* ed. Leonard Carmichael, 452–630. New York: Wiley.

McCarthy, Michael. 1991. *Discourse Analysis for Teachers.* Cambridge: Cambridge University Press.

Milroy, James. 1992. *Linguistic Variation and Change: On the Historical Sociolinguistics of English.* Oxford: Blackwell.

Milroy, James, and Lesley Milroy. 1985. *Authority in Language: Investigating Language Prescription and Standardisation.* London: Routledge and Kegan Paul.

Milroy, Lesley. 1987. *Observing and Analyzing Natural Language.* Oxford: Blackwell.

Monk, Ray. 1990. *Ludwig Wittgenstein: The Duty of Genius.* London: Cape.

Mühlhäuser, Peter, and Rom Harré. 1990. *Pronouns and People: The Linguistic Construction of Social and Personal Identity.* Oxford: Blackwell.

Munro, Pamela, ed. 1989. *U.C.L.A. Slang: A Dictionary of Slang Words and Expressions used at U.C.L.A.* Los Angeles: Department of Linguistics, University of California.

Murray, Stephen O. 1998. *American Sociolinguistics: Theorists and Theory Groups.* Amsterdam: John Benjamins.

Newmeyer, Frederick J. 1996. *Generative Linguistics: A Historical Perspective.* London: Routledge.

———. 1998. *Language Form and Language Function.* Cambridge, MA: MIT Press.

Nida, Eugene A. 1949. *Morphology: The Descriptive Analysis of Words.* 2d ed. Ann Arbor: University of Michigan Press.

Nofsinger, Robert E. 1991. *Everyday Conversation.* Newbury Park, Calif.: Sage.

Ochs, Elinor. 1988. *Culture and Language Development: Language Acquisition and Language Socialization in a Samoan Village.* Cambridge: Cambridge University Press.

Oller, D. Kimborough. 2000. *The Emergence of the Speech Capacity.* Mahwah, N.J.: Erlbaum.

Oller, D. Kimborough and Ulrike Griebel, eds. 2004. *Evolution of Communication Systems: A Comparative Approach.* Cambridge, Mass.: MIT Press.

Ong, Walter J. 1982. *Orality and Literacy: The Technologizing of the Word.* London: Methuen.

Opie, Iona, and Peter Opie. 1959. *The Lore and Language of Schoolchildren.* London: Oxford University Press.

Orwell, George. 1945. "Politics and the English Language." In *Shooting an Elephant and Other Essays.* New York: Harcourt Brace Jovanovich.

Partridge, Eric. 1959. *Origins: A Short Etymological Dictionary of Modern English.* New York: Macmillan.

Piaget, Jean. 1959. *The Language and Thought of the Child.* London: Routledge and Kegan Paul.

Pinker, Steven. 1994. *The Language Instinct.* New York: Morrow.

Postman, Neil. 1970. "The Politics of Reading." *Harvard Educational Journal* 40:244–52.

Pound, Louise. 1949. *Selected Writings.* Lincoln: University of Nebraska Press.

Preston, Dennis R. 1989. *Sociolinguistics and Second Language Acquisition.* Oxford: Blackwell.

Quirk, Randolph, Sidney Greenbaum, Geoffrey Leech, and Jan Svartvik. 1985. *A Comprehensive Grammar of the English Language.* London: Longman.

Rickford, John. 1987. *Dimensions of a Creole Continuum: History, Texts, and Linguistic Analysis of a Guyanese Creole.* Stanford, Calif.: Stanford University Press.

Robinson, Mairi, ed. 1985. *The Concise Scots Dictionary.* Aberdeen: Aberdeen University Press.

Romaine, Suzanne. 1984. *The Language of Children and Adolescents: The Acquisition of Communicative Competence.* Oxford: Blackwell.

———. 1988. *Pidgin and Creole Languages.* London: Longman.

———. 1989. *Bilingualism.* Oxford: Blackwell.

Sacks, Harvey, Emanuel Schegloff, and Gail Jefferson. 1974. "A Simplest Systematics for the Organization of Turn-taking for Conversation." *Language* 50:696–735.

Sankoff, Gillian. 1980. *The Social Life of Language.* Philadelphia: University of Pennsylvania Press.

Sapir, Edward. 1921. *Language.* New York: Harcourt, Brace and World.

Saussure, Ferdinand de. 1959. *Course in General Linguistics.* Translated by W. Baskin. New York: McGraw-Hill.

Schieffelin, Bambi B. 1990. *The Give and Take of Everyday Life: Language Socialization of Kaluli Children.* Cambridge: Cambridge University Press.

Schiffrin, Deborah. 1987. *Discourse Markers.* Cambridge: Cambridge University Press.

School of Barbiana. 1970. *Letter to a Teacher.* New York: Random House.

Scollon, Ronald. 1976. *Conversations with a One-Year-Old.* Honolulu: University of Hawaii Press.

Siegel, Jeff. 1987. *Language Contact in a Plantation Environment: A Sociolinguistic History of Fiji.* Cambridge: Cambridge University Press.

Sledd, James. 1969. "Bi-dialectalism: The Linguistics of White Supremacy." *English Journal* 58:1306–15.

Slobin, Dan, ed. 1985. *A Cross-cultural Study of Language Acquisition.* Hillsdale, N.J.: Erlbaum.

Snow, Catherine E. 1977. "The Development of Conversation between Mothers and Babies." *Journal of Child Language* 4:1–22.

Snow, Catherine E., and Charles A. Ferguson, eds. 1977. *Talking to Children: Language Input and Acquisition.* Cambridge: Cambridge University Press.

Stern, J. P. 1959. *Lichtenberg: A Doctrine of Scattered Occasions.* Bloomington: Indiana University Press.

Stockwell, Robert P., J. D. Bowen, and J. W. Martin. 1965. *The Grammatical Structures of English and Spanish.* Chicago: University of Chicago Press.

Stubbs, Michael. 1983. *Discourse Analysis.* Oxford: Blackwell.

Sutton-Smith, Brian. 1972. *The Folkgames of Children.* Publications of the American Folklore Society, Bibliographical and Special Series, vol. 24. Austin: University of Texas Press.

Taine, Hippolyte. 1877. "Acquisition of Language by Children." *Mind* 2:252–59.

Tannen, Deborah. 1989. *Talking Voices: Repetition, Dialogue, and Imagery in Conversational Discourse.* Cambridge: Cambridge University Press.

Todd, Loreto. 1984. *Modern Englishes: Pidgins and Creoles.* Oxford: Blackwell.

Tomasello, Michael. 2003. *Constructing a Language: A Usage-based Theory of Language Acquisition.* Cambridge, Mass.: Harvard University Press.

Tomasello, Michael, and Dan Isaac Slobin, eds. 2005. *Beyond Nature-nurture: Essays in Honor of Elizabeth Bates.* Mahwah, N.J.: Erlbaum.

Tomlin, Russell S. 1986. *Basic Word Order: Functional Principles.* London: Croom Helm.

Tough, Joan. 1977. *The Development of Meaning.* New York: Wiley.

Trudgill, Peter. 1974. *Sociolinguistics: An Introduction.* Baltimore: Penguin Books.

———. 1990. *The Dialects of England.* Oxford: Blackwell.

Trudgill, Peter, and J. K. Chambers, eds. 1991. *Dialects of English: Studies in Grammatical Variation.* London: Longman.

Twain, Mark. 1891. "The Awful German Language." In *A Tramp Abroad,* 538–53. London: Chatto and Windus.

Veblen, Thorstein. 1934. *The Theory of the Leisure Class.* New York: Modern Library.

Watson-Gegeo, Karen A., and Geoffrey M. White, eds. 1990. *Disentangling: Conflict Discourse in Pacific Societies.* Stanford, Calif.: Stanford University Press.

Whorf, Benjamin Lee. 1956. *Language, Thought and Reality: Collected Writings,* ed. J. B. Carroll. Cambridge, Mass.: MIT Press.

Williams, Frederick. 1976. *Explorations of the Linguistic Attitudes of Teachers.* Rowley, Mass.: Newbury House.

Wilson, John. 1990. *Politically Speaking: The Pragmatic Analysis of Political Language.* Oxford: Blackwell.

Wray, Alison, ed. 2002. *The Transition to Language.* New York: Oxford University Press.

Yule, George. 1985. *The Study of Language.* Cambridge: Cambridge University Press.

Index

(Items in bold are explained in the glossary)